MW00605425

React 17 Design Patterns and Best Practices

Best Practices

Third Edition

Design, build, and deploy production-ready web applications using industry-standard practices

Carlos Santana Roldán

BIRMINGHAM - MUMBAI

React 17 Design Patterns and Best Practices
Third Edition

Copyright © 2021 Packt Publishing

Group Product Manager: Pavan Ramchandani
Publishing Product Manager: Rohit Rajkumar
Senior Editor: Hayden Edwards
Content Development Editor: Abhishek Jadhav
Technical Editor: Saurabh Kadave
Copy Editor: Safis Editing
Project Coordinator: Manthan Patel
Proofreader: Safis Editing
Indexer: Tejal Soni
Production Designer: Roshan Kawale

First published: January 2017
Second edition: March 2019
Third published: May 2021

Production reference: 1140521

Published by Packt Publishing Ltd.
Livery Place
35 Livery Street
Birmingham
B3 2PB, UK.

ISBN 978-1-80056-044-4

www.packt.com

To my lovely wife, Cristina, for her patience and support.

– Carlos Santana

About the author

Carlos Santana Roldán is a senior web developer with more than 13 years of experience. Currently, he is working as a senior software engineer at Snapchat. He is the founder of `http://js.education`, where he teaches people web technologies such as React, Node.js, JavaScript, and TypeScript.

About the reviewers

Phily Austria is a hands-on software engineering manager with a professional degree and 15 years of experience. He is currently a software engineering manager at Endpoint Closing, Inc. and still works hands-on in React.js. At this moment, he is interested in FinTech, PropTech, and blockchain.

Phily lives in Los Angeles with his wife, Ashley, and his very cute daughter, Chalida.

Before he became an engineering manager, Phily got a graduate degree in computer software engineering from Cal State Fullerton. He was a frontend engineer for 10 years, working with VanillaJS, jQuery, BackboneJS, EmberJS, AngularJS, and now React.js.

> *I would like to thank Packt and Carlos, the author, for the opportunity to review this book. Anyone who reads this book will become a React expert who can deploy their code to production. Not only are the fundamental React topics written about in detail here, but you will also find practical code and a step-by-step guide to ensure you understand everything about React with up-to-date information. Last but not least, thank you for picking up this book. I hope it makes you a React expert.*

Kirill Ezhemenskii is an experienced software engineer, a frontend and mobile developer, a solution architect, and the CTO at a healthcare company. He's a functional programming advocate and an expert in the React stack, GraphQL, and TypeScript. He's also a React Native mentor.

Emmanuel Demey works with the JavaScript ecosystem on a daily basis. He spends his time sharing his knowledge with anyone and everyone. His first goal at work is to help the people he works with. He has spoken at French conferences (such as Devfest Nantes, Devfest Toulouse, Sunny Tech, and Devoxx France) about topics related to the web platform, such as JavaScript frameworks (Angular, React.js, and Vue.js), accessibility, and Nest.js. He has been a trainer for 10 years at Worldline and Zenika (two French consulting companies). He also the co-leader of the Google Developer of Lille group and the co-organizer of the Devfest Lille conference.

Table of Contents

Preface

React is an open source, adaptable JavaScript library for building complex user interfaces from small, detached bits called **components**. This book will help you to use React effectively to make your applications more flexible, easier to maintain, and improve their performance while giving your workflow a huge boost by improving speed without affecting quality.

You'll start by understanding the internals of React, before gradually moving on to writing maintainable and clean code. The chapters that follow will show you how to build components that are reusable across the application, how to structure applications, and how to create forms that actually work. Later, you will build on your knowledge by exploring how to style React components and optimize them to make applications faster and more responsive. Finally, you'll learn how to write tests effectively and learn how to contribute to React and its ecosystem.

By the end of this book, you'll be able to avoid the process of trial and error and developmental headaches, and instead have the skills you need to efficiently build and deploy real-world React web applications.

Who this book is for

This book is for web developers who want to increase their understanding of React and apply it to real-life app development. Intermediate-level experience with React and JavaScript is assumed.

What this book covers

Chapter 1, Taking Your First Steps with React, covers some basic concepts that are important for following the rest of the book, and that are crucial to working with React daily. We will learn how to write declarative code and will gain a clear understanding of the difference between the components we create and the elements React uses to display instances on the screen. We'll then learn the reasons behind the choice of co-locating logic and templates together, and why that unpopular decision has been a big win for React. We will go through the reasons why it is common to feel fatigued in the JavaScript ecosystem, but we'll also see how to avoid those problems by following an iterative approach. Finally, we will see what the new `create-react-app` CLI is, and with that, we'll be ready to start writing some real code.

Chapter 2, Cleaning Up Your Code, teaches you a great deal about how JSX works and how to use it in the right way in our components. We start from the basics of the syntax to create a solid knowledge base that will enable us to master JSX and its features. We will look at how ESLint and its plugins can help us find problems faster and enforce a consistent style guide across our code base. Finally, we will go through the basics of functional programming to understand the important concepts to use when writing a React application. Now that our code is clean, we are ready to start digging deeper into React and learn how to write truly reusable components.

Chapter 3, React Hooks, teaches you how to use the new React Hooks and how to build your own Hooks.

Chapter 4, Exploring Popular Composition Patterns, explains how to compose our reusable components and make them communicate effectively. Then, we will go through some of the most interesting composition patterns in React. We will also see how React tried to solve the problem of sharing functionalities between components with mixins. We'll then learn how to deal with context without needing to couple our components to it, thanks to HOCs. Finally, we'll see how we can compose components dynamically by following the *FunctionAsChild* pattern.

Chapter 5, Understanding GraphQL with a Real Project, explains how to use GraphQL queries and mutations with a real project, where you will learn how to build an authentication system with GraphQL, JWT tokens, and Node.js.

Chapter 6, Managing Data, goes through some of the most common patterns to make a child and parent communicate using callbacks. We'll then learn how we can use a common parent to share data across components that are not directly connected. We will start with a simple component, which will be able to load data from GitHub, and we'll make it reusable with HOCs, and then go on to learn how we can use `react-refetch` to apply data fetching patterns to our components and avoid reinventing the wheel. Finally, we'll learn how to use the new Context API.

Chapter 7, Writing Code for the Browser, looks at different things we can do when we target the browser with React, from form creation to events; from animations to SVGs. React gives us a declarative way to manage all the aspects we need to deal with when we create a web application. React gives us access to the actual DOM nodes in a way that we can perform imperative operations with them, which is useful if we need to integrate React with an existing imperative library.

Chapter 8, Making Your Components Look Beautiful, studies the reasons why regular CSS may not be the best approach for styling components, along with the various alternative solutions. Moving through the chapter, we'll learn to use inline styles in React, along with the downsides of this, which can be fixed by using the Radium library. At the end, a new library, `styled-components`, will be introduced, along with an outline of the modern approach that it offers.

Chapter 9, Server-Side Rendering for Fun and Profit, invites you to follow certain steps to set up a server-side rendered application. By the end of this chapter, we will be able to build a universal application and be aware of its pros and cons.

Chapter 10, Improving the Performance of Your Applications, takes a quick look at the basic components of the performance of React, and how we can use some APIs to help the library find the optimal path to update the DOM without degrading the user experience. We will also learn how to monitor performance and find bottlenecks using some tools that we can import into our code base. At the end, we'll see how immutability and *PureComponent* are the perfect tools to build fast React applications.

Chapter 11, Testing and Debugging, explains why it is important to test our applications, along with an outline of the most popular tools that we could use to create tests with React. We will also learn to set up a Jest environment to test components using Enzyme, along with a discussion of what Enzyme is and why it is a must for testing React applications. By covering all these topics, at the end of the chapter, we will be able to create a test environment from scratch and write tests for our application's components.

Chapter 12, React Router, looks at certain steps that will help us to implement React Router in our application. Moving ahead, as we complete each section, we will add dynamic routes and understand how exactly React Router works. We will learn how to install and configure React Router, along with adding a component, exact prop, and parameters to routes.

Chapter 13, Anti-Patterns to be Avoided, is all about the common anti-patterns we should avoid when using React. We will study why mutating the state is harmful to performance. Choosing the right keys and helping the reconciler will also be covered in this chapter, along with the reason why spreading props on DOM elements is bad and how we can avoid doing that.

Chapter 14, Deploying to Production, covers how to deploy our React application using Node.js and nginx on an Ubuntu server from Google Cloud, along with configuring nginx, PM2, and a domain. Implementing CircleCI for continuous integration will also be covered.

Chapter 15, Next Steps, demonstrates how we can contribute to the React library by opening issues and pull requests, and explains why it is important to give back to the community and share our code. At the end, we will cover the most important aspects to keep in mind when pushing open source code, along with how we can publish an npm package and how to use semantic versioning.

To get the most out of this book

To master React, you need to have a fundamental knowledge of JavaScript and Node.js. This book is mostly targeted at web developers, and, at the time of writing, the following assumptions were made of the reader:

- The reader knows how to install the latest version of Node.js.
- The reader is an intermediate developer who can understand JavaScript ES6 syntax.
- The reader has some experience of CLI tools and Node.js syntax.

Download the example code files

You can download the example code files for this book from GitHub at `https://github.com/PacktPublishing/React-17-Design-Patterns-and-Best-Practices-Third-Edition`. In case there's an update to the code, it will be updated on the existing GitHub repository.

We also have other code bundles from our rich catalog of books and videos available at `https://github.com/PacktPublishing/`. Check them out!

Download the color images

We also provide a PDF file that has color images of the screenshots/diagrams used in this book. You can download it here: `https://static.packt-cdn.com/downloads/9781800560444_ColorImages.pdf`.

Conventions used

There are a number of text conventions used throughout this book.

`CodeInText`: Indicates code words in text, database table names, folder names, filenames, file extensions, pathnames, dummy URLs, user input, and Twitter handles. Here is an example: "Mount the downloaded `WebStorm-10*.dmg` disk image file as another disk in your system."

A block of code is set as follows:

```
html, body, #map {
 height: 100%;
 margin: 0;
 padding: 0
}
```

When we wish to draw your attention to a particular part of a code block, the relevant lines or items are set in bold:

```
const name = `Carlos`
const multilineHtml = `<p>
 This is a multiline string
 </p>`
console.log(`Hi, my name is ${name}`)
```

Any command-line input or output is written as follows:

```
npm install -g @babel/preset-env @babel/preset-react
```

Bold: Indicates a new term, an important word, or words that you see onscreen. For example, words in menus or dialog boxes appear in the text like this. Here is an example: "Select **System info** from the **Administration** panel."

 Warnings or important notes appear like this.

 Tips and tricks appear like this.

Get in touch

Feedback from our readers is always welcome.

General feedback: If you have questions about any aspect of this book, mention the book title in the subject of your message and email us at customercare@packtpub.com.

Errata: Although we have taken every care to ensure the accuracy of our content, mistakes do happen. If you have found a mistake in this book, we would be grateful if you would report this to us. Please visit www.packtpub.com/support/errata, selecting your book, clicking on the Errata Submission Form link, and entering the details.

Piracy: If you come across any illegal copies of our works in any form on the Internet, we would be grateful if you would provide us with the location address or website name. Please contact us at copyright@packt.com with a link to the material.

If you are interested in becoming an author: If there is a topic that you have expertise in and you are interested in either writing or contributing to a book, please visit authors.packtpub.com.

Reviews

Please leave a review. Once you have read and used this book, why not leave a review on the site that you purchased it from? Potential readers can then see and use your unbiased opinion to make purchase decisions, we at Packt can understand what you think about our products, and our authors can see your feedback on their book. Thank you!

For more information about Packt, please visit packt.com.

1
Hello React!

The objective of this section is to explain to you the basic concepts of declarative programming, React elements, and how to use TypeScript.

We will cover the following chapters in this section:

- *Chapter 1, Taking Your First Steps with React*
- *Chapter 2, Cleaning Up Your Code*

Taking Your First Steps with React

1

Hello, readers!

This book assumes that you already know what React is and what problems it can solve for you. You may have written a small/medium application with React, and you want to improve your skills and answer all of your open questions. You should know that React is maintained by the developers at Facebook and hundreds of contributors within the JavaScript community. React is one of the most popular libraries for creating UIs, and it is well known to be fast, thanks to its smart way of working with the **Document Object Model (DOM)**. It comes with JSX, a new syntax for writing markup in JavaScript, which requires you to change your thinking regarding the separation of concerns. It has many cool features, such as server-side rendering, which gives you the power to write universal applications.

In this first chapter, we will go through some basic concepts that are essential to master in order to use React effectively, but are straightforward enough for beginners to figure out:

- The difference between imperative and declarative programming
- React components and their instances, and how React uses elements to control the UI flow
- How React changed the way we build web applications, enforcing a different new concept of separation of concerns, and the reasons behind its unpopular design choice
- Why people feel JavaScript fatigue, and what you can do to avoid the most common errors developers make when approaching the React ecosystem
- How TypeScript changed the game

Technical requirements

In order to follow this book, you need to have some minimal experience using the terminal to run a few Unix commands. Also, you need to install Node.js. You have two options. The first one is to download Node.js directly from the official website, `https://nodejs.org`, and the second option (recommended) is to install **Node Version Manager** (**NVM**) from `https://github.com/nvm-sh/nvm`.

If you decide to go with NVM, you can install any version of Node.js you want and switch the versions with the `nvm install` command:

```
# "node" is an alias for the latest version:
nvm install node

# You can also install a global version of node (will install the latest
from that version):
nvm install 10
nvm install 9
nvm install 8
nvm install 7
nvm install 6

# Or you can install a very specific version:
nvm install 6.14.3
```

After you have installed the different versions, you can switch them by using the `nvm use` command:

```
nvm use node # for latest version
nvm use 10
nvm use 6.14.3
```

Finally, you can specify a default `node` version by running the following command:

```
nvm alias default node
nvm alias default 10
nvm alias default 6.14.3
```

In short, here is a list of the requirements to complete the chapter:

- **Node.js (12+)**: https://nodejs.org
- **NVM**: https://github.com/nvm-sh/nvm
- **VS Code**: https://code.visualstudio.com
- **TypeScript**: https://www.npmjs.com/package/typescript

You can find the code for this chapter in the book's GitHub repository: https://github.com/PacktPublishing/React-17-Design-Patterns-and-Best-Practices-Third-Edition.

Differentiating between declarative and imperative programming

When reading the React documentation or blog posts about React, you will have undoubtedly come across the term **declarative**. One of the reasons why React is so powerful is that it enforces a declarative programming paradigm.

Therefore, to master React, it is essential to understand what declarative programming means and what the main differences between imperative and declarative programming are. The easiest way to approach this is to think about imperative programming as a way of describing how things work, and declarative programming as a way of describing what you want to achieve.

Entering a bar for a beer is a real-life example in the imperative world, where normally you will give the following instructions to the bartender:

1. Find a glass and collect it from the shelf.
2. Place the glass under the tap.
3. Pull down the handle until the glass is full.
4. Hand me the glass.

In the declarative world, you would just say "Can I have a beer, please?"

The declarative approach assumes that the bartender already knows how to serve a beer, an important aspect of the way declarative programming works.

Let's move into a JavaScript example. Here we will write a simple function that, given an array of lowercase strings, returns an array with the same strings in uppercase:

```
toUpperCase(['foo', 'bar']) // ['FOO', 'BAR']
```

An imperative function to solve the problem would be implemented as follows:

```
const toUpperCase = input => {
  const output = []
  for (let i = 0; i < input.length; i++) {
    output.push(input[i].toUpperCase())
  }
  return output
}
```

First of all, an empty array to contain the result is created. Then, the function loops through all the elements of the input array and pushes the uppercase values into the empty array. Finally, the output array is returned.

A declarative solution would be as follows:

```
const toUpperCase = input => input.map(value => value.toUpperCase())
```

The items of the input array are passed to a map function that returns a new array containing the uppercase values. There are some significant differences to note: the former example is less elegant and it requires more effort to be understood. The latter is terser and easier to read, which makes a huge difference in big code bases, where maintainability is crucial.

Another aspect worth mentioning is that in the declarative example, there is no need to use variables, nor to keep their values updated during the execution. Declarative programming tends to avoid creating and mutating a state.

As a final example, let's see what it means for React to be declarative. The problem we will try to solve is a common task in web development: creating a toggle button.

Imagine a simple UI component such as a toggle button. When you click it, it turns green (on) if it was previously gray (off), and switches to gray (off) if it was previously green (on).

The imperative way of doing this would be as follows:

```
const toggleButton = document.querySelector('#toggle')

toggleButton.addEventListener('click', () => {
  if (toggleButton.classList.contains('on')) {
    toggleButton.classList.remove('on')
    toggleButton.classList.add('off')
  } else {
    toggleButton.classList.remove('off')
    toggleButton.classList.add('on')
  }
})
```

It is imperative because of all the instructions needed to change the classes. In contrast, the declarative approach using React would be as follows:

```
// To turn on the Toggle
<Toggle on />

// To turn off the toggle
<Toggle />
```

In declarative programming, developers only describe what they want to achieve, and there's no need to list all the steps to make it work. The fact that React offers a declarative approach makes it easy to use, and consequently, the resulting code is simple, which often leads to fewer bugs and more maintainability.

In the next section, you will learn how React elements work and you will get more context on how `props` are being passed on a React component.

How React elements work

This book assumes that you are familiar with components and their instances, but there is another object you should know about if you want to use React effectively – the element.

Whenever you call `createClass`, extend `Component`, or declare a stateless function, you are creating a component. React manages all the instances of your components at runtime, and there can be more than one instance of the same component in memory at a given point in time.

As mentioned previously, React follows a declarative paradigm, and there's no need to tell it how to interact with the DOM; you declare what you want to see on the screen, and React does the job for you.

As you might have already experienced, most other UI libraries work the other way round: they leave the responsibility of keeping the interface updated to the developer, who has to manage the creation and destruction of the DOM elements manually.

To control the UI flow, React uses a particular type of object, called an **element**, which describes what has to be shown on the screen. These immutable objects are much simpler compared to the components and their instances and contain only the information that is strictly needed to represent the interface.

The following is an example of an element:

```
{
  type: Title,
  props: {
    color: 'red',
    children: 'Hello, Title!'
  }
}
```

Elements have `type`, which is the most important attribute, and some properties. There is also a particular property, called `children`, that is optional and represents the direct descendant of the element.

`type` is important because it tells React how to deal with the element itself. If `type` is a string, the element represents a DOM node, while if `type` is a function, the element is a component.

DOM elements and components can be nested with each other as follows, to represent the render tree:

```
{
  type: Title,
  props: {
    color: 'red',
    children: {
      type: 'h1',
      props: {
        children: 'Hello, H1!'
      }
    }
  }
}
```

When the type of the element is a function, React calls the function, passing `props` to get back the underlying elements. It keeps on performing the same operation recursively on the result until it gets a tree of DOM nodes that React can render on the screen. This process is called **reconciliation**, and it is used by both React DOM and React Native to create the UIs of their respective platforms.

React is a game-changer, so at the beginning, the React syntax might seem weird to you, but once you understand how it works, you will love it, and for this, you need to unlearn everything you know so far.

Unlearning everything

Using React for the first time usually requires an open mind because it is a new way of designing web and mobile applications. React tries to innovate the way we build UIs following a path that breaks most of the well-known best practices.

In the last two decades, we learned that the separation of concerns is important, and we used to think about it as separating the logic from the templates. Our goal has always been to write the JavaScript and the HTML in different files. Various templating solutions have been created to help developers achieve this.

The problem is that most of the time, that kind of separation is just an illusion and the truth is that the JavaScript and the HTML are tightly coupled, no matter where they live.

Let's see an example of a template:

```
{{#items}}
  {{#first}}
    <li><strong>{{name}}</strong></li>
  {{/first}}
  {{#link}}
    <li><a href="{{url}}">{{name}}</a></li>
  {{/link}}
{{/items}}
```

The preceding snippet is taken from the Mustache website, one of the most popular templating systems.

The first row tells Mustache to loop through a collection of items. Inside the loop, there is some conditional logic to check whether the `#first` and `#link` properties exist and, depending on their values, a different piece of HTML is rendered. Variables are wrapped in curly braces.

If your application only has to display some variables, a templating library could represent a good solution, but when it comes to starting to work with complex data structures, things change. Templating systems and their **Domain-Specific Language** (**DSL**) offer a subset of features, and they try to provide the functionalities of a real programming language without reaching the same level of completeness. As shown in the example, templates highly depend on the models they receive from the logic layer to display the information.

On the other hand, JavaScript interacts with the DOM elements rendered by the templates to update the UI, even if they are loaded from separate files. The same problem applies to styles – they are defined in a different file, but they are referenced in the templates, and the CSS selectors follow the structure of the markup, so it is almost impossible to change one without breaking the other, which is the definition of **coupling**. That is why the classic separation of concerns ended up being more the separation of technologies, which is, of course, not a bad thing, but it doesn't solve any real problems.

React tries to move a step forward by putting the templates where they belong – next to the logic. The reason it does that is that React suggests you organize your applications by composing small bricks called components. The framework should not tell you how to separate the concerns because every application has its own, and only the developers should decide how to limit the boundaries of their applications.

The component-based approach drastically changes the way we write web applications, which is why the classic concept of separation of concerns is gradually being taken over by a much more modern structure. The paradigm enforced by React is not new, and it was not invented by its creators, but React has contributed to making the concept mainstream and, most importantly, popularized it in such a way that it is easier to understand for developers with different levels of expertise.

Rendering of a React component looks like this:

```
return (
  <button style={{ color: 'red' }} onClick={this.handleClick}>
    Click me!
  </button>
)
```

We all agree that it seems a bit weird in the beginning, but that is just because we are not used to that kind of syntax. As soon as we learn it and we realize how powerful it is, we understand its potential. Using JavaScript for both logic and templating not only helps us separate our concerns in a better way, but it also gives us more power and more expressivity, which is what we need to build complex UIs.

That is why even if the idea of mixing JavaScript and HTML sounds weird in the beginning, it is vital to give React 5 minutes. The best way to get started with new technology is to try it on a small side project and see how it goes. In general, the right approach is always to be ready to unlearn everything and change your mindset if the long-term benefits are worth it.

There is another concept that is pretty controversial and hard to accept, and that the engineers behind React are trying to push to the community: moving the styling logic inside the component, too. The end goal is to encapsulate every single technology used to create our components and separate the concerns according to their domain and functionalities.

Here is an example of a style object taken from the React documentation:

```
const divStyle = {
  color: 'white',
  backgroundImage: `url(${imgUrl})`,
  WebkitTransition: 'all', // note the capital 'W' here
  msTransition: 'all' // 'ms' is the only lowercase vendor prefix
}
ReactDOM.render(<div style={divStyle}>Hello World!</div>, mountNode)
```

This set of solutions, where developers use JavaScript to write their styles, is known as #CSSinJS, and we will talk about it extensively in *Chapter 8, Making Your Components Look Beautiful*.

In the next section, we will see how to avoid JavaScript fatigue, which is caused by the large number of configurations that are needed to run a React application (webpack mainly).

Understanding JavaScript fatigue

There is a prevailing opinion that React consists of a vast set of technologies and tools, and if you want to use it, you are forced to deal with package managers, transpilers, module bundlers, and an infinite list of different libraries. This idea is so widespread and shared among people that it has been clearly defined, and has been given the name **JavaScript fatigue**.

It is not hard to understand the reasons behind this. All the repositories and libraries in the React ecosystem are made using shiny new technologies, the latest version of JavaScript, and the most advanced techniques and paradigms.

Moreover, there is a massive number of React boilerplate on GitHub, each with tens of dependencies to offer solutions for any problems. It is straightforward to think that all these tools are required to start using React, but this is far from the truth. Despite this common way of thinking, React is a pretty tiny library, and it can be used inside any page (or even inside JSFiddle) in the same way everyone used to use jQuery or Backbone, just by including the script on the page before the closing body element.

There are two scripts because React is split into two packages:

- `react`: Implements the core features of the library
- `react-dom`: Contains all the browser-related features

The reason behind this is that the core package is used to support different targets, such as React DOM in browsers and React Native on mobile devices. Running a React application inside a single HTML page does not require any package manager or complex operation. You can just download the distribution bundle and host it yourself (or use `https://unpkg.com/`), and you are ready to get started with React and its features in a few minutes.

Here are the URLs to be included in the HTML to start using React:

- `https://unpkg.com/react@17.0.1/umd/react.production.min.js`
- `https://unpkg.com/react-dom@17.0.1/umd/react-dom.production.min.js`

If we add the core React library only, we cannot use JSX because it is not a standard language supported by the browser; but the whole point is to start with the bare minimum set of features and add more functionalities as soon as they are needed. For a simple UI, we could just use `createElement` (`_jsx` on React 17) and only when we start building something more complex can we include a transpiler to enable JSX and convert it into JavaScript. As soon as the app grows a bit more, we may need a router to handle different pages and views, and we can include that as well.

At some point, we may want to load data from some API endpoints, and if the application keeps growing, we will reach the point where we need some external dependencies to abstract complex operations. Only at that very moment should we introduce a package manager. Then, the time will come to split our application into separate modules and organize our files in the right way. At that point, we should start thinking about using a module bundler.

Following this simple approach, there's no fatigue. Starting with a boilerplate that has 100 dependencies and tens of `npm` packages of which we know nothing is the best way to get lost. It is important to note that every programming-related job (and frontend engineering in particular) requires continuous learning. It is the nature of the web to evolve at a breakneck pace and change according to the needs of both users and developers. This is the way our environment has worked since the beginning and is what makes it very exciting.

As we gain experience working on the web, we learn that we cannot master everything and we should find the right way to keep ourselves updated to avoid fatigue. We are able to follow all the new trends without jumping into the new libraries for the sake of it unless we have time for a side project.

It is astonishing how, in the JavaScript world, as soon as a specification is announced or drafted, someone in the community implements it as a transpiler plugin or a polyfill, letting everyone else play with it while the browser vendors agree and start supporting it.

This is something that makes JavaScript and the browser a completely different environment compared to any other language or platform. The downside of it is that things change quickly, but it is just a matter of finding the right balance between betting on new technologies versus staying safe.

In any case, Facebook developers care a lot about the **Developer Experience (DX)**, and they listen carefully to the community. So, even if it is not true that to use React we are required to learn hundreds of different tools, they realized that people were feeling the fatigue and they released a CLI tool that makes it incredibly easy to scaffold and run a real React application.

The only requirement is to use a `node.js/npm` environment and install the CLI tool globally as follows:

```
npm install -g create-react-app
```

When the executable is installed, we can use it to create our application, passing a folder name:

```
create-react-app hello-world --template typescript
```

Finally, we move into the folder of our application with `cd hello-world`, and we just run the following command:

```
npm start
```

Magically, our application is running with a single dependency, but with all the features needed to build a complete React application using the most advanced techniques. The following screenshot shows the default page of an application created with `create-react-app`:

This is basically your first React application.

Introducing TypeScript

TypeScript is a typed superset of JavaScript that is compiled to JavaScript, which means **TypeScript** is **JavaScript** with some additional features. TypeScript was designed by Anders Hejlsberg (the designer of C#) at Microsoft and is open source.

Let's see what the features of TypeScript are and how to convert JavaScript to TypeScript.

TypeScript features

This section will try to summarize the most important features you should be taking advantage of:

- **TypeScript is JavaScript**: Any JavaScript code you write will work with TypeScript, which means if you already know how to use JavaScript basically you have all you need to do TypeScript; you just need to learn how to add types to your code. All the TypeScript code is transformed into JavaScript at the end.
- **JavaScript is TypeScript**: This just means that you can rename any valid .js file with the .ts extension, and it will work.
- **Error checking**: TypeScript compiles the code and checks for errors, which helps a lot to highlight errors before we run our code.
- **Strong typing**: By default, JavaScript is not strongly typed. With TypeScript, you can add types to all your variables and functions, and you can even specify the returned value types.
- **Object-oriented programming supported**: It supports concepts such as classes, interfaces, inheritance, and so on.

Converting JavaScript code into TypeScript

In this section, we will see how to transform some JavaScript code into TypeScript.

Let's suppose we have to check whether a word is a palindrome. The JavaScript code for this algorithm will be as follows:

```
function isPalindrome(word) {
  const lowerCaseWord = word.toLowerCase()
  const reversedWord = lowerCaseWord.split('').reverse().join('')

  return lowerCaseWord === reversedWord
}
```

You can name this file palindrome.ts.

As you can see, we are receiving a `string` variable (`word`), and we are returning a `boolean` value, so how will this be translated to TypeScript?

```
function isPalindrome(word: string): boolean {
  const lowerCaseWord = word.toLowerCase()
  const reversedWord = lowerCaseWord.split('').reverse().join('')

  return lowerCaseWord === reversedWord
}
```

You're probably thinking great, I just specified the `string` type as `word` and `boolean` type to the function returned value, but now what?

If you try to run the function with some value that is different from a string, you will get a TypeScript error:

```
console.log(isPalindrome('Level')) // true
console.log(isPalindrome('Anna')) // true
console.log(isPalindrome('Carlos')) // false
console.log(isPalindrome(101)) // TS Error
console.log(isPalindrome(true)) // TS Error
console.log(isPalindrome(false)) // TS Error
```

So, if you try to pass a number to the function, you will get the following error:

```
console.log(isPalindrome(    Argument of type 'number' is not assignable to parameter of type
console.log(isPalindrome(    'string'. ts(2345)
console.log(isPalindrome(    Peek Problem (⌥F8)    No quick fixes available
console.log(isPalindrome(101)) // TS Error
console.log(isPalindrome(true)) // TS Error
console.log(isPalindrome(false)) // TS Error
```

That's why TypeScript is very useful because it will force you to be more strict and explicit with your code.

Types

In the last example, we saw how to specify some primitive types for our function parameter and returned value, but you're probably wondering how you can describe an object or array with more details. **Types** can help us to describe our objects or arrays in a better way. For example, let's suppose you want to describe a User type to save the information into the database:

```
type User = {
  username: string
  email: string
  name: string
  age: number
  website: string
  active: boolean
}

const user: User = {
  username: 'czantany',
  email: 'carlos@milkzoft.com',
  name: 'Carlos Santana',
  age: 33,
  website: 'http://www.js.education',
  active: true
}

// Let's suppose you will insert this data using Sequelize...
models.User.create({ ...user }}
```

We get the following error if you forget to add one of the nodes or put an invalid value in one of them:

```
type User = {
    username: string
    email: string
    name: string
    age: number
    we
    ac  const user: User

}       Property 'age' is missing in type '{ username: string; email: string; name: string; website:
        string; active: true; }' but required in type 'User'. ts(2741)

        user.ts(19, 5): 'age' is declared here.

        Peek Problem (⌥F8)   No quick fixes available
const user: User = {
    username: 'czantany',
    email: 'carlos@milkzoft.com',
    name: 'Carlos Santana',
    website: 'http://www.js.education',
    active: true
}
```

If you need optional nodes, you can always put a `?` next to the name of the node, as shown in the following code block:

```
type User = {
  username: string
  email: string
  name: string
  age?: number
  website: string
  active: boolean
}
```

> You can name `type` as you want, but a good practice to follow is to add a prefix of `T`, so, for example, the `User` type will become `TUser`. In this way, you can quickly recognize that it is `type` and you don't get confused thinking it is a class or a React component.

Interfaces

Interfaces are very similar to types and sometimes developers don't know the differences between them. Interfaces can be used to describe the shape of an object or function signature just like types, but the syntax is different:

```
interface User {
  username: string
  email: string
  name: string
  age?: number
  website: string
  active: boolean
}
```

 You can name an interface as you want, but a good practice to follow is to add a prefix of I, so, for example, the User interface will become IUser. In this way, you can quickly recognize that it is an interface and you don't get confused thinking it is a class or a React component.

An interface can also be extended, implemented, and merged.

Extending

An interface or type can also be extended, but again the syntax will differ, as shown in the following code block:

```
// Extending an interface
interface IWork {
  company: string
  position: string
}

interface IPerson extends IWork {
  name: string
  age: number
}

// Extending a type
type TWork = {
  company: string
  position: string
}

type TPerson = TWork & {
  name: string
```

```
    age: number
}

// Extending an interface into a type
interface IWork {
  company: string
  position: string
}

type TPerson = IWork & {
  name: string
  age: number
}
```

As you can see, by using the & character, you can extend a type, while you extend an interface using the `extends` keyword.

Implementing

A class can implement an interface or type alias in the same exact way. But it cannot implement (or extend) a type alias that names a union type, for example:

```
// Implementing an interface
interface IWork {
  company: string
  position: string
}

class Person implements IWork {
  name: 'Carlos'
  age: 33
}

// Implementing a type
type TWork = {
  company: string
  position: string
}

class Person2 implements TWork {
  name: 'Cristina'
  age: 32
}

// You can't implement a union type
type TWork2 = { company: string; position: string } | { name: string; age:
```

```
number }

class Person3 implements TWork2 {
  company: 'Google'
  position: 'Senior Software Engineer'
}
```

If you write that code, you will get the following error in your editor:

```
// You can't implement a union type
type TWork2 = { company: string; position: string } | { name: string; age: number }

class Person3 implements TWork2 {
  company: 'Google'                    type TWork2 = {
  position: 'Senior Softw                  company: string;
}                                          position: string;
                                       } | {
                                           name: string;
                                           age: number;
                                       }

                                       A class can only implement an object type or intersection of object types with statically
                                       known members. ts(2422)

                                       Peek Problem (⌥F8)    No quick fixes available
```

As you can see, you are not able to implement a union type.

Declaration merging

Unlike a type, an interface can be defined multiple times and will be treated as a single interface (all declarations will be merged), as shown in the following code block:

```
interface IUser {
  username: string
  email: string
  name: string
  age?: number
  website: string
  active: boolean
}

interface IUser {
  country: string
}

const user: IUser = {
  username: 'czantany',
  email: 'carlos@milkzoft.com',
```

```
    name: 'Carlos Santana',
    country: 'Mexico',
    age: 33,
    website: 'http://www.js.education',
    active: true
}
```

This is very useful when you need to extend your interfaces in different scenarios by just re-defining the same interface.

Summary

In this first chapter, we have learned some basic concepts that are very important for following the rest of the book, and that are crucial to working with React daily. We now know how to write declarative code, and we have a clear understanding of the difference between the components we create and the elements that React uses to display their instances on the screen.

We learned the reasons behind the choice of locating logic and templates together, and why that unpopular decision has been a big win for React. We went through the reasons why it is common to feel fatigued in the JavaScript ecosystem, but we have also seen how to avoid those problems by following an iterative approach.

We learned how to use TypeScript to create some basic types and interfaces. Finally, we have seen what the new `create-react-app` CLI is, and we are now ready to start writing some real code.

In the next chapter, you will learn how to use JSX/TSX code and apply very useful configurations to improve your code style.

Cleaning Up Your Code

2

This chapter assumes that you already have experience with JSX and you want to improve your skills to use it effectively. To use JSX/TSX without any problems or unexpected behaviors, it is essential to understand how it works under the hood, and the reasons why it is a useful tool for building UIs.

Our goal is to write clean JSX/TSX code, maintain it, and know where it comes from, how it gets translated to JavaScript, and what features it provides.

In this chapter, we will cover the following topics:

- What is JSX and why should we use it?
- What is Babel and how can we use it to write modern JavaScript code?
- The main features of JSX and the differences between HTML and JSX
- Best practices to write JSX in an elegant and maintainable way
- How linting, and ESLint in particular, can make our JavaScript code consistent across applications and teams
- The basics of functional programming and why following a functional paradigm will make us write better React components

Technical requirements

To complete this chapter, you will need the following:

- Node.js 12+
- Visual Studio Code

Using JSX

In the previous chapter, we saw how React changes the concept of separation of concerns, moving the boundaries inside components. We also learned how React uses the elements returned by the components to display the UI on the screen.

Let's now look at how we can declare our elements inside our components.

React provides two ways to define our elements. The first one is by using JavaScript functions, and the second one is by using JSX, an optional XML-like syntax. The following is a screenshot of the examples section of the official React.js website (`https://reactjs.org/#examples`):

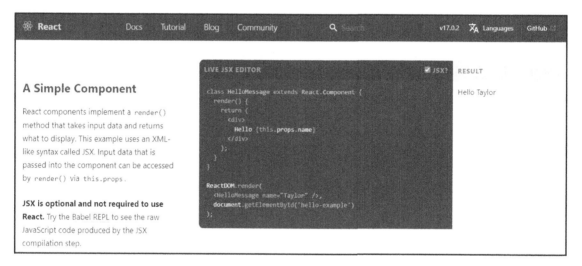

To begin with, JSX is one of the main reasons why people fail to approach React, because looking at the examples on the home page and seeing JavaScript mixed with HTML for the first time can seem strange to most of us.

As soon as we get used to it, we realize that it is very convenient, precisely because it is similar to HTML and looks very familiar to anyone who has already created UIs on the web. The opening and closing tags make it easier to represent nested trees of elements, something that would have been unreadable and hard to maintain using plain JavaScript.

Let's take a look at JSX in more detail in the following sub-sections.

Babel 7

To use JSX (and some features of ES6) in our code, we have to install the new Babel 7. Babel is a popular JavaScript compiler widely adopted within the React community.

First of all, it is important to clearly understand the problems it can solve for us and why we need to add a step to our process. The reason is that we want to use features of the language that have not yet been added in the browser, our target environment. Those advanced features make our code cleaner for developers, but the browser cannot understand and execute it.

The solution is to write our scripts in JSX and ES6 and, when we are ready to ship, we compile the sources into ES5, the standard specification implemented in major browsers today.

Babel can compile ES6 code into ES5 JavaScript, as well as compile JSX into JavaScript functions. This process is called **transpilation** because it compiles the source into a new source rather than into an executable.

In older versions of Babel 6.x, you installed the `babel-cli` package and you got `babel-node` and `babel-core`, and now everything is separated: `@babel/core`, `@babel/cli`, `@babel/node`, and so on.

To install Babel, we need to install `@babel/core` and `@babel/node` as follows:

```
npm install -g @babel/core @babel/node
```

If you do not want to install it globally (developers usually tend to avoid this), you can install Babel locally to a project and run it through an `npm` script, but for this chapter, a global instance is fine.

When the installation is complete, we can run the following command to compile any JavaScript file:

```
babel source.js -o output.js
```

One of the reasons why Babel is so powerful is because it is highly configurable. Babel is just a tool to transpile a source file into an output file, but to apply some transformations, we need to configure it.

Luckily, there are some very useful presets of configurations that we can easily install and use:

```
npm install -g @babel/preset-env @babel/preset-react
```

Once the installation is complete, we create a configuration file called .babelrc in the root folder, and put the following lines into it to tell Babel to use those presets:

```
{
  "presets": [
    "@babel/preset-env",
    "@babel/preset-react"
  ]
}
```

From this point on, we can write ES6 and JSX in our source files and execute the output files in the browser.

Creating our first element

Now that our environment has been set up to support JSX, we can dive into the most basic example: generating a div element. This is how you would create a div element with the _jsx function:

```
_jsx('div', {})
```

This is the JSX for creating a div element:

```
<div />
```

It looks similar to regular HTML.

The big difference is that we are writing the markup inside a .js file, but it is important to note that JSX is only syntactic sugar, and it gets transpiled into JavaScript before being executed in the browser.

In fact, our <div /> element is translated into _jsx('div', {}) when we run Babel, which is something we should always keep in mind when we write our templates.

In React 17, React.createElement('div') is deprecated, now internally using react/jsx-runtime to render the JSX, meaning that we will have something such as _jsx('div', {}). Basically, this means that you don't need to import the React object anymore in order to write JSX code.

DOM elements and React components

With JSX, we can create both HTML elements and React components; the only difference is whether or not they start with a capital letter.

For example, to render an HTML button, we use `<button />`, while to render the `Button` component, we use `<Button />`. The first button is transpiled into the following:

```
_jsx('button', {})
```

The second one is transpiled into the following:

```
_jsx(Button, {})
```

The difference here is that in the first call, we are passing the type of the DOM element as a string, while in the second call, we are passing the component itself, which means that it should exist in the scope to work.

As you may have noticed, JSX supports self-closing tags, which are pretty good for keeping the code terse and do not require us to repeat unnecessary tags.

Props

JSX is very convenient when your DOM elements or React components have props. Using XML is pretty easy to set attributes on elements:

```
<img src="https://www.js.education/images/logo.png" alt="JS Education" />
```

The equivalent in JavaScript would be as follows:

```
_jsx("img", {
  src: "https://www.js.education/images/logo.png",
  alt: "JS Education"
})
```

This is far less readable, and even with only a couple of attributes, it is harder to read without a bit of reasoning.

Children

JSX allows you to define children to describe the tree of elements and compose complex UIs. A basic example is a link with text inside it, as follows:

```
<a href="https://js.education">Click me!</a>
```

This would be transpiled into the following:

```
_jsx(
  "a",
  { href: "https://www.js.education" },
  "Click me!"
)
```

Our link can be enclosed inside a `div` element for some layout requirements, and the JSX snippet to achieve that is as follows:

```
<div>
  <a href="https://www.js.education">Click me!</a>
</div>
```

The JavaScript equivalent is as follows:

```
_jsx(
  "div",
  null,
  _jsx(
    "a",
    { href: "https://www.js.education" },
    "Click me!"
  )
)
```

It should now be clear how the *XML-like* syntax of JSX makes everything more readable and maintainable, but it is always important to know the JavaScript parallel to our JSX has control over the creation of elements. The good part is that we are not limited to having elements as children of elements, but we can use JavaScript expressions, such as functions or variables.

To do this, we have to enclose the expression within curly braces:

```
<div>
  Hello, {variable}.
  I'm a {() => console.log('Function')}.
</div>
```

The same applies to non-string attributes, as follows:

```
<a href={this.createLink()}>Click me!</a>
```

As you see, any variable or function should be enclosed with curly braces.

Differences with HTML

So far, we have looked at the similarities between JSX and HTML. Let's now look at the little differences between them and the reasons they exist.

Attributes

We must always keep in mind that JSX is not a standard language and that it gets transpiled into JavaScript. Because of this, some attributes cannot be used.

For example, instead of class, we have to use className, and instead of for, we have to use htmlFor, as follows:

```
<label className="awesome-label" htmlFor="name" />
```

The reason for this is that class and for are reserved words in JavaScript.

Style

A pretty significant difference is the way the style attribute works. We will look at how to use it in more detail in *Chapter 8, Making Your Components Look Beautiful*, but now we will focus on the way it works.

The style attribute does not accept a CSS string as the HTML parallel does, but it expects a JavaScript object where the style names are *camelCased*:

```
<div style={{ backgroundColor: 'red' }} />
```

As you can see, you can pass an object to the style prop, meaning you can even have your styles in a separate variable if you want:

```
const styles = {
  backgroundColor: 'red'
}

<div style={styles} />
```

This is the best way to have better control of your inline styles.

Root

One important difference with HTML worth mentioning is that since JSX elements get translated into JavaScript functions, and you cannot return two functions in JavaScript, whenever you have multiple elements at the same level, you are forced to wrap them in a parent.

Let's look at a simple example:

```
<div />
<div />
```

This gives us the following error:

```
Adjacent JSX elements must be wrapped in an enclosing tag.
```

On the other hand, the following works:

```
<div>
  <div />
  <div />
</div>
```

Before, React forced you to return an element wrapped with an `<div>` element or any other tag; since React 16.2.0, it is possible to return an array directly as follows:

```
return [
  <li key="1">First item</li>,
  <li key="2">Second item</li>,
  <li key="3">Third item</li>
]
```

Or you can even return a string directly, as shown in the following code block:

```
return 'Hello World!'
```

Also, React now has a new feature called `Fragment` that also works as a special wrapper for elements. It can be specified with `React.Fragment`:

```
import { Fragment } from 'react'

return (
  <Fragment>
    <h1>An h1 heading</h1>
    Some text here.
```

```
      <h2>An h2 heading</h2>
      More text here.
      Even more text here.
    </Fragment>
  )
```

Or you can use empty tags (<></>):

```
  return (
    <>
      <ComponentA />
      <ComponentB />
      <ComponentC />
    </>
  )
```

Fragment won't render anything visible on the DOM; it is just a helper tag to wrap your React elements or components.

Spaces

There's one thing that could be a little bit tricky in the beginning and, again, it concerns the fact that we should always keep in mind that JSX is not HTML, even if it has XML-like syntax. JSX handles the spaces between text and elements differently from HTML, in a way that's counter-intuitive.

Consider the following snippet:

```
  <div>
    <span>My</span>
    name is
    <span>Carlos</span>
  </div>
```

In a browser that interprets HTML, this code would give you My name is Carlos, which is exactly what we expect.

In JSX, the same code would be rendered as MynameisCarlos, which is because the three nested lines get transpiled as individual children of the div element, without taking the spaces into account. A common solution to get the same output is putting a space explicitly between the elements, as follows:

```
  <div>
    <span>My</span>
    {' '}
    name is
```

```
  {' '}
  <span>Carlos</span>
</div>
```

As you may have noticed, we are using an empty string wrapped inside a JavaScript expression to force the compiler to apply a space between the elements.

Boolean attributes

A couple more things are worth mentioning before really starting regarding the way you define Boolean attributes in JSX. If you set an attribute without a value, JSX assumes that its value is `true`, following the same behavior as the HTML `disabled` attribute, for example.

This means that if we want to set an attribute to `false`, we have to declare it explicitly as false:

```
<button disabled />
React.createElement("button", { disabled: true })
```

The following is another example of the Boolean attribute:

```
<button disabled={false} />
React.createElement("button", { disabled: false })
```

This can be confusing in the beginning, because we may think that omitting an attribute would mean `false`, but it is not like that. With React, we should always be explicit to avoid confusion.

Spread attributes

An important feature is the **spread attribute** operator (. . .), which comes from the rest/spread properties for ECMAScript proposal, and is very convenient whenever we want to pass all the attributes of a JavaScript object to an element.

A common practice that leads to fewer bugs is not to pass entire JavaScript objects down to children by reference, but to use their primitive values, which can be easily validated, making components more robust and error-proof.

Let's see how it works:

```
const attrs = {
  id: 'myId',
  className: 'myClass'
}
return <div {...attrs} />
```

The preceding code gets transpiled into the following:

```
var attrs = {
  id: 'myId',
  className: 'myClass'
}

return _jsx('div', attrs)
```

Template literals

Templates literals are string literals allowing embedded expressions. You can use multiline strings and string interpolation features with them.

Template literals are enclosed by the backtick (` `` `) character instead of double or single quotes. Also, template literals can contain placeholders. You can add them using the dollar sign and curly braces (`${expression}`):

```
const name = `Carlos`
const multilineHtml = `<p>
  This is a multiline string
  </p>`
console.log(`Hi, my name is ${name}`)
```

Common patterns

Now that we know how JSX works and can master it, we are ready to see how to use it in the right way following some useful conventions and techniques.

Multiline

Let's start with a very simple one. As stated previously, one of the main reasons we should prefer JSX over React's `_jsx` function is because of its XML-like syntax, and because balanced opening and closing tags are perfect to represent a tree of nodes.

Therefore, we should try to use it in the right way and get the most out of it. One example is as follows; whenever we have nested elements, we should always go multiline:

```
<div>
  <Header />
  <div>
    <Main content={...} />
  </div>
</div>
```

This is preferable to the following:

```
<div><Header /><div><Main content={...} /></div></div>
```

The exception is if the children are not elements such as text or variables. In that case, it makes sense to remain on the same line and avoid adding noise to the markup, as follows:

```
<div>
  <Alert>{message}</Alert>
  <Button>Close</Button>
</div>
```

Always remember to wrap your elements inside parentheses when you write them on multiple lines. JSX always gets replaced by functions, and functions written on a new line can give you an unexpected result because of automatic semicolon insertion. Suppose, for example, that you are returning JSX from your render method, which is how you create UIs in React.

The following example works fine because the div element is on the same line as the return:

```
return <div />
```

The following, however, is not right:

```
return
  <div />
```

The reason for this is that you would then have the following:

```
return
_jsx("div", null)
```

This is why you have to wrap the statement in parentheses, as follows:

```
return (
  <div />
)
```

Multi-properties

A common problem in writing JSX comes when an element has multiples attributes. One solution is to write all the attributes on the same line, but this would lead to very long lines that we do not want in our code (see the following section for how to enforce coding style guides).

A common solution is to write each attribute on a new line, with one level of indentation, and then align the closing bracket with the opening tag:

```
<button
  foo="bar"
  veryLongPropertyName="baz"
  onSomething={this.handleSomething}
/>
```

Conditionals

Things get more interesting when we start working with **conditionals**, for example, if we want to render some components only when certain conditions are matched. The fact that we can use JavaScript in our conditions is a big plus, but there are many different ways to express conditions in JSX, and it is important to understand the benefits and problems of each one of these to write code that is both readable and maintainable.

Suppose we want to show a logout button only if the user is currently logged in to our application.

A simple snippet to start with is as follows:

```
let button
if (isLoggedIn) {
  button = <LogoutButton />
}
return <div>{button}</div>
```

This works, but it is not very readable, especially if there are multiple components and multiple conditions.

In JSX, we can use an inline condition:

```
<div>
  {isLoggedIn && <LoginButton />}
</div>
```

This works because if the condition is `false`, nothing gets rendered, but if the condition is `true`, the `createElement` function of `LoginButton` gets called, and the element is returned to compose the resulting tree.

If the condition has an alternative (the classic `if...else` statement) and we want, for example, to show a logout button if the user is logged in and a login button otherwise, we can use JavaScript's `if...else` statement as follows:

```
let button

if (isLoggedIn) {
  button = <LogoutButton />
} else {
  button = <LoginButton />
}
return <div>{button}</div>
```

Alternatively, and better still, we can use a ternary condition that makes the code more compact:

```
<div>
  {isLoggedIn ? <LogoutButton /> : <LoginButton />}
</div>
```

You can find the ternary condition used in popular repositories, such as the Redux real-world example (`https://github.com/reactjs/redux/blob/master/examples/real-world/src/components/List.js#L28`), where the ternary is used to show a **Loading** label if the component is fetching the data, or **Load More** inside a button depending on the value of the `isFetching` variable:

```
<button [...]>
  {isFetching ? 'Loading...' : 'Load More'}
</button>
```

Let's now look at the best solution for when things get more complicated and, for example, we have to check more than one variable to determine whether to render a component or not:

```
<div>
  {dataIsReady && (isAdmin || userHasPermissions) &&
    <SecretData />
  }
</div>
```

In this case, it is clear that using the inline condition is a good solution, but the readability is strongly impacted. Instead, we can create a helper function inside our component and use it in JSX to verify the condition:

```
const canShowSecretData = () => {
  const { dataIsReady, isAdmin, userHasPermissions } = props
  return dataIsReady && (isAdmin || userHasPermissions)
}
return (
  <div>
    {this.canShowSecretData() && <SecretData />}
  </div>
```

As you can see, this change makes the code more readable and the condition more explicit. If you look at this code in 6 months, you will still find it clear just by reading the name of the function.

The same applies to computed properties. Suppose you have two single properties for currency and value. Instead of creating the price string inside render, you can create a function:

```
const getPrice = () => {
  return `${props.currency}${props.value}`
}
return <div>{getPrice()}</div>
```

This is better because it is isolated and you can easily test it if it contains logic.

Going back to conditional statements, other solutions require using external dependencies. A good practice is to avoid external dependencies as much as we can to keep our bundle smaller, but it may be worth it in this particular case because improving the readability of our templates is a big win.

The first solution is render-if, which we can install with the following:

```
npm install --save render-if
```

We can then easily use it in our projects, as follows:

```
const { dataIsReady, isAdmin, userHasPermissions } = props

const canShowSecretData = renderIf(
  dataIsReady && (isAdmin || userHasPermissions)
);
return (
  <div>
```

```
      {canShowSecretData(<SecretData />)}
    </div>
  );
```

Here, we wrap our conditions inside the `renderIf` function.

The utility function that gets returned can be used as a function that receives the JSX markup to be shown when the condition is `true`.

One goal is to never add too much logic inside our components. Some of them will require a bit of it, but we should try to keep them as simple as possible so that we can easily spot and fix errors.

We should at least try to keep the `renderIf` method as clean as possible and to do that, we can use another utility library, called `react-only-if`, which lets us write our components as if the condition is always `true` by setting the conditional function using a **Higher-Order Component (HOC)**.

We will talk about HOCs extensively in *Chapter 4, Exploring Popular Composition Patterns*, but for now, you just need to know that they are functions that receive a component and return an enhanced one by adding some properties or modifying their behavior.

To use the library, we need to install it as follows:

```
npm install --save react-only-if
```

Once it is installed, we can use it in our apps in the following way:

```
import onlyIf from 'react-only-if'

const SecretDataOnlyIf = onlyIf(
  ({ dataIsReady, isAdmin, userHasPermissions }) => dataIsReady &&
  (isAdmin || userHasPermissions)
)(SecretData)

const MyComponent = () => (
  <div>
    <SecretDataOnlyIf
      dataIsReady={...}
      isAdmin={...}
      userHasPermissions={...}
    />
  </div>
)

export default MyComponent
```

As you can see here, there is no logic at all inside the component itself.

We pass the condition as the first parameter of the `onlyIf` function, and when the condition is matched, the component is rendered.

The function used to validate the condition receives the props, state, and context of the component.

In this way, we avoid polluting our component with conditionals so that it is easier to understand and reason about.

Loops

A very common operation in UI development is to display lists of items. When it comes to showing lists, using JavaScript as a template language is a very good idea.

If we write a function that returns an array inside our JSX template, each element of the array gets compiled into an element.

As we have seen before, we can use any JavaScript expressions inside curly braces, and the most common way to generate an array of elements, given an array of objects, is to use `map`.

Let's dive into a real-world example. Suppose you have a list of users, each one with a name property attached to it.

To create an unordered list to show the users, you can do the following:

```
<ul>
  {users.map(user => <li>{user.name}</li>)}
</ul>
```

This snippet is incredibly simple and incredibly powerful at the same time, where the power of HTML and JavaScript converge.

Control statements

Conditionals and loops are very common operations in UI templates, and you may feel wrong using the JavaScript ternary or the `map` function to perform them. JSX has been built in such a way that it only abstracts the creation of the elements, leaving the logic parts to real JavaScript, which is great except that sometimes, the code becomes less clear.

In general, we aim to remove all the logic from our components, and especially from our render methods, but sometimes we have to show and hide elements according to the state of the application, and very often we have to loop through collections and arrays.

If you feel that using JSX for that kind of operation will make your code more readable, there is a Babel plugin available to do just that: `jsx-control-statements`.

This follows the same philosophy as JSX, and it does not add any real functionality to the language; it is just syntactic sugar that gets compiled into JavaScript.

Let's see how it works.

First of all, we have to install it:

```
npm install --save jsx-control-statements
```

Once it is installed, we have to add it to the list of our Babel plugins in our `.babelrc` file:

```
"plugins": ["jsx-control-statements"]
```

From now on, we can use the syntax provided by the plugin and Babel will transpile it together with the common JSX syntax.

A conditional statement written using the plugin looks like the following snippet:

```
<If condition={this.canShowSecretData}>
  <SecretData />
</If>
```

This gets transpiled into a ternary expression as follows:

```
{canShowSecretData ? <SecretData /> : null}
```

The `If` component is great, but if, for some reason, you have nested conditions in your render method, it can easily become messy and hard to follow. This is where the `Choose` component comes in handy:

```
<Choose>
  <When condition={...}>
    <span>if</span>
  </When>
  <When condition={...}>
    <span>else if</span>
  </When>
  <Otherwise>
    <span>else</span>
  </Otherwise>
</Choose>
```

Please note that the preceding code gets transpiled into multiple ternaries.

Finally, there is a component (always remember that we are not talking about real components but just syntactic sugar) to manage the loops that is also very convenient:

```
<ul>
  <For each="user" of={this.props.users}>
    <li>{user.name}</li>
  </For>
</ul>
```

The preceding code gets transpiled into a `map` function – no magic there.

If you are used to using **linters**, you might wonder why the linter is not complaining about that code. The `user` variable does not exist before the transpilation, nor is it wrapped in a function. To avoid those linting errors, there is another plugin to install: `eslint-plugin-jsx-control-statements`.

If you did not understand the previous sentence, don't worry; we will talk about linting in the upcoming section.

Sub-rendering

It is worth stressing that we always want to keep our components very small and our render methods very clean and simple.

However, that is not an easy goal, especially when you are creating an application iteratively, and in the first iteration, you are not sure exactly how to split the components into smaller ones. So, what should we be doing when the render method becomes too big to maintain? One solution is to split it into smaller functions in a way that lets us keep all the logic in the same component.

Let's look at an example:

```
const renderUserMenu = () => {
  // JSX for user menu
}
const renderAdminMenu = () => {
  // JSX for admin menu
}
return (
  <div>
    <h1>Welcome back!</h1>
    {userExists && renderUserMenu()}
    {userIsAdmin && renderAdminMenu()}
  </div>
)
```

This is not always considered best practice because it seems more obvious to split the component into smaller ones. However, sometimes it helps to keep the render method cleaner. For example, in the Redux real-world examples, a sub-render method is used to render the *load more* button.

Now that we are JSX power users, it is time to move on and see how to follow a style guide within our code to make it consistent.

Styling code

In this section, you will learn how to implement EditorConfig and ESLint to improve your code quality by validating your code style. It is important to have a standard code style in your team and avoid using different code styles.

EditorConfig

EditorConfig helps developers to maintain consistent coding styles between different IDEs.

EditorConfig is supported by a lot of editors. You can check whether your editor is supported or not on the official website, `https://www.editorconfig.org`.

You need to create a file called `.editorconfig` in your `root` directory – the configuration I use is this one:

```
root = true

[*]
indent_style = space
indent_size = 2
end_of_line = lf
charset = utf-8
trim_trailing_whitespace = true
insert_final_newline = true

[*.html]
indent_size = 4

[*.css]
indent_size = 4

[*.md]
trim_trailing_whitespace = false
```

You can affect all the files with `[*]`, and specific files with `[.extension]`.

Prettier

Prettier is an opinionated code formatter, supported by many languages that can be integrated with most editors. This plugin is really useful because you can format the code on saving and you don't need to discuss the code style in code reviews, which will save you a lot of time and energy.

If you work with Visual Studio Code, you have to install the Prettier extension first:

Then, if you want to configure the option to format when you save a file, you need to go to **Settings**, search `Format on Save`, and check that option:

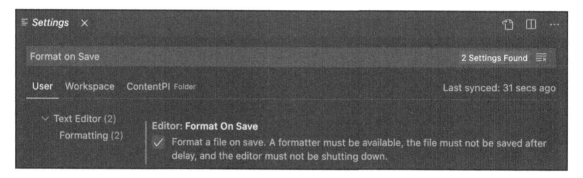

This will affect all your projects because it is a global setting. If you want to apply this option just in a specific project, you have to create a `.vscode` folder inside your project and a `settings.json` file with the following code:

```
{
    "editor.defaultFormatter": "esbenp.prettier-vscode",
    "editor.formatOnSave": true
}
```

Then you can configure the options you want in your `.prettierrc` file – this is the configuration I normally use:

```
{
    "arrowParens": "avoid",
    "bracketSpacing": true,
    "jsxSingleQuote": false,
    "printWidth": 100,
    "quoteProps": "as-needed",
    "semi": false,
    "singleQuote": true,
```

```
    "tabWidth": 2,
    "trailingComma": "none",
    "useTabs": false
  }
```

This will help you or your team to standardize the code style.

ESLint

We always try to write the best code possible, but sometimes errors happen, and spending a few hours catching a bug due to a typo is very frustrating. Luckily, some tools can help us check the correctness of our code as soon as we type it. These tools are not able to tell us whether our code is going to do what it's supposed to do, but they can help us to avoid syntactical errors.

If you come from a static language, such as C#, you are used to getting that kind of warning inside your IDE. Douglas Crockford made linting popular in JavaScript with JSLint (initially released in 2002) a few years ago; then we had JSHint, and finally, the de facto standard in the React world nowadays is ESLint.

ESLint is an open-source project released in 2013 that became popular thanks to the fact that it is highly configurable and extensible.

In the JavaScript ecosystem, where libraries and techniques change very quickly, it is crucial to have a tool that can be easily extended with plugins, and rules that can be enabled and disabled when needed. Most importantly, nowadays we use transpilers, such as Babel, and experimental features that are not part of the standard version of JavaScript, so we need to be able to tell our linter which rules we are following in our source files. Not only does a linter help us to make fewer errors, or at least find those errors sooner, but it enforces some common coding style guides, which is important especially in big teams with many developers, each one with their favorite coding style.

It is very hard to read the code in a code base where different files, or even various functions, are written using inconsistent styles. For that reason, let's look at ESLint in more detail.

Installation

First of all, we have to install ESLint and some plugins as follows:

```
npm install -g eslint eslint-config-airbnb eslint-config-prettier eslint-
plugin-import eslint-plugin-jsx-a11y eslint-plugin-prettier eslint-plugin-
react
```

Once the executable is installed, we can run it with the following command:

```
eslint source.ts
```

The output will tell us if there are errors within the file.

When we install and run it for the first time, we do not see any errors because it is completely configurable and it does not come with any default rules.

Configuration

Let's start configuring ESLint. It can be configured using a `.eslintrc` file that lives in the root folder of the project. To add some rules, let's create a `.eslintrc` file configured for TypeScript and add one basic rule:

```
{
  "parser": "@typescript-eslint/parser",
  "plugins": ["@typescript-eslint", "prettier"],
  "extends": [
    "airbnb",
    "eslint:recommended",
    "plugin:@typescript-eslint/eslint-recommended",
    "plugin:@typescript-eslint/recommended",
    "plugin:prettier/recommended"
  ],
  "settings": {
    "import/extensions": [".js", ".jsx", ".ts", ".tsx"],
    "import/parsers": {
      "@typescript-eslint/parser": [".ts", ".tsx"]
    },
    "import/resolver": {
      "node": {
        "extensions": [".js", ".jsx", ".ts", ".tsx"]
      }
    }
  },
  "rules": {
    "semi": [2, "never"]
```

```
        }
    }
```

This configuration file needs a bit of explanation: `"semi"` is the name of the rule and `[2, "never"]` is the value. It is not very intuitive the first time you see it.

ESLint rules have three levels that determine the severity of the problem:

- `off` (or 0): The rule is disabled.
- `warn` (or 1): The rule is a warning.
- `error` (or 2): The rule throws an error.

We are using the 2 value because we want ESLint to throw an error every time our code does not follow the rule. The second parameter tells ESLint that we want the semicolon to never be used (the opposite is *always*). ESLint and its plugins are very well documented, and for any single rule, you can find the description of the rule and some examples of when it passes and when it fails.

Now create an `index.ts` file with the following content:

```
const foo = 'bar';
```

If we run `eslint index.js`, we get the following:

```
Extra semicolon (semi)
```

This is great; we set up the linter and it is helping us follow our first rule.

Here are other rules that I prefer to turn off or change:

```
"rules": {
    "semi": [2, "never"],
    "@typescript-eslint/class-name-casing": "off",
    "@typescript-eslint/interface-name-prefix": "off",
    "@typescript-eslint/member-delimiter-style": "off",
    "@typescript-eslint/no-var-requires": "off",
    "@typescript-eslint/ban-ts-ignore": "off",
    "@typescript-eslint/no-use-before-define": "off",
    "@typescript-eslint/ban-ts-comment": "off",
    "@typescript-eslint/explicit-module-boundary-types": "off",
    "no-restricted-syntax": "off",
    "no-use-before-define": "off",
    "import/extensions": "off",
    "import/prefer-default-export": "off",
    "max-len": [
      "error",
```

```
      {
        "code": 100,
        "tabWidth": 2
      }
    ],
    "no-param-reassign": "off",
    "no-underscore-dangle": "off",
    "react/jsx-filename-extension": [
      1,
      {
        "extensions": [".tsx"]
      }
    ],
    "import/no-unresolved": "off",
    "consistent-return": "off",
    "jsx-a11y/anchor-is-valid": "off",
    "sx-a11y/click-events-have-key-events": "off",
    "jsx-a11y/no-noninteractive-element-interactions": "off",
    "jsx-a11y/click-events-have-key-events": "off",
    "jsx-a11y/no-static-element-interactions": "off",
    "react/jsx-props-no-spreading": "off",
    "jsx-a11y/label-has-associated-control": "off",
    "react/jsx-one-expression-per-line": "off",
    "no-prototype-builtins": "off",
    "no-nested-ternary": "off",
    "prettier/prettier": [
      "error",
      {
        "endOfLine": "auto"
      }
    ]
  ]
}
```

Git Hooks

To avoid having unlinted code in our repository, what we can do is add ESLint at one point of our process using Git Hooks. For example, we can use husky to run our linter in a Git Hook called pre-commit, and it is also useful to run our unit tests on the Hook called pre-push.

To install husky, you need to run the following command:

```
npm install --save-dev husky
```

Then, in our `package.json` file, we can add this node to configure the tasks we want to run in the Git Hooks:

```json
{
  "scripts": {
    "lint": "eslint --ext .tsx,.ts src",
    "lint:fix": "eslint --ext .tsx,.ts --fix src",
    "test": "jest src"
  },
  "husky": {
    "hooks": {
      "pre-commit": "npm lint",
      "pre-push": "npm test"
    }
  }
}
```

There is a special option (flag) for the ESlint command called `--fix` – with this option, ESLint will try to fix all our linter errors automatically (not all of them). Be careful with this option because sometimes it can affect a little bit of our code style. Another useful flag is `--ext` to specify the extensions of the files we want to validate, in this case just the `.tsx` and `.ts` files.

In the next section, you will learn about how **Functional Programming (FP)** works and topics such as first-class objects, purity, immutability, currying, and composition.

Functional programming

Apart from following the best practices when we write JSX and using a linter to enforce consistency and find errors earlier, there is one more thing we can do to clean up our code: follow an FP style.

As discussed in *Chapter 1, Taking Your First Steps with React*, React has a declarative programming approach that makes our code more readable. FP is a declarative paradigm, where side effects are avoided and data is considered immutable to make the code easier to maintain and reason about.

Don't consider the following sub-sections as an exhaustive guide to FP; it is only an introduction to get started with some concepts that are commonly used in React of which you should be aware.

First-class functions

JavaScript has first-class functions because they are treated like any other variable, meaning you can pass a function as a parameter to other functions, or it can be returned by another function and be assigned as a value to a variable.

This allows us to introduce the concept of **Higher-Order Functions (HoFs)**. HoFs are functions that take a function as a parameter, and optionally some other parameters, and return a function. The returned function is usually enhanced with some special behaviors.

Let's look at an example:

```
const add = (x, y) => x + y

const log = fn => (...args) => {
  return fn(...args)
}

const logAdd = log(add)
```

Here, a function is adding two numbers that enhance a function that logs all the parameters and then executes the original function.

This concept is pretty important to understand because in the React world, a common pattern is to use HOCs to treat our components as functions, and to enhance them with common behaviors. We will see HOCs and other patterns in *Chapter 4, Exploring Popular Composition Patterns*.

Purity

An important aspect of FP is to write pure functions. You will encounter this concept very often in the React ecosystem, especially if you look into libraries such as Redux.

What does it mean for a function to be pure?

A function is pure when there are no side effects, which means that the function does not change anything that is not local to the function itself.

For example, a function that changes the state of an application, or modifies variables defined in the upper scope, or a function that touches external entities, such as the **Document Object Model (DOM)**, is considered impure. Impure functions are harder to debug, and most of the time it is not possible to apply them multiple times and expect to get the same result.

For example, the following function is pure:

```
const add = (x, y) => x + y
```

It can be run multiple times, always getting the same result, because nothing is stored anywhere and nothing gets modified.

The following function is not pure:

```
let x = 0
const add = (y) => (x = x + y)
```

Running add(1) twice, we get two different results. The first time we get 1, but the second time we get 2, even if we call the same function with the same parameter. The reason we get that behavior is that the global state gets modified after every execution.

Immutability

We have seen how to write pure functions that don't mutate the state, but what if we need to change the value of a variable? In FP, a function, instead of changing the value of a variable, creates a new variable with a new value and returns it. This way of working with data is called **immutability**.

An immutable value is a value that cannot be changed.

Let's look at an example:

```
const add3 = arr => arr.push(3)
const myArr = [1, 2]

add3(myArr); // [1, 2, 3]
add3(myArr); // [1, 2, 3, 3]
```

The preceding function doesn't follow immutability because it changes the value of the given array. Again, if we call the same function twice, we get different results.

We can change the preceding function to make it immutable using concat, which returns a new array without modifying the given one:

```
const add3 = arr => arr.concat(3)
const myArr = [1, 2]
const result1 = add3(myArr) // [1, 2, 3]
const result2 = add3(myArr) // [1, 2, 3]
```

After we have run the function twice, myArr still has its original value.

Currying

A common technique in FP is currying. **Currying** is the process of converting a function that takes multiple arguments into a function one argument at a time and returning another function. Let's look at an example to clarify the concept.

Let's start with the `add` function we have seen before and transform it into a curried function.

Say we have the following code:

```
const add = (x, y) => x + y
```

We can instead define the function as follows:

```
const add = x => y => x + y
```

We use it in the following way:

```
const add1 = add(1)
add1(2); // 3
add1(3); // 4
```

This is a pretty convenient way of writing functions because, since the first value is stored after the application of the first parameter, we can reuse the second function multiple times.

Composition

Finally, an important concept in FP that can be applied to React is **composition**. Functions (and components) can be combined to produce new functions with more advanced features and properties.

Consider the following functions:

```
const add = (x, y) => x + y
const square = x => x * x
```

These functions can be composed together to create a new function that adds two numbers and then doubles the result:

```
const addAndSquare = (x, y) => square(add(x, y))
```

Following this paradigm, we end up with small, simple, testable pure functions that can be composed together.

FP and UIs

The last step is to learn how we can use FP to build UIs, which is what we use React for.

We can think about a UI as a function to which the state of the application is applied as follows:

```
UI = f(state)
```

We expect this function to be idempotent so that it returns the same UI given the same state of the application.

Using React, we create our UIs using components we can consider functions, as we will see in the following chapters.

Components can be composed to form the final UI, which is a property of FP.

There are a lot of similarities in the way we build UIs with React and the principles of FP, and the more we are aware of it, the better our code will be.

Summary

In this chapter, we learned a great deal about how JSX works and how to use it in the right way in our components. We started from the basics of the syntax to create a solid knowledge base that will enable us to master JSX and its features.

In the second part, we looked at how to configure Prettier and how ESLint and its plugins can help us find problems faster and enforce a consistent style guide across our code base.

Finally, we went through the basics of FP to understand the important concepts to use when writing a React application.

Now that our code is clean, we are ready to start digging deeper into React and learn how to write truly reusable components in the next chapter.

2
How React Works

This section explains how to use the new React Hooks, their rules, and how you can create your own Hooks. Also covered will be how you can migrate your current React class components applications to the new React Hooks.

We will cover the following chapters in this section:

- *Chapter 3, React Hooks*
- *Chapter 4, Exploring Popular Composition Patterns*
- *Chapter 5, Understanding GraphQL with a Real Project*
- *Chapter 6, Managing Data*
- *Chapter 7, Writing Code for the Browser*

3
React Hooks

React is evolving really quickly and since React 16.8, the new React Hooks have been introduced, which are a game-changer as regards React development in that they will boost the speed of coding and improve the performance of our applications. React enables us to write React applications using only functional components, meaning there is no longer any need to use class components.

In this chapter, we will cover the following topics:

- The new React Hooks and how to use them
- The rules of the Hooks
- How to migrate a class component to React Hooks
- Understanding the component life cycle with Hooks and effects
- How to fetch data with Hooks
- How to memorize components, values, and functions with `memo`, `useMemo`, and `useCallback`
- How to implement `useReducer`

Technical requirements

To complete this chapter, you will require the following:

- Node.js 12+
- Visual Studio Code

You can find the code for this chapter in the book's GitHub repository at `https://github.com/PacktPublishing/React-17-Design-Patterns-and-Best-Practices-Third-Edition/tree/main/Chapter03`.

Introducing React Hooks

React Hooks are a new addition in React 16.8. They let you use state and other React features without writing a React class component. React Hooks are also backward-compatible, which means it does not contain any breaking change and it does not replace your knowledge of React concepts. Over the course of this chapter, we will see an overview of Hooks for experienced React users, and we are also going to learn some of the most common React Hooks such as `useState, useEffect, useMemo, useCallback` and `memo`.

No breaking changes

Many people think that with the new React Hooks, class components are now obsolete in React, but this statement is incorrect. There are no plans to remove classes from React. The Hooks don't replace your knowledge of React concepts. Instead, Hooks provide a more direct API to the React concepts, such as props, state, context, refs, and life cycle, which you already know.

Using the State Hook

You probably know how to use the component state by using it in a class with `this.setState`. Now you can use the component state by using the new React `useState` Hook.

First, you need to extract the `useState` Hook from React:

```
import { useState } from 'react'
```

 Since React 17, the React object is no longer required to render JSX code.

Then you need to declare the state you want to use by defining the state and the setter for this specific state:

```
const Counter = () => {
  const [counter, setCounter] = useState<number>(0)
}
```

As you can see, we are declaring the counter state with the `setCounter` setter and we are specifying that we will only accept numbers, and finally, we set the initial value with zero.

In order to test our state, we need to create a method that will be triggered by the `onClick` event:

```
const Counter = () => {
  const [counter, setCounter] = useState<number>(0)
  const handleCounter = (operation) => {
    if (operation === 'add') {
      return setCounter(counter + 1)
    }
    return setCounter(counter - 1)
  }
}
```

Finally, we can render the `counter` state and some buttons to increase or decrease the `counter` state:

```
return (
  <p>
    Counter: {counter} <br />
    <button onClick={() => handleCounter('add')}>+ Add</button>
    <button onClick={() => handleCounter('subtract')}>- Subtract</button>
  </p>
)
```

If you click on the **+ Add** button one time, you should see **1** for **Counter**:

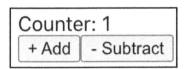

And if you click the **- Subtract** button twice, then you should see **-1** for **Counter**:

Counter: -1
+ Add | - Subtract

As you can see, the `useState` Hook is a game-changer in React and makes it very easy to handle the state in a functional component.

Rules of Hooks

React Hooks are basically JavaScript functions, but there are two rules that you need to follow in order to use them. React provides a linter plugin to enforce those rules for you, which you can install by running the following command:

```
npm install --save-dev eslint-plugin-react-hooks
```

Let's look at these two rules.

Rule 1: Only call Hooks at the top level

From the official React documentation (`https://reactjs.org/docs/hooks-rules.html`):

> *"**Don't call Hooks inside loops, conditions, or nested functions**. Instead, always use Hooks at the top level of your React function. By following this rule, you ensure that Hooks are called in the same order each time a component renders. That's what allows React to correctly preserve the state of Hooks between multiple useState and useEffect calls."*

Rule 2: Only call Hooks from React Functions

From the official React documentation (`https://reactjs.org/docs/hooks-rules.html`):

> *"Don't call Hooks from regular JavaScript functions. Instead, you can:*

- Call Hooks from React function components.
- Call Hooks from custom Hooks (we'll learn about them on the next page).

> *By following this rule, you ensure that all stateful logic in a component is clearly visible from its source code."*

In the next section, we will learn how to migrate a class component to use the new React Hooks.

Migrating a class component to React Hooks

Let's transform a code that is currently using class components and is also using some life cycle methods. In this example, we are fetching the issues from a GitHub repository and listing them.

For this example, you will need to install `axios` to perform the fetch:

```
npm install axios
```

This is the class component version:

```
// Dependencies
import { Component } from 'react'
import axios from 'axios'

// Types
type Issue = {
  number: number
  title: string
  state: string
}
type Props = {}
type State = { issues: Issue[] };

class Issues extends Component<Props, State> {
  constructor(props: Props) {
    super(props)

    this.state = {
      issues: []
    }
  }

  componentDidMount() {
    axios
      .get('https://api.github.com/repos/ContentPI/ContentPI/issues')
      .then((response: any) => {
        this.setState({
          issues: response.data
        })
      })
  }

  render() {
```

```
    const { issues = [] } = this.state

    return (
      <>
        <h1>ContentPI Issues</h1>

        {issues.map((issue: Issue) => (
          <p key={issue.title}>
            <strong>#{issue.number}</strong> {' '}
            <a href=
{`https://github.com/ContentPI/ContentPI/issues/${issue.number}`}
              target="_blank">{issue.title}</a> {' '}
            {issue.state}
          </p>
        ))}
      </>
    )
  }
}

export default Issues
```

If you render this component, you should see something like this:

ContentPI Issues

#99 Fix Playground open

#97 CPI-35 - Added Drag-n-Drop Functionality to sort fields open

#81 Edit Reference Field open

#80 Edit Dropdown Field open

#75 Page for empty Content (when you don't have any model) open

#74 Page for empty Schema (create your first model) open

#73 Remove all any on ContentPI open

#71 Remove all any in @contentpi/ui open

#69 Create a Toast Alert open

#62 Removing a reference field should also remove the reference and its values open

#61 When a user removes a field we need to make sure we are removing all the related values first open

#60 Validate that a model does not have content before delete it open

#52 Add Italian Translations open

#51 Add Deutsch Translation open

#50 Add Chinese Translation open

#49 Add French Translations open

#48 Settings: User profile open

#47 Settings: Analytics (Limits) open

#46 Settings: Stages (Environments) open

#45 Settings: Teams open

#44 Settings: Create roles for users open

#43 Settings: Users page (list all registered users) open

#42 Settings: Danger Zone page to delete an Application open

#41 Add Settings page open

#40 Remove Publish and Unpublish options for I18n entries, just Delete option should be there open

#39 Edit I18n entry open

#38 Create new I18n entry open

#35 Order fields by drag and drop open

#28 Fix Breadcrumbs open

#26 Docker implementation open

Now, let's transform our code to be a functional component using React Hooks. The first thing we need to do is to import some React functions and types:

```
// Dependencies
import { FC, useState, useEffect } from 'react'
import axios from 'axios'
```

Now we can remove the `Props` and `State` types we created previously and just leave the `Issue` type:

```
// Types
type Issue = {
  number: number
  title: string
  state: string
}
```

After this, you can change the class definition to use a functional component:

```
const Issues: FC = () => {...}
```

The `FC` type is used to define a **Functional Component** in React. If you need to pass some props to the component, you can pass them like this:

```
type Props = {
  propX: string
  propY: number
  propZ: boolean
}

const Issues: FC<Props> = () => {...}
```

The next thing we need to do is to replace our constructor and our state definition by using the `useState` Hook:

```
// The useState hook replace the this.setState method
const [issues, setIssues] = useState<Issue[]>([])
```

We have used the life cycle method called `componentDidMount` before, which is executed when the component is mounted and is going to run just once. The new React Hook, called `useEffect`, will now handle all the life cycle methods using different syntax for each one, but for now, let's see how we can get the same *effect* of `componentDidMount` into our new functional component:

```
// When we use the useEffect hook with an empty array [] on the
// dependencies (second parameter)
// this represents the componentDidMount method (will be executed when the
```

```
// component is mounted).
useEffect(() => {
  axios
    .get('https://api.github.com/repos/ContentPI/ContentPI/issues')
    .then((response: any) => {
      // Here we update directly our issue state
      setIssues(response.data)
    })
}, [])
```

And finally, we just render our JSX code:

```
return (
  <>
    <h1>ContentPI Issues</h1>

    {issues.map((issue: Issue) => (
      <p key={issue.title}>
        <strong>#{issue.number}</strong> {' '}
        <a href=
          {`https://github.com/ContentPI/ContentPI/issues/${issue.number}`}
            target="_blank">{issue.title}</a> {' '}
        {issue.state}
      </p>
    ))}
  </>
)
```

As you can see, the new Hooks help us to simplify our code a lot and makes more sense. Also, we reduced our code by 10 lines (the class component code has 53 lines and the functional component has 43 lines).

Understanding React effects

In this section, we will learn the difference between the component life cycle methods that we used on class components and the new React effects. Even if you have read in other places that they are the same, just with a different syntax, this is not correct.

Understanding useEffect

When you work with `useEffect`, you need to *think in effects*. If you want to perform the equivalent method of `componentDidMount` using `useEffect`, you can do the following:

```
useEffect(() => {
  // Here you perform your side effect
}, [])
```

The first parameter is the callback of the effect that you want to execute, and the second parameter is the dependencies array. If you pass an empty array (`[]`) on the dependencies, the state and props will have their original initial values.

However, it is important to mention that even though this is the closest equivalent for `componentDidMount`, it does not have the same behavior. Unlike `componentDidMount` and `componentDidUpdate`, the function that we pass to `useEffect` fires after layout and paint, during a deferred event. This normally works for many common side effects, such as setting up subscriptions and event handlers, because most types of work shouldn't block the browser from updating the screen.

However, not all effects can be deferred. For example, you would get a blink if you need to mutate the **Document Object Model (DOM)**. This is the reason why you must fire the event synchronously before the next paint. React provides one Hook called `useLayoutEffect`, which works in the exact same way as `useEffect`.

Firing an effect conditionally

If you need to fire an effect conditionally, then you should add a dependency to the array of dependencies, otherwise, you will execute the effect multiple times and this may cause an infinite loop. If you pass an array of dependencies, the `useEffect` Hook will only run if one of those dependencies changes:

```
useEffect(() => {
  // When you pass an array of dependencies the useEffect hook will only
  // run
  // if one of the dependencies changes.
}, [dependencyA, dependencyB])
```

 If you understand how the React class life cycle methods works, basically, `useEffect` behaves in the same way as `componentDidMount`, `componentDidUpdate`, and `componentWillUnmount` combined.

The effects are very important, but let's also explore some other important new Hooks, including useCallback, useMemo, and memo.

Understanding useCallback, useMemo, and memo

In order to understand the difference between useCallback, useMemo and memo, we will do a to-do list example. You can create a basic application by using create-react-app and typescript as a template:

```
create-react-app todo --template typescript
```

Right after that, you can remove all the extra files (App.css, App.test.ts, index.css, logo.svg, reportWebVitals.ts, and setupTests.ts). You just need to keep the App.tsx file, which will contain the following code:

```tsx
// Dependencies
import { useState, useEffect, useMemo, useCallback } from 'react'

// Components
import List, { Todo } from './List'

const initialTodos = [
  { id: 1, task: 'Go shopping' },
  { id: 2, task: 'Pay the electricity bill'}
]

function App() {
  const [todoList, setTodoList] = useState(initialTodos)
  const [task, setTask] = useState('')

  useEffect(() => {
    console.log('Rendering <App />')
  })

  const handleCreate = () => {
    const newTodo = {
      id: Date.now(),
      task
    }
    // Pushing the new todo to the list
    setTodoList([...todoList, newTodo])
    // Resetting input value
    setTask('')
```

```
    }

    return (
      <>
        <input
          type="text"
          value={task}
          onChange={(e) => setTask(e.target.value)}
        />

        <button onClick={handleCreate}>Create</button>

        <List todoList={todoList} />
      </>
    )
  }

export default App
```

Basically, we are defining some initial tasks and creating the todoList state, which we will pass to the list component. Then you need to create the List.tsx file with the following code:

```
// Dependencies
import { FC, useEffect } from 'react'

// Components
import Task from './Task'

// Types
export type Todo = {
  id: number
  task: string
}

interface Props {
  todoList: Todo[]
}

const List: FC<Props> = ({ todoList }) => {
  useEffect(() => {
    // This effect is executed every new render
    console.log('Rendering <List />')
  })

  return (
    <ul>
      {todoList.map((todo: Todo) => (
```

```
      <Task key={todo.id} id={todo.id} task={todo.task} />
    ))}
  </ul>
  )
}

export default List
```

As you can see, we are rendering each task of the `todoList` array by using the `Task` component and we pass `task` as a prop. I also added a `useEffect` Hook to see how many renders we are performing.

Finally, we create our `Task.tsx` file with the following code:

```
import { FC, useEffect } from 'react'

interface Props {
  id: number
  task: string
}

const Task: FC<Props> = ({ task }) => {
  useEffect(() => {
    console.log('Rendering <Task />', task)
  })

  return (
    <li>{task}</li>
  )
}

export default Task
```

This is how we should see the to-do list:

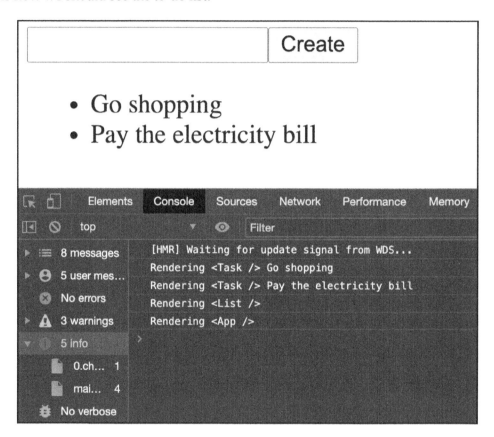

As you can see, when we render our to-do list, by default, we are performing two renders of the Task component, one render for List, and the other for the App component.

Now, if we try to write a new task in the input, we can see that for each letter we write, we will again see all of those renders:

As you can see, by just writing `Go`, we have two new batches of renders, so we can determine that this component does not have good performance, and this is where `memo` can help us to improve performance. In the next sections, we are going to learn how to implement `memo`, `useMemo`, and `useCallback` to memoize a component, a value, and a function.

Memoizing a component with memo

The `memo` **High Order Component (HOC)** is similar to `PureComponent` of a React class because it performs a shallow comparison of the props (meaning a superficial check), so if we try to render a component with the same props all the time, the component will render just once and will memorize. The only way to re-render the component is when a prop changes its value.

In order to fix our components to avoid the multiple renders when we write in the input, we need to wrap our components on the `memo` HOC.

The first component we will fix is our `List` component, and you just need to effect `import memo` and wrap the component on `export default`:

```
import { FC, useEffect, memo } from 'react'

...

export default memo(List)
```

Then you need to do the same with the `Task` component:

```
import { FC, useEffect, memo } from 'react'

...

export default memo(Task)
```

Now, when we try to write `Go` again in the input, let's see how many renders we get this time:

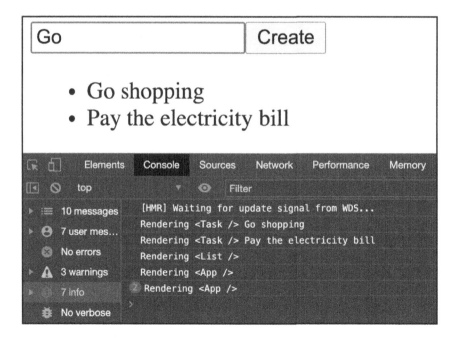

Now, we just get the first batch of renders the first time, and then, when we write `Go`, we just get two more renders of the `App` component, which is totally fine because the task state (input value) that we are changing is actually part of the `App` component.

Also, we can see how many renders we are performing when we create a new task by clicking on the **Create** button:

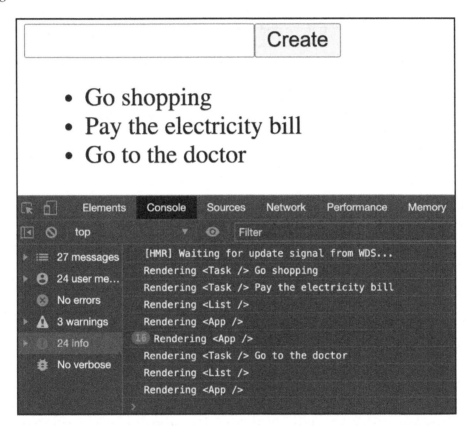

If you see, the first 16 renders are the word counting of the **Go to the doctor** string, and then, when you click on the **Create** button, you should see one render of the `Task` component, one render of `List`, and one render of the `App` component. As you can see, we have improved performance a lot, and we are just performing the exact need that it renders.

At this point, you're probably thinking that the correct way is to always add memo to our components, or maybe you're thinking why React doesn't do this by default for us?

The reason is **performance**, which means **it is not a good idea to add** memo **to all our components unless it is totally necessary**, otherwise, the process of shallow comparisons and memorization will have inferior performance than if we don't use it.

I have a rule when it comes to establishing whether it is a good idea to use memo, and this rule is straightforward: **just don't use it.** Normally, when we have small components or basic logic, we don't need this unless you're working with **large data from some API or your component needs to perform a lot of renders (normally huge lists), or when you notice that your app is going slow**. Only in that case would I recommend using memo.

Memoizing a value with useMemo

Let's suppose that we now want to implement a search feature in our to-do list. The first thing we need to do is to add a new state called term to the App component:

```
const [term, setTerm] = useState('')
```

Then we need to create a function called handleSearch:

```
const handleSearch = () => {
  setTerm(task)
}
```

Right before the return, we will create filterTodoList, which will filter the to-dos based on the task, and we will add a console there to see how many times it is being rendered:

```
const filteredTodoList = todoList.filter((todo: Todo) => {
  console.log('Filtering...')
  return todo.task.toLowerCase().includes(term.toLocaleLowerCase())
})
```

Finally, we need to add a new button next to the **Create** button that already exists:

```
<button onClick={handleSearch}>Search</button>
```

At this point, I recommend that you remove or comment `console.log` in the `List` and `Task` components so that we can focus on the performance of filtering:

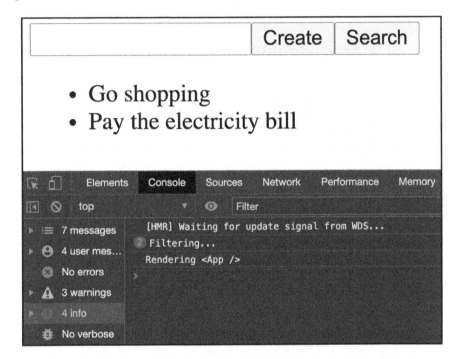

When you run the application again, you will see that filtering is being executed twice, and then the App component as well, and everything looks good here, but what's the problem with this? Try to write Go to the doctor again in the input and let's see how many **Rendering** and **Filtering** you get:

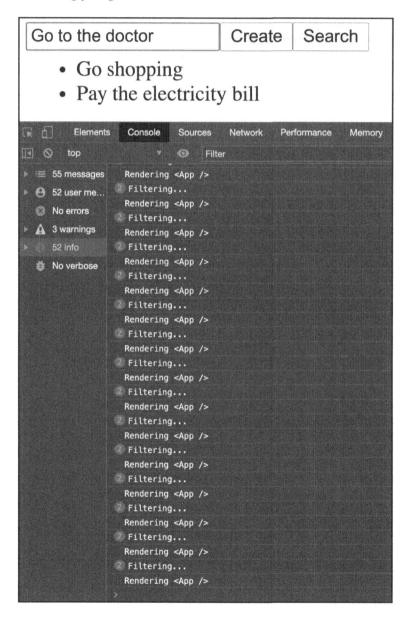

As you can see, for each letter you write, you will get two filtering calls and one `App` render and you don't need to be a genius to see that this is bad performance; and not to mention that if you are working with a large data array, this will be worse, so how can we fix this issue?

The `useMemo` Hook is our hero in this situation, and basically, we need to move our filter inside `useMemo`, but first let's see the syntax:

```
const filteredTodoList = useMemo(() => SomeProcessHere, [])
```

The `useMemo` Hook will memorize the result (value) of a function and will have some dependencies to listen to. Let's see how we can implement it:

```
const filteredTodoList = useMemo(() => todoList.filter((todo: Todo) => {
  console.log('Filtering...')
  return todo.task.toLowerCase().includes(term.toLowerCase())
}), [])
```

Now, if you write something again in the input, you will see that filtering won't be executed all the time, as was the case previously:

This is great, but there is still one small problem. If you try to click on the **Search** button, it won't filter, and this is because we missed the dependencies. Actually, if you see the console warnings, you will see this warning:

```
⚠ ▸ src/App.tsx                                    webpackHotDevClient.js:138
    Line 38:7:  React Hook useMemo has missing dependencies: 'term'
  and 'todoList'. Either include them or remove the dependency array
  react-hooks/exhaustive-deps
>
```

You need to add the `term` and `todoList` dependencies to the array:

```
const filteredTodoList = useMemo(() => todoList.filter((todo: Todo) => {
  console.log('Filtering...')
  return todo.task.toLowerCase().includes(term.toLocaleLowerCase())
}), [term, todoList])
```

It should now work if you write `Go` and click on the **Search** button:

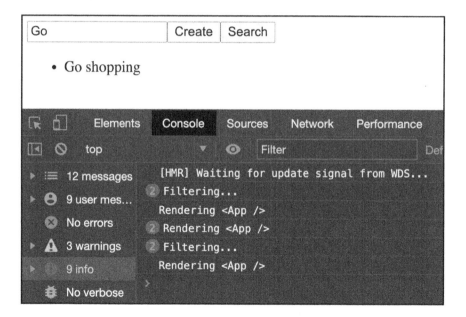

Here, we have to use the same rule that we used for memo; **just don't use it until absolutely necessary.**

Memoizing a function definition with useCallback

Now we will add a delete task feature to learn how `useCallback` works. The first thing we need to do is to create a new function called `handleDelete` in our `App` component:

```
const handleDelete = (taskId: number) => {
  const newTodoList = todoList.filter((todo: Todo) => todo.id !== taskId)
  setTodoList(newTodoList)
}
```

And then you need to pass this function to the `List` component as a prop:

```
<List todoList={filteredTodoList} handleDelete={handleDelete} />
```

Then, in our `List` component, you need to add the prop to the `Props` interface:

```
interface Props {
  todoList: Todo[]
  handleDelete: any
}
```

Next, you need to pull it from the props and pass it down to the `Task` component:

```
const List: FC<Props> = ({ todoList, handleDelete }) => {
  useEffect(() => {
    // This effect is executed every new render
    console.log('Rendering <List />')
  })

  return (
    <ul>
      {todoList.map((todo: Todo) => (
        <Task
          key={todo.id}
          id={todo.id}
          task={todo.task}
          handleDelete={handleDelete}
        />
      ))}
    </ul>
  )
}
```

In the `Task` component, you need to create a button that will execute `handleDelete` onClick:

```
interface Props {
  id: number
  task: string
  handleDelete: any
}

const Task: FC<Props> = ({ id, task, handleDelete }) => {
  useEffect(() => {
    console.log('Rendering <Task />', task)
  })

  return (
    <li>{task} <button onClick={() => handleDelete(id)}>X</button></li>
  )
}
```

At this point, I recommend that you remove or comment `console.log` in the `List` and `Task` components, so we can focus on the performance of filtering. Now you should see the **X** button next to the task:

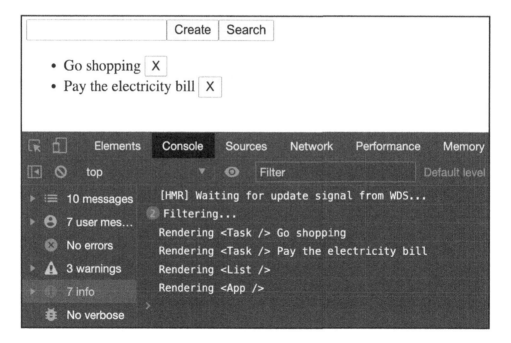

If you click on the **X** for **Go shopping,** you should be able to remove it:

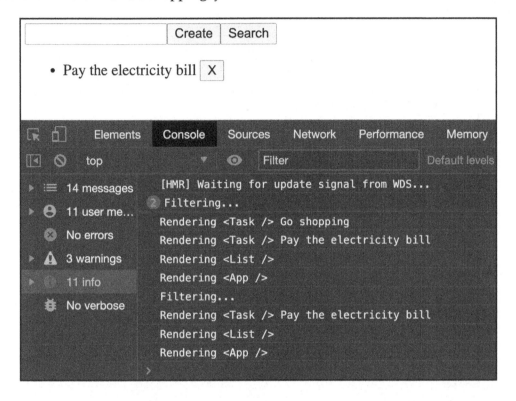

So far, so good, right? But again we have a little issue with this implementation. If you now try to write something in the input, such as Go to the doctor, let's see what happens:

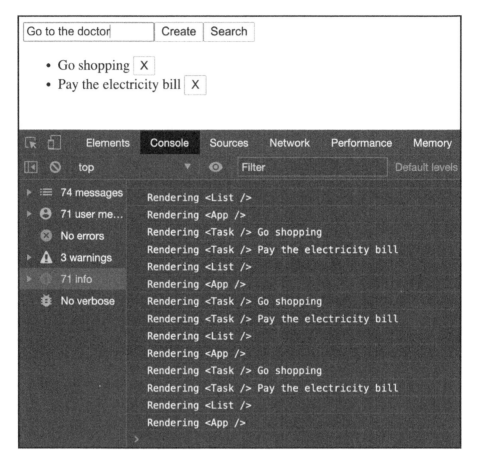

If you see, we are performing **71** renders of all the components again. At this point, you are probably thinking about, *what is going on if we have already implemented the memo HOC to memorize the components*? But the problem now is that our handleDelete function is being passed in two components, from App to List and to Task, and the issue is that this function is regenerated every time we have a new re-render, in this case, every time we write something. So how do we fix this problem?

The `useCallback` Hook is the hero in this case and is very similar to `useMemo` in the syntax, but the main difference is that instead of memorizing the result value of a function, as `useMemo` does, it is memorizing the **function definition** instead:

```
const handleDelete = useCallback(() => SomeFunctionDefinition, [])
```

Our `handleDelete` function should be like this:

```
const handleDelete = useCallback((taskId: number) => {
  const newTodoList = todoList.filter((todo: Todo) => todo.id !== taskId)
  setTodoList(newTodoList)
}, [todoList])
```

Now, it should work just fine if we write `Go to the doctor` again:

Now, instead of 71 renders, we just have 23, which is normal, and we are also able to delete tasks:

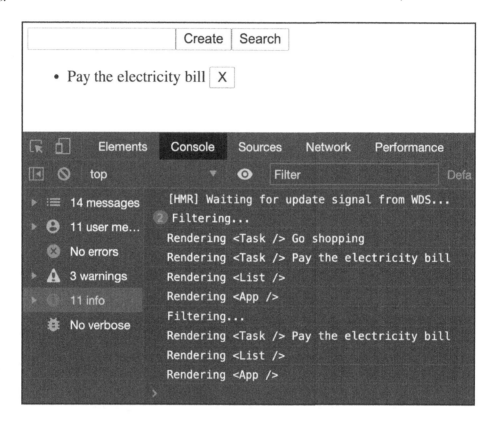

As you can see, the useCallback Hook helps us to improve performance significantly. In the next section, you will learn how to memorize a function passed as an argument in the useEffect Hook.

Memoizing function passed as an argument in effect

There is a special case where we will need to use the useCallback Hook, and this is when we pass a function as an argument in a useEffect Hook, for example, in our App component. Let's create a new useEffect block:

```
const printTodoList = () => {
  console.log('Changing todoList')
```

```
}

useEffect(() => {
  printTodoList()
}, [todoList])
```

In this case, we are listening for changes on the `todoList` state. If you run this code and you create or remove a task, it will work just fine (remember to remove all the other consoles first):

Everything works fine, but let's add `todoList` to the console:

```
const printTodoList = () => {
  console.log('Changing todoList', todoList)
}
```

If you're using Visual Studio Code, you will get the following warning:

```
useEffect(() => {
  // console.log('Rendering <App />')
})
    React Hook useEffect has a missing dependency: 'printTodoList'. Either include it or remove
    the dependency array. eslint(react-hooks/exhaustive-deps)
use
  p  Peek Problem (⌥F8)   Quick Fix... (⌘.)
}, [todoList])
```

Basically, it is asking us to add the `printTodoList` function to the dependencies:

```
useEffect(() => {
  printTodoList()
}, [todoList, printTodoList])
```

But now, after we do that, we get another warning:

```
▲ ▸ src/App.tsx                                                          webpackHotDevClient.js:138
    Line 17:9:  The 'printTodoList' function makes the dependencies of useEffect Hook (at line 27)
  change on every render. Move it inside the useEffect callback. Alternatively, wrap the
  definition of 'printTodoList' in its own useCallback() Hook   react-hooks/exhaustive-deps
  ⟩
```

The reason why we get this warning is that we are now manipulating a state (consoling the state), which is why we need to add a `useCallback` Hook to this function to fix this issue:

```
const printTodoList = useCallback(() => {
  console.log('Changing todoList', todoList)
}, [todoList])
```

Now, when we delete a task, we can see that `todoList` updated correctly:

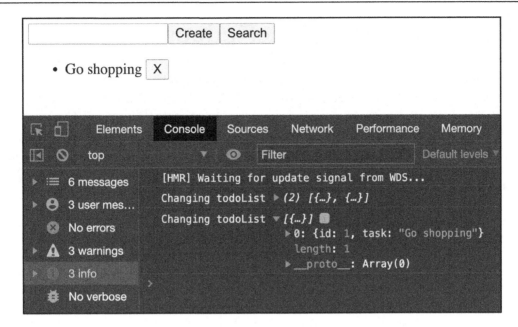

At this point, this may be information overload for you, so let's have a quick recap:

memo:

- Memorizes a **component**
- Re-memorizes when props change
- Avoids re-renders

useMemo:

- Memorizes a **calculated value**
- For computed properties
- For heavy processes

useCallback:

- Memorizes a **function definition** to avoid redefining it on each render.
- Use it whenever a function is passed as an effect argument.
- Use it whenever a function is passed by props to a memorized component.

And finally, do not forget the golden rule: **Do not use them until absolutely necessary.**

In the next section, we are going to learn how to use the new useReducer Hook.

Understanding the useReducer Hook

You probably have some experience of using Redux (`react-redux`) with class components, and if that is the case, then you will understand how `useReducer` works. The concepts are basically the same: actions, reducers, dispatch, store, and state. Even if, in general, it seems very similar to `react-redux`, they have some differences. The main difference is that `react-redux` provides middleware and wrappers such as thunk, sagas, and many more besides, while `useReducer` just gives you a `dispatch` method that you can use to dispatch plain objects as actions. Also, `useReducer` does not have a store by default; instead, you can create one using `useContext`, but this is just reinventing the wheel.

Let's create a basic application to understand how `useReducer` works. You can start by creating a new React app:

```
create-react-app reducer --template typescript
```

Then, as always, you can delete all files in your `src` folder except `App.tsx` and `index.tsx` to start a brand-new application.

We will create a basic `Notes` application where we can list, delete, create, or update our notes using `useReducer`. The first thing you need to do is import the `Notes` component, which we will create later, into your `App` component:

```
import Notes from './Notes'

function App() {
  return (
    <Notes />
  )
}

export default App
```

Now, in our `Notes` component, you first need to import `useReducer` and `useState`:

```
import { useReducer, useState, ChangeEvent } from 'react'
```

Then we need to define some TypeScript types that we need to use for our Note object, the Redux action, and the action types:

```typescript
type Note = {
  id: number
  note: string
}

type Action = {
  type: string
  payload?: any
}

type ActionTypes = {
  ADD: 'ADD'
  UPDATE: 'UPDATE'
  DELETE: 'DELETE'
}

const actionType: ActionTypes = {
  ADD: 'ADD',
  DELETE: 'DELETE',
  UPDATE: 'UPDATE'
}
```

After this, we need to create initialNotes (also known as initialState) with some dummy notes:

```typescript
const initialNotes: Note[] = [
  {
    id: 1,
    note: 'Note 1'
  },
  {
    id: 2,
    note: 'Note 2'
  }
]
```

If you remember how the reducers work, then this will seem very similar to how we handle the reducer using a `switch` statement, so as to perform basic operations such as ADD, DELETE, and UPDATE:

```
const reducer = (state: Note[], action: Action) => {
  switch (action.type) {
    case actionType.ADD:
      return [...state, action.payload]

    case actionType.DELETE:
      return state.filter(note => note.id !== action.payload)
    case actionType.UPDATE:
      const updatedNote = action.payload
      return state.map((n: Note) => n.id === updatedNote.id ?
        updatedNote : n)
    default:
      return state
  }
}
```

Finally, the component is very straightforward. Basically, you get the notes and the `dispatch` method from the `useReducer` Hook (similar to `useState`), and you need to pass the `reducer` function and `initialNotes` (`initialState`):

```
const Notes = () => {
  const [notes, dispatch] = useReducer(reducer, initialNotes)
  const [note, setNote] = useState('')
  ...
}
```

Then, we have a `handleSubmit` function to create a new note when we write something in the input. Then, we press *Enter:*

```
const handleSubmit = (e: ChangeEvent<HTMLInputElement>) => {
  e.preventDefault()

  const newNote = {
    id: Date.now(),
    note
  }

  dispatch({ type: actionType.ADD, payload: newNote })
}
```

Finally, we render our Notes list with `map`, and we also create two buttons, one for delete and one for update, and then the input should be wrapped into a `<form>` tag:

```
return (
  <div>
    <h2>Notes</h2>

    <ul>
      {notes.map((n: Note) => (
        <li key={n.id}>
          {n.note} {' '}
          <button
            onClick={() => dispatch({
              type: actionType.DELETE,
              payload: n.id
            })}
          >
            X
          </button>

          <button
            onClick={() => dispatch({
              type: actionType.UPDATE,
              payload: {...n, note}
            })}
          >
            Update
          </button>
        </li>
      ))}
    </ul>
    <form onSubmit={handleSubmit}>
      <input
        placeholder="New note"
        value={note}
        onChange={e => setNote(e.target.value)}
      />
    </form>
  </div>
)

export default Notes
```

If you run the application, you should see the following output:

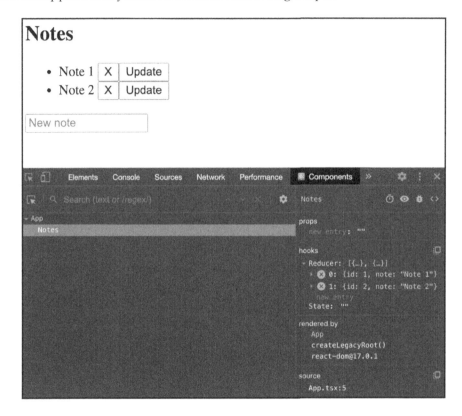

As you can see in the React DevTools, the `Reducer` object contains the two notes that we have defined as our initial state. Now, if you write something in the input and you press *Enter*, you should be able to create a new note:

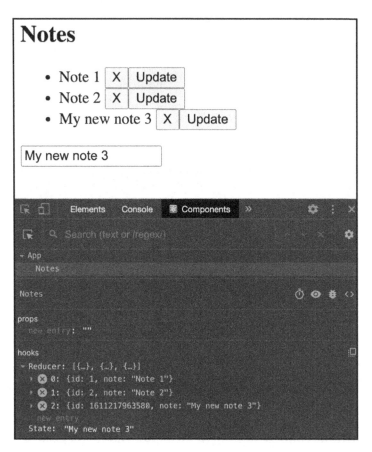

Then, if you want to delete a note, you just need to click on the **X** button. Let's remove **Note 2**:

Finally, you can write anything you want in the input, and if you click on the **Update** button, you will change the note value:

Nice, huh? As you can see the `useReducer` Hook is pretty much the same as redux in terms of the dispatch method, actions, and reducers, but the main difference is that this is limited just to the context of your component and its child, so if you need a global store to be accessible from your entire application then you should use `react-redux` instead.

Summary

I hope you enjoyed reading this chapter, which is full of very good information pertaining to the new React Hooks. So far, you have learned how the new React Hooks work, how to fetch data with Hooks, how to migrate a class component to React Hooks, how the effects work, the difference between `memo`, `useMemo`, and `useCallback`, and finally, you learned how the `useReducer` Hook works and the main difference compared with `react-redux`. This will help you to improve the performance of your React components.

In the next chapter, we will go through some of the most popular composition patterns and tools.

4
Exploring Popular Composition Patterns

Now, it's time to learn how to make components communicate with each other effectively. React is powerful because it lets you build complex applications comprising small, testable, and maintainable components. Applying this paradigm, you can take control of every single part of the application.

In this chapter, we will go through some of the most popular composition patterns and tools.

We will cover the following topics:

- How components communicate with each other using props and children
- The container and presentational patterns and how they can make our code more maintainable
- What **higher-order components** (**HOCs**) are and how, thanks to them, we can structure our applications in a better way
- What the function of the child component pattern is and what its benefits are

Technical requirements

To complete this chapter, you will need the following:

- Node.js 12+
- Visual Studio Code

You can find the code for this chapter in the book's GitHub Repository at https://github.com/PacktPublishing/React-17-Design-Patterns-and-Best-Practic es-Third-Edition/tree/main/Chapter04.

Communicating components

Reusing functions is one of our goals as developers, and in the previous chapter, we saw how React makes it easy to create reusable components. **Reusable components** can be shared across multiple domains of your application to avoid duplication.

Small components with a clean interface can be composed together to create complex applications that are powerful and maintainable at the same time.

Composing React components is pretty straightforward; you just have to include them in the render:

```
const Profile = ({ user }) => (
  <>
    <Picture profileImageUrl={user.profileImageUrl} />
    <UserName name={user.name} screenName={user.screenName} />
  </>
)
```

For example, you can create a `Profile` component by simply composing a `Picture` component to display the profile image and a `UserName` component to display the name and the screen name of the user.

In this way, you can produce new parts of the user interface very quickly, writing only a few lines of code. Whenever you compose components, as in the preceding example, you share data between them using props. Props are the way a parent component can pass its data down the tree to every component that needs it (or part of it).

When a component passes some props to another component, it is called the **owner**, irrespective of the parent-child relationship between them. For example, in the preceding snippet, `Profile` is not the direct parent of `Picture` (the `div` tag is), but `Profile` owns `Picture` because it passes down the props to it.

In the next section, you will learn about the `children` prop and how to use it correctly.

Using the children prop

There is a special prop that can be passed from the owners to the components defined inside their render—`children`.

In the React documentation, it is described as **opaque** because it is a property that does not tell you anything about the value it contains. Subcomponents defined inside the render of a parent component usually receive props that are passed as attributes of the component itself in JSX, or as a second parameter of the _jsx function. Components can also be defined with nested components inside them, and they can access those children using the children prop.

Consider that we have a Button component that has a text property representing the text of the button:

```
const Button = ({ text }) => (
  <button className="btn">{text}</button>
)
```

The component can be used in the following way:

```
<Button text="Click me!" />
```

And this will render the following code:

```
<button class="btn">Click me!</button>
```

Now, suppose we want to use the same button with the same class name in multiple parts of our application, and we also want to be able to display more than a simple string. Our UI consists of buttons with text, buttons with text and icons, and buttons with text and labels.

In most cases, a good solution would be to add multiple parameters to Button or to create different versions of Button, each one with its single specialization, for example, IconButton.

However, we should realize that Button could just be a wrapper, and we are able to render any element inside it and use the children property:

```
const Button = ({ children }) => (
  <button className="btn">{children}</button>
)
```

By passing the children prop, we are not limited to a simple single text property, but we can pass any element to Button, and it is rendered in place of the children property.

In this case, any element that we wrap inside the Button component will be rendered as a child of the button element with btn as the class name.

For example, if we want to render an image inside the button and some text wrapped into a `span` tag, we can do this:

```
<Button>
  <img src="..." alt="..." />
  <span>Click me!</span>
</Button>
```

The preceding snippet gets rendered in the browser as follows:

```
<button class="btn">
  <img src="..." alt="..." />
  <span>Click me!</span>
</button>
```

This is a pretty convenient way to allow components to accept any `children` elements and wrap those elements inside a predefined parent.

Now, we can pass images, labels, and even other React components inside the `Button` component, and they will be rendered as its children. As you can see in the preceding example, we defined the `children` property as an array, which means that we can pass any number of elements as the component's children.

We can pass a single child, as shown in the following code:

```
<Button>
  <span>Click me!</span>
</Button>
```

Let's now explore the container and the presentational pattern in the next section.

Exploring the container and presentational patterns

In the last chapter, we saw how to take a coupled component and make it reusable step by step. Now we will see how to apply a similar pattern to our components to make them clearer and more maintainable.

React components typically contain a mix of *logic* and *presentation.* By logic, we refer to anything that is unrelated to the UI, such as API calls, data manipulation, and event handlers. The presentation is the part inside `render` where we create the elements to be displayed on the UI.

In React, there are simple and powerful patterns, known as **container** and **presentational**, which we can apply when creating components that help us to separate those two concerns.

Creating well-defined boundaries between logic and presentation not only makes components more reusable, but also provides many other benefits, which you will learn about in this section. Again, one of the best ways to learn new concepts is by seeing practical examples, so let's delve into some code.

Suppose we have a component that uses geolocation APIs to get the position of the user and displays the latitude and longitude on the page in the browser.

First, we create a `Geolocation.tsx` file in our `components` folder and define the `Geolocation` component using a functional component:

```
import { useState, useEffect } from 'react'

const Geolocation = () => {}

export default Geolocation
```

We then define our states:

```
const [latitude, setLatitude] = useState<number | null>(null)
const [longitude, setLongitude] = useState<number | null>(null)
```

Now, we can use the `useEffect` Hook to fire the request to the APIs:

```
useEffect(() => {
  if (navigator.geolocation) {
    navigator.geolocation.getCurrentPosition(handleSuccess)
  }
}, [])
```

When the browser returns the data, we store the result into the state using the following function (place this function before the `useEffect` Hook):

```
const handleSuccess = ({
  coords: {
    latitude,
    longitude
  }
}: { coords: { latitude: number; longitude: number }}) => {
  setLatitude(latitude)
  setLongitude(longitude)
}
```

Finally, we show the `latitude` and `longitude` values:

```
return (
  <div>
    <h1>Geolocation:</h1>
    <div>Latitude: {latitude}</div>
    <div>Longitude: {longitude}</div>
  </div>
)
```

It is important to note that, during the first `render`, `latitude` and `longitude` are `null` because we asked the browser for the coordinates when the component was mounted. In a real-world component, you might want to display a spinner until the data gets returned. To do that, you can use one of the conditional techniques we saw in *Chapter 2, Cleaning Up Your Code*.

Now, this component does not have any problems, and it works as expected. Wouldn't it be nice to separate it from the part where the position gets requested and loaded to iterate faster on it?

We will use the container and presentational patterns to isolate the presentational part. In this pattern, every component is split into two smaller ones, each one with its clear responsibilities. The container knows everything about the logic of the component and is where the APIs are called. It also deals with data manipulation and event handling.

The presentational component is where the UI is defined, and it receives data in the form of props from the container. Since the presentational component is usually logic-free, we can create it as a functional, stateless component.

There are no rules that say that the presentational component must not have a state (for example, it could keep a UI state inside it). In this case, we need a component to display the latitude and longitude, so we are going to use a simple function.

First of all, we should rename our `Geolocation` component to `GeolocationContainer`:

```
const GeolocationContainer = () => {...}
```

We will also change the filename
from `Geolocation.tsx` to `GeolocationContainer.tsx`.

This rule is not strict, but it is a best practice that's widely used in the React community to append `Container` to the end of the `Container` component name and give the original name to the presentational one.

We also have to change the implementation of `render` and remove all the UI parts of it, as follows:

```
return (
  <Geolocation latitude={latitude} longitude={longitude} />
)
```

As you can see in the preceding snippet, instead of creating the HTML elements inside the `return` of the container, we just use the presentational one (which we will create next), and we pass the state to it. The states are `latitude` and `longitude`, which are `null` by default, and they contain the real position of the user when the browser fires the callback.

Let's create a new file, called `Geolocation.tsx`, where we define the functional component as follows:

```
import { FC } from 'react'

type Props = {
  latitude: number
  longitude: number
}

const Geolocation: FC<Props> = ({ latitude, longitude }) => (
  <div>
    <h1>Geolocation:</h1>
    <div>Latitude: {latitude}</div>
    <div>Longitude: {longitude}</div>
  </div>
)

export default Geolocation
```

Functional components are an incredibly elegant way to define UIs. They are pure functions that, given a `state`, return the elements of it. In this case, our function receives `latitude` and `longitude` from the owner, and it returns the markup structure to display it.

If you run the components in the browser the first time, the browser will require your permission to allow it to know about your location:

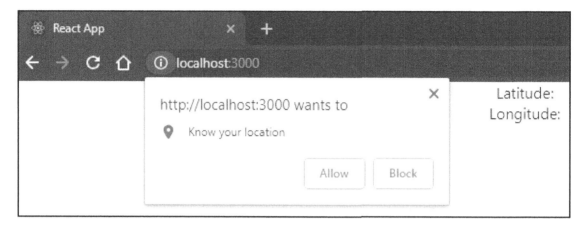

After you allow the browser to know your location, you will see something like this:

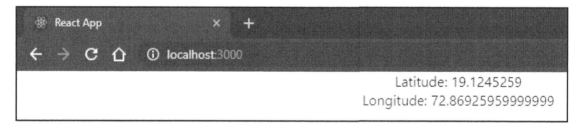

Following the container and presentational pattern, we created a dumb reusable component that we can put in our Style Guide so that we can pass fake coordinates to it. If in some other parts of the application we need to display the same data structure, we do not have to create a new component; we just wrap this one into a new container that, for example, could load the latitude and longitude from a different endpoint.

At the same time, other developers in our team can improve the container that uses geolocation by adding some error-handling logic, without affecting its presentation. They can even build a temporary presentational component just to display and debug data and then replace it with the real presentational component when it is ready.

Being able to work in parallel on the same component is a big win for teams, especially for those companies where building interfaces is an iterative process.

This pattern is simple but very powerful, and when applied to big applications, it can make a difference when it comes to the speed of development and the maintainability of the project. On the other hand, applying this pattern without a real reason can give us the opposite problem and make the **code base** less useful as it involves the creation of more files and components.

So, we should think carefully when we decide that a component has to be refactored following the container and presentational patterns. In general, the right path to follow is starting with a single component and splitting it only when the logic and the presentation become too coupled where they shouldn't be.

In our example, we began from a single component, and we realized that we could separate the API call from the markup. Deciding what to put in the container and what goes into the presentation is not always straightforward; the following points should help you make that decision:

The following are the characteristics of container components:

- They are more concerned with behavior.
- They render their presentational components.
- They make API calls and manipulate data.
- They define event handlers.

The following are the characteristics of presentational components:

- They are more concerned with the visual representation.
- They render the HTML markup (or other components).
- They receive data from the parents in the form of props.
- They are often written as stateless functional components.

As you can see, these patterns form a really powerful tool that will help you to develop your web applications faster. Let's see what HOCs are in the next section.

Understanding HOCs

In the *Functional programming* section of *Chapter 2, Cleaning Up Your Code*, we mentioned the concept of **higher-order functions (HOFs)**, which are functions that, given a function, enhance it with some extra behaviors, returning a new one. When we apply the idea of HOFs to components, we call these **higher-order components** (or **HOCs** for brevity).

First of all, let's see what HoC looks like:

```
const HoC = Component => EnhancedComponent
```

HOCs are functions that take a component as input and return an enhanced one as the output.

Let's start with a very simple example to understand what an enhanced component looks like.

Suppose, for whatever reason, you need to attach the same className property to every component. You could go and change all the render methods by adding the className property to each of them, or you could write an HOC such as the following:

```
const withClassName = Component => props => (
  <Component {...props} className="my-class" />
)
```

In the React community, it is very common to have the prefix with for HOCs.

The preceding code can be a little difficult to understand initially; let's go through it together.

We declare a withClassName function that takes a Component and returns another function. The returned function is a functional component that receives some props and renders the original component. The collected props are spread, and a className property with the "my-class" value is passed to the functional component.

The reason why HOCs usually spread the props they receive on the component is because they tend to be transparent and only add the new behavior.

This is pretty simple and not very useful, but it should give you a better understanding of what HOCs are and what they look like. Let's now see how we can use the withClassName HOC in our components.

First of all, we create a stateless functional component that receives the class name and applies it to a div tag:

```
const MyComponent = ({ className }) => (
  <div className={className} />
)
```

Instead of using the component directly, we pass it to an HOC, as follows:

```
const MyComponentWithClassName = withClassName(MyComponent)
```

Wrapping our components into the withClassName function, we ensure that it receives the className property.

Now, let's move on to something more exciting, and let's create an HOC to detect the InnerWidth. First of all, we have to create a function that receives a Component:

```
import { useEffect, useState } from 'react'

const withInnerWidth = Component => props => {
  return <Component {...props} />
}
```

You may have spotted a pattern in the way HOCs are named. It is a common practice to prefix HOCs that provide some information to the components they enhance using the with pattern.

Now you need to define the innerWidth state and the handleResize function:

```
const withInnerWidth = Component => props => {
  const [innerWidth, setInnerWidth] = useState(window.innerWidth)

  const handleResize = () => {
    setInnerWidth(window.innerWidth)
  }

  return <Component {...props} />
}
```

Then we add the effects:

```
useEffect(() => {
  window.addEventListener('resize', handleResize)

  return () => { // <<< This emulates the componentWillUnmount
    window.removeEventListener('resize', handleResize)
  }
}, []) // <<< This emulates the componentDidMount
```

Finally, the original component gets rendered in the following way:

```
return <Component {...props} innerWidth={innerWidth} />
```

As you may note here, we are spreading the props as we saw before, but we are also passing the `innerWidth` state.

We are storing the `innerWidth` value as a state to achieve the original behavior, but we do not pollute the state of the component; we use props instead.

Using props is always a good solution to enforce reusability.

Now, using an HOC and getting the `innerWidth` value is pretty straightforward.

 The new React Hooks can easily replace an HOC by creating custom Hooks.

We create a functional component that expects `innerWidth` as a property:

```
const MyComponent = ({ innerWidth }) => {
  console.log('window.innerWidth', innerWidth)
  ...
}
```

We enhance it as follows:

```
const MyComponentWithInnerWidth = withInnerWidth(MyComponent)
```

First of all, we do not pollute any state, and we do not require the component to implement any function. This means that the component and the HOC are not coupled, and they can both be reused across the application.

Again, using props instead of state lets us make our component dumb so that we can use it in our Style Guide, ignoring any complex logic and just passing down the props.

In this particular case, we could create a component for each of the different `innerWidth` sizes we support.

Consider the following example:

```
<MyComponent innerWidth={320} />
```

Or consider the following:

```
<MyComponent innerWidth={960} />
```

As you can see, by using the HOCs we can pass a component and then return a new component with extra functionalities. Some of the most common HOCs are `connect` from Redux and `createFragmentContainer` from Relay.

Understanding FunctionAsChild

There is a pattern that is gaining consensus within the React community, known as `FunctionAsChild`. It is widely used in the popular `react-motion` library, which we will see in *Chapter 7, Writing Code for the Browser*.

The main concept is that, instead of passing a child in the form of a component, we define a function that can receive parameters from the parent. Let's see what it looks like:

```
const FunctionAsChild = ({ children }) => children()
```

As you can see, `FunctionAsChild` is a component that has a `children` property defined as a function and, instead of being used as a JSX expression, it gets called.

The preceding component can be used in the following way:

```
<FunctionAsChild>
  {() => <div>Hello, World!</div>}
</FunctionAsChild>
```

It is as simple as it looks: the children function is fired in the `render` method of the parent, and it returns the `Hello, World!` text wrapped in a `div` tag, which is displayed on the screen.

Let's delve into a more meaningful example where the parent component passes some parameters to the `children` function.

Create a `Name` component that expects a function as `children` and passes it the `World` string:

```
const Name = ({ children }) => children('World')
```

The preceding component can be used in the following way:

```
<Name>
  {name => <div>Hello, {name}!</div>}
</Name>
```

The snippet renders `Hello, World!` again, but this time the name has been passed by the parent. It should be clear how this pattern works, so let's look at the advantages of this approach.

The first benefit is that we can wrap components, passing the variables at runtime rather than fixed properties, as we do with HOCs.

A good example is a `Fetch` component that loads some data from an API endpoint and returns it to the `children` function:

```
<Fetch url="...">
  {data => <List data={data} />}
</Fetch>
```

Secondly, composing components with this approach does not force `children` to use some predefined prop names. Since the function receives variables, their names can be decided by the developers who use the component. That makes the `FunctionAsChild` solution more flexible.

Last but not least, the wrapper is highly reusable because it does not make any assumptions about `children` it receives—it just expects a function. Due to this, the same `FunctionAsChild` component can be used in different parts of the application, serving various `children` components.

Summary

In this chapter, we learned how to compose our reusable components and make them communicate effectively. Props are a way to decouple components from each other and create a clean and well-defined interface.

Then, we went through some of the most interesting composition patterns in React. The first one was the so-called container and the other was the presentational pattern. These patterns helped us to separate the logic from the presentation and create more specialized components with a single responsibility.

We learned how to deal with context without needing to couple our components to it, thanks to HOCs. Finally, we saw how we could compose components dynamically by following the `FunctionAsChild` pattern.

In the next chapter, we will learn about GraphQL and how to create JWT tokens, perform a login, and create models with Sequelize.

Understanding GraphQL with a Real Project

5

GraphQL is a query language for APIs that helps them work with your existing data. It provides a complete description of the data in your API, and you can only request the exact data you need and nothing more. It also makes it easier to improve APIs if they need it and has very powerful developer tools.

In this chapter, we are going to learn how to use GraphQL in a real project by creating a basic login and user registration system.

We will cover the following topics in this chapter:

- Installing PostgreSQL
- Creating environment variables with a `.env` file
- Configuring Apollo Server
- Defining GraphQL queries and mutations
- Working with resolvers
- Creating Sequelize models
- Implementing JWTs
- Using GraphQL Playground
- Performing authentication

Technical requirements

To complete this chapter, you will need the following:

- Node.js 12+
- Visual Studio Code

- PostgreSQL
- Homebrew (`https://brew.sh`)
- pgAdmin 4 (`https://www.pgadmin.org/download/`)
- OmniDB (`https://omnidb.org`)

You can find the code for this chapter in this book's GitHub repository: `https://github.com/PacktPublishing/React-17-Design-Patterns-and-Best-Practices-Third-Edition/tree/main/Chapter05`.

Installing PostgreSQL

For this example, we will use a PostgreSQL database, so you'll need to install PostgreSQL to be able to run this project on your machine.

If you have a macOS machine, the easiest way to install PostgreSQL is by doing so with Homebrew. You just need to run the following command:

```
brew install postgres
```

Once you've installed it, you need to run the following command:

```
ln -sfv /usr/local/opt/postgresql/*.plist ~/Library/LaunchAgents
```

Then, you can create two new aliases to start and stop your PostgreSQL server:

```
alias pg_start="launchctl load ~/Library/LaunchAgents"
alias pg_stop="launchctl unload ~/Library/LaunchAgents"
```

Now, you should be able to start your PostgreSQL server by using `pg_start` or stop it with `pg_stop`.

After this, you need to create your first database, like so:

```
createdb `whoami`
```

Now, you can connect to PostgreSQL using the `psql` command.

If you get an error stating `role "postgresql" does not exist`, you can fix it by running the following command:

```
createuser -s postgres
```

If you did everything correctly, you should see something like this:

```
→ backend git:(main) psql
psql (13.2)
Type "help" for help.

czantany=#
```

 If you use Windows, you can download PostgreSQL at https://www. postgresql.org/download/windows/ and for those that use Linux (Ubuntu), you can download it from https://www.postgresql.org/ download/linux/ubuntu/.

Best tools for PostgreSQL database management

One of the bests tools for PostgreSQL database management is **pgAdmin 4** (https://www. pgadmin.org/download/). I like this tool as it can be used to create new servers, users, and databases. The other tool I like to use to perform SQL queries and work with data is **OmniDB** (https://omnidb.org). I highly recommend that you install both tools.

Remember to create a database in order to use it in this example.

 Sometimes, you may get an error when you start your PostgreSQL server that could say something like
FATAL: lock file "postmaster.pid" already exists.

If you get this error, you can easily fix it by running the rm /usr/local/var/postgres/postmaster.pid command. Then, you will be able to start your PostgreSQL server.

Creating our .env file and configuration files

First, you need to create a backend directory in your GraphQL project (graphql/backend), after that let's review the huge list of NPM packages you will need to install (the most relevant):

```
npm init --yes

npm install @contentpi/lib @graphql-tools/load-files @graphql-tools/merge
apollo-server dotenv express jsonwebtoken pg pg-hstore sequelize ts-node
```

```
npm install --save-dev husky jest prettier sequelize-mock ts-jest ts-node-
dev typescript eslint @types/jsonwebtoken
```

The scripts you should have in your `package.json` file should be as follows:

```
"scripts": {
  "dev": "ts-node-dev src/index.ts",
  "start": "ts-node dist/index.js",
  "build": "tsc -p .",
  "lint": "eslint . --ext .js,.tsx,.ts",
  "lint:fix": "eslint . --fix --ext .js,.tsx,.ts",
  "test": "jest src"
}
```

In the next section, we are going to configure our environment variables.

Configuring our .env file

A `.env` file (also known as `dotenv`) is a configuration file to specify your application's environment variables. Normally your application won't change from development, staging, or production environments but they normally need a different configuration: the most common variables to change are the base URL, API URL, or even your API keys.

Before we jump into the actual login code, we need to create a file called `.env` (normally, this file is ignored by `.gitignore`), which will allow us to use private data, such as the database connection and security secrets. A file already exists in the repository called `.env.example`; you just need to rename it and put your connection data inside it. This will look something like this:

```
DB_DIALECT=postgres
DB_PORT=5432
DB_HOST=localhost
DB_DATABASE=<your-database>
DB_USERNAME=<your-username>
DB_PASSWORD=<your-password>
```

Creating a basic config file

For this project, we need to create a config file, which should be created at `/backend/config/config.json`. Here, we will define some basic configurations, such as our server's port and some security information:

```
{
  "server": {
    "port": 5000
  },
  "security": {
    "secretKey": "C0nt3ntP1",
    "expiresIn": "7d"
  }
}
```

Then, you need to create an `index.ts` file. This will bring in all the database connection information we defined in the `.env` file using the `dotenv` package and then export three configuration variables called `$db`, `$security`, and `$server`:

```
// Dependencies
import dotenv from 'dotenv'

// Configuration
import config from './config.json'

// Loading .env vars
dotenv.config()

// Types
type Db = {
  dialect: string
  host: string
  port: string
  database: string
  username: string
  password: string
}

type Security = {
  secretKey: string
  expiresIn: string
}

type Server = {
  port: number
}

// Extracting data from .env file
const {
  DB_DIALECT = '',
  DB_PORT = '',
  DB_HOST = '',
  DB_DATABASE = '',
```

```
  DB_USERNAME = '',
  DB_PASSWORD = '',
} = process.env

const db: Db = {
  dialect: DB_DIALECT,
  port: DB_PORT,
  host: DB_HOST,
  database: DB_DATABASE,
  username: DB_USERNAME,
  password: DB_PASSWORD
}

// Configuration
const { security, server } = config

export const $db: Db = db
export const $security: Security = security
export const $server: Server = server
```

If your `.env` file is not at the root or does not exist, all your variables are going to be `undefined`.

Configuring Apollo Server

Apollo Server is the most popular open source library that works with GraphQL (server and client). It has a lot of documentation and is really easy to implement.

The following diagram explains how Apollo Server works in the client and the server:

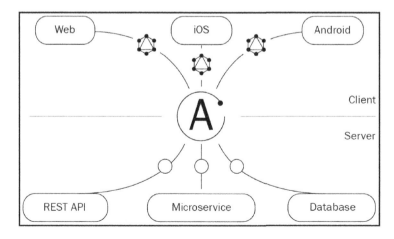

We are going to use Express to set up our Apollo Server and Sequelize ORM to handle our PostgreSQL database. So, initially, we need to do some imports. The required file can be found at `/backend/src/index.ts`:

```
// Dependencies
import { ApolloServer, makeExecutableSchema } from 'apollo-server'

// Models
import models from './models'

// Type Definitions & Resolvers
import resolvers from './graphql/resolvers'
import typeDefs from './graphql/types'

// Configuration
import { $server } from '../config'
```

First, we need to create our schema using `makeExecutableSchema` by passing `typeDefs` and `resolvers`:

```
// Schema
const schema = makeExecutableSchema({
  typeDefs,
  resolvers
})
```

Then, we need to create an instance of `ApolloServer`, where we need to pass the schema and the models in the context:

```
// Apollo Server
const apolloServer = new ApolloServer({
  schema,
  context: {
    models
  }
})
```

Finally, we need to synchronize Sequelize. Here, we are passing some optional variables (`alter` and `force`). If `force` is `true` and you change your Sequelize models, **this will delete your tables, including their values**, and force you to create the tables again, while if `force` is `false` and `alter` is `true`, **then you will only update the table fields, without this affecting your values**. So, you need to be careful with this option as you can lose all your data by accident. Then, after the sync, we must run our Apollo Server, which is listening to port 5000 (`$server.port`):

```
const alter = true
```

```
const force = false

models.sequelize.sync({ alter, force }).then(() => {
  apolloServer
    .listen($server.port)
    .then(({ url }) => {
      // eslint-disable-next-line no-console
      console.log(`Running on ${url}`)
    })
})
```

This will help us synchronize our database with our models so that any time we make a change to the models, the tables are going to be updated.

Defining our GraphQL types, queries, and mutations

Now that you've created your Apollo Server instance, you need to create your GraphQL types. In this case, we will create some types, queries, and mutations for users.

The first thing you need to do is define your scalar types at /backend/src/graphql/types/Scalar.graphql:

```
scalar UUID
scalar Datetime
scalar JSON
```

Now, let's create our User.graphql file with our initial User type:

```
type User {
  id: UUID!
  username: String!
  password: String!
  email: String!
  privilege: String!
  active: Boolean!
  createdAt: Datetime!
  updatedAt: Datetime!
}
```

As you can see, we are using some scalar types such as UUID and Datetime to define some fields in our User type. In this case, when you define a type in GraphQL, you need to do so with the type keyword, followed by the type's name capitalized. Then, you can define your fields inside the curly braces, {}.

There are some primitive data types in GraphQL such as `String`, `Boolean`, `Float`, and `Int`. You can define custom scalar types as we did with `UUID`, `Datetime`, and `JSON`, and you can also define custom types such as the `User` type and specify whether we want an array of that type; for example, `[User]`.

 The `!` character after the types means the field is **non-nullable**.

Queries

GraphQL queries are used to read or fetch values from a data store.

Now that you know how to define custom types, let's define our `Query` type. Here, we are going to define `getUsers` and `getUserData`. The first will retrieve a list of users, while the second will bring us the data of the specific user:

```
type Query {
 getUsers: [User!]
 getUserData(at: String!): User!
}
```

In this case, our `getUsers` query is going to return an array of users (`[User!]`), while our `getUserData` query, which requires the `at` (**access token**) attribute, will return a single `User!`. Remember that with any query you add here, you will need to define it under your resolvers later (we will do that in the next section).

Mutations

Mutations are used to write or post values – that is, to modify data in the data store – and return a value if you want to do some comparisons with REST, such as perform any POST, PUT, or DELETE actions. The `Mutation` type works exactly the same as the `Query` type in there you need to define your mutations and specify what arguments you will receive and what data you will return:

```
type Mutation {
  createUser(input: CreateUserInput): User!
  login(input: LoginInput): AuthPayload!
}
```

As you can see, we have defined two mutations. The first is `createUser`, to register or create a new user in our data store, while the second one is to perform a `login`. As you may have noticed, both are receiving the `input` argument with some different values (`CreateUserInput` and `LoginInput`), called **input types**, which are used as query or mutation parameters. Finally, they will return the `User!` type and `AuthPayload!`, respectively. Let's learn how to define those inputs:

```
input CreateUserInput {
  username: String!
  password: String!
  email: String!
  privilege: String!
  active: Boolean!
}

input LoginInput {
  email: String!
  password: String!
}

type AuthPayload {
  token: String!
}
```

The inputs are normally used with mutations, but you can also use them with queries.

Merging our type definitions

Now that we've defined all our types, queries, and mutations, we need to merge all our GraphQL files to create our GraphQL schema, which is basically one big file containing all our GraphQL definitions.

For this, you need to create a file called `/backend/src/graphql/types/index.ts` that contains the following code:

```
import path from 'path'
import { loadFilesSync } from '@graphql-tools/load-files'
import { mergeTypeDefs } from '@graphql-tools/merge'

const typesArray = loadFilesSync(path.join(__dirname, './'), { extensions:
['graphql'] })

export default mergeTypeDefs(typesArray)
```

We are using `@graphql-tools` packages to load our GraphQL files and merging them into `typesArray` using the `mergeTypesDefs` method.

Creating our resolvers

A resolver is a function that's responsible for generating data for a field in your GraphQL schema. It can normally generate the data in any way you want, in that it can fetch data from a database or by using a third-party API.

To create our user resolvers, you need to create a file called `/backend/src/graphql/resolvers/user.ts`. Let's create a skeleton of what our resolver should look like. Here, we need to specify the functions that are defined under `Query` and `Mutation` in our GraphQL schema. So, your resolver should look like this:

```
export default {
  Query: {
    getUsers: () => {},
    getUserData: () => {},
  },
  Mutation: {
    createUser: () => {},
    login: () => {}
  }
}
```

As you can see, we are returning an object with two main nodes called `Query` and `Mutation`, and we are mapping the queries and the mutations we defined in our GraphQL schema (the `User.graphql` file). Of course, we need to make some changes to receive some parameters and return some data, but I wanted to show you the basic skeleton of a resolver file first.

The first thing you need to do is add some imports to the file:

```
// Lib
import { getUserData } from '../../lib/jwt'

// Interfaces
import {
  IUser,
  ICreateUserInput,
  IModels,
  ILoginInput,
  IAuthPayload
} from '../../types'
```

```
// Utils
import { doLogin, getUserBy } from '../../lib/auth'
```

We will create the doLogin and getUserBy functions in the next section.

Creating the getUsers query

Our first method will be the getUsers query. Let's see how we need to define it:

```
getUsers: (
  _: any,
  args: any,
  ctx: { models: IModels }
): IUser[] => ctx.models.User.findAll(),
```

In any query or mutation method, we always receive four parameters: the parent (defined as _), arguments (defined as args), the context (defined as ctx), and info (which is optional).

If you want to simplify the code a little bit, you can destructure the context, like this:

```
getUsers: (
  _: any,
  args: any,
  { models }: { models: IModels }
): IUser[] => models.User.findAll(),
```

In our next resolver function, we are going to destructure our arguments as well. Just as a reminder, the context is being passed in our Apollo Server setup (we did this previously):

```
// Apollo Server
const apolloServer = new ApolloServer({
  schema,
  context: {
    models
  }
})
```

The context is very important when we need to share something globally in our resolvers.

Creating the getUserData query

This function needs to be async because we need to perform some asynchronous operations, such as getting the connected user via an at (access token) if a user already has a valid session. Then, we can validate whether this is a real user by looking at our database. This helps stop people from modifying the cookies or trying to do some form of injection. If we don't find a connected user, then we return an object of the user that contains empty data:

```
getUserData: async (
  _: any,
  { at }: { at: string },
  { models }: { models: IModels }
): Promise<any> => {
  // Get current connected user
  const connectedUser = await getUserData(at)

  if (connectedUser) {
    // Validating if the user is still valid
    const user = await getUserBy(
      {
        id: connectedUser.id,
        email: connectedUser.email,
        privilege: connectedUser.privilege,
        active: connectedUser.active
      },
      models
    )

    if (user) {
      return connectedUser
    }
  }

  return {
    id: '',
    username: '',
    password: '',
    email: '',
    privilege: '',
    active: false
  }
}
```

Creating the mutations

Our mutations are very simple – we just need to execute some functions and pass all our arguments by spreading the input value (this is coming from our GraphQL schema). Let's see what our Mutation node should look like:

```
Mutation: {
  createUser: (
    _: any,
    { input }: { input: ICreateUserInput },
    { models }: { models: IModels }
  ): IUser => models.User.create({ ...input }),
  login: (
    _: any,
    { input }: { input: ILoginInput },
    { models }: { models: IModels }
  ): Promise<IAuthPayload> => doLogin(input.email, input.password, models)
}
```

You need to pass the email, password, and models to the doLogin function.

Merging our resolvers

As we did with our types definitions, we need to merge all our resolvers using the @graphql-tools packages. You need to create the following file at /backend/src/graphql/resolvers/index.ts:

```
import path from 'path'
import { loadFilesSync } from '@graphql-tools/load-files'
import { mergeResolvers } from '@graphql-tools/merge'

const resolversArray = loadFilesSync(path.join(__dirname, './'))
const resolvers = mergeResolvers(resolversArray)

export default resolvers
```

This will combine all your resolvers into an array of resolvers.

Creating Sequelize models

Before we jump into the authentication functions, we need to create our `User` model in Sequelize. For this, we need to create a file at `/backend/src/models/User.ts`. Our model will have the following fields:

- `id`
- `username`
- `password`
- `email`
- `privilege`
- `active`

Let's see the code:

```
// Dependencies
import { encrypt } from '@contentpi/lib'

// Interfaces
import { IUser, IDataTypes } from '../types'

export default (sequelize: any, DataTypes: IDataTypes): IUser => {
  const User = sequelize.define(
    'User',
    {
      id: {
        primaryKey: true,
        allowNull: false,
        type: DataTypes.UUID,
        defaultValue: DataTypes.UUIDV4()
      },
      username: {
        type: DataTypes.STRING,
        allowNull: false,
        unique: true,
        validate: {
          isAlphanumeric: {
            args: true,
            msg: 'The user just accepts alphanumeric characters'
          },
          len: {
            args: [4, 20],
            msg: 'The username must be from 4 to 20 characters'
          }
        }
      }
```

```
      },
      password: {
        type: DataTypes.STRING,
        allowNull: false
      },
      email: {
        type: DataTypes.STRING,
        allowNull: false,
        unique: true,
        validate: {
          isEmail: {
            args: true,
            msg: 'Invalid email'
          }
        }
      },
      privilege: {
        type: DataTypes.STRING,
        allowNull: false,
        defaultValue: 'user'
      },
      active: {
        type: DataTypes.BOOLEAN,
        allowNull: false,
        defaultValue: false
      }
    },
    {
      hooks: {
        beforeCreate: (user: IUser): void => {
          user.password = encrypt(user.password)
        }
      }
    }
  )

  return User
}
```

As you can see, we are defining a Sequelize Hook called `beforeCreate`, which helps us encrypt (using `sha1`) the user password right before the data is saved. Finally, we return the `User` model.

Connecting Sequelize to a PostgreSQL database

Now that we've created the user model, we need to connect Sequelize to our PostgreSQL database and put all our models together. You need to add the following code to the `/backend/src/models/index.ts` file:

```
// Dependencies
import { Sequelize } from 'sequelize'

// Configuration
import { $db } from '../../config'

// Interfaces
import { IModels } from '../types'

// Db Connection
const { dialect, port, host, database, username, password } = $db

// Connecting to the database
const uri =
`${dialect}://${username}:${password}@${host}:${port}/${database}`
const sequelize = new Sequelize(uri)

// Models
const models: IModels = {
  User: require('./User').default(sequelize, Sequelize),
  sequelize
}

export default models
```

Authentication functions

Step by step, we are putting all the puzzle pieces together. Now, let's look at the authentication functions we are using to validate whether a user is connected or not and get the user's data. For this, we need to use **JSON Web Tokens (JWTs)**.

What is JSON Web Token?

JWT is an open standard – RFC 7519 (`https://tools.ietf.org/html/rfc7519`) – which is useful for transmitting information between parties as a JSON object. The advantage of JWTs is that they are digitally signed, which is why they can be verified and trusted. It uses the HMAC algorithm to sign the token by using a secret or a public key pair using RSA or ECDSA.

JWT functions

Let's create some functions that will help verify a JWT and get the user data. For this, we need to create the `jwtVerify`, `getUserData`, and `createToken` functions. This file should be created at `/backend/src/lib/jwt.ts`:

```
// Dependencies
import jwt from 'jsonwebtoken'
import { encrypt, setBase64, getBase64 } from '@contentpi/lib'

// Configuration
import { $security } from '../../config'

// Interface
import { IUser } from '../types'

const { secretKey } = $security

export function jwtVerify(accessToken: string, cb: any): void {
  // Verifiying our JWT token using the accessToken and the secretKey
  jwt.verify(
    accessToken,
    secretKey,
    (error: any, accessTokenData: any = {}) => {
      const { data: user } = accessTokenData

      // If we get an error or the user is not found we return false
      if (error || !user) {
        return cb(false)
      }

      // The user data is on base64 and getBase64 will retreive the
      // information as JSON object
      const userData = getBase64(user)

      return cb(userData)
    }
```

```
    )
  }

  export async function getUserData(accessToken: string): Promise<any> {
    // We resolve the jwtVerify promise to get the user data
    const UserPromise = new Promise(resolve =>
      jwtVerify(accessToken, (user: any) => resolve(user))
    )

    // This will get the user data or false (if the user is not connected)
    const user = await UserPromise

    return user
  }

  export const createToken = async (user: IUser): Promise<string[]> => {
    // Extracting the user data
    const { id, username, password, email, privilege, active } = user

    // Encrypting our password by combining the secretKey and the password
    // and converting it to base64
    const token = setBase64(`${encrypt($security.secretKey)}${password}`)

    // The "token" is an alias for password in this case
    const userData = {
      id,
      username,
      email,
      privilege,
      active,
      token
    }

    // We sign our JWT token and we save the data as Base64
    const _createToken = jwt.sign(
      { data: setBase64(userData) },
      $security.secretKey,
      { expiresIn: $security.expiresIn }
    )

    return Promise.all([_createToken])
  }
```

As you can see, `jwt.sign` is used to create a new JWT, while `jwt.verify` is used to validate our JWT.

Creating authentication functions

Now that we've created the JWT functions, we need to create some functions that will help us log in at /backend/src/lib/auth.ts:

```ts
// Dependencies
import { AuthenticationError } from 'apollo-server'

// Utils
import { encrypt, isPasswordMatch } from '@contentpi/lib'

// Interface
import { IUser, IModels, IAuthPayload } from '../types'

// JWT
import { createToken } from './jwt'

export const getUserBy = async (
  where: any,
  models: IModels
): Promise<IUser> => {
  // We find a user by a WHERE condition
  const user = await models.User.findOne({
    where,
    raw: true
  })

  return user
}

export const doLogin = async (
  email: string,
  password: string,
  models: IModels
): Promise<IAuthPayload> => {
  // Finding a user by email
  const user = await getUserBy({ email }, models)

  // If the user does not exists we return Invalid Login
  if (!user) {
    throw new AuthenticationError('Invalid Login')
  }

  // We verify that our encrypted password is the same as the user.password
  // value
  const passwordMatch = isPasswordMatch(encrypt(password), user.password)

  // We validate that the user is active
```

```
const isActive = user.active

// If the password does not match we return invalid login
if (!passwordMatch) {
  throw new AuthenticationError('Invalid Login')
}

// If the account is not active we return an error
if (!isActive) {
  throw new AuthenticationError('Your account is not activated yet')
}

// If the user exists, the password is correct and the account is active
// then we create the JWT token
const [token] = await createToken(user)

// Finally we return the token to Graphql
return {
  token
}
}
```

Here, we are validating whether the user exists by email, whether the password is correct, and whether the account is active in order to create the JWT.

Types and interfaces

Finally, we need to define our types and interfaces for all our Sequelize models and GraphQL inputs. For this, you need to create a file at /backend/src/types/types.ts:

```
export type User = {
  username: string
  password: string
  email: string
  privilege: string
  active: boolean
}

export type Sequelize = {
  _defaults?: any
  name?: string
  options?: any
  associate?: any
}
```

Now, let's create our interfaces at `/backend/src/types/interfaces.ts`:

```
// Types
import { User, Sequelize } from './types'

// Sequelize
export interface IDataTypes {
  UUID: string
  UUIDV4(): string
  STRING: string
  BOOLEAN: boolean
  TEXT: string
  INTEGER: number
  DATE: string
  FLOAT: number
}

// User
export interface IUser extends User, Sequelize {
  id: string
  token?: string
  createdAt?: Date
  updatedAt?: Date
}

export interface ICreateUserInput extends User {}

export interface ILoginInput {
  email: string
  password: string
}

export interface IAuthPayload {
  token: string
}

// Models
export interface IModels {
  User: any
  sequelize: any
}
```

Finally, we need to export both files in `/backend/src/types/index.ts`:

```
export * from './interfaces'
export * from './types'
```

When you need to add more models, remember to always add your types and interfaces to those files.

Finally, you need to create your `tsconfig.json` file at the root directory:

```
{
  "compilerOptions": {
    "baseUrl": "./src",
    "esModuleInterop": true,
    "module": "commonjs",
    "noImplicitAny": true,
    "outDir": "dist",
    "resolveJsonModule": true,
    "sourceMap": true,
    "target": "es6",
    "typeRoots": ["./src/@types", "./node_modules/@types"]
  },
  "include": ["src/**/*.ts"],
  "exclude": ["node_modules"]
}
```

In the next section, we are going to run our project and create our tables.

Running our project for the first time

If you followed the previous sections correctly and run the `npm run dev` command, you should be able to see that the `Users` table is being created and that Apollo Server is running on port `5000`:

Now, let's say that you want to modify your user model and change the `"username"` field to `"username2"`. Let's see what will happen:

```
[INFO] 23:45:16 Restarting: /Users/czantany/projects/React-Design-Patterns-
and-Best-Practices-Third-
Edition/Chapter05/graphql/backend/src/models/User.ts has been modified
Executing (default): CREATE TABLE IF NOT EXISTS "Users" ("id" UUID NOT NULL
, "username2" VARCHAR(255) NOT NULL UNIQUE, "password" VARCHAR(255) NOT
NULL, "email" VARCHAR(255) NOT NULL UNIQUE, "privilege" VARCHAR(255) NOT
NULL DEFAULT 'user', "active" BOOLEAN NOT NULL DEFAULT false, "createdAt"
TIMESTAMP WITH TIME ZONE NOT NULL, "updatedAt" TIMESTAMP WITH TIME ZONE NOT
NULL, PRIMARY KEY ("id"));
Executing (default): ALTER TABLE "public"."Users" ADD COLUMN "username2"
VARCHAR(255) NOT NULL UNIQUE;
Executing (default): ALTER TABLE "Users" ALTER COLUMN "password" SET NOT
NULL;ALTER TABLE "Users" ALTER COLUMN "password" DROP DEFAULT;ALTER TABLE
"Users" ALTER COLUMN "password" TYPE VARCHAR(255);
Executing (default): ALTER TABLE "Users" ALTER COLUMN "email" SET NOT
NULL;ALTER TABLE "Users" ALTER COLUMN "email" DROP DEFAULT;ALTER TABLE
"Users" ADD UNIQUE ("email");ALTER TABLE "Users" ALTER COLUMN "email" TYPE
VARCHAR(255) ;
Executing (default): ALTER TABLE "Users" ALTER COLUMN "privilege" SET NOT
NULL;ALTER TABLE "Users" ALTER COLUMN "privilege" SET DEFAULT 'user';ALTER
TABLE "Users" ALTER COLUMN "privilege" TYPE VARCHAR(255);
Executing (default): ALTER TABLE "Users" ALTER COLUMN "active" SET NOT
NULL;ALTER TABLE "Users" ALTER COLUMN "active" SET DEFAULT false;ALTER
TABLE "Users" ALTER COLUMN "active" TYPE BOOLEAN;
Executing (default): ALTER TABLE "Users" ALTER COLUMN "createdAt" SET NOT
NULL;ALTER TABLE "Users" ALTER COLUMN "createdAt" DROP DEFAULT;ALTER TABLE
"Users" ALTER COLUMN "createdAt" TYPE TIMESTAMP WITH TIME ZONE;
Running on http://localhost:5000/
```

This will execute the following SQL query:

```
Executing (default): ALTER TABLE "public"."Users" ADD COLUMN "username2"
VARCHAR(255) NOT NULL UNIQUE;
Executing (default): ALTER TABLE "public"."Users" DROP COLUMN "username";
```

Now, let's suppose you changed the `force` constant in your `index.ts` file to `true`. The following will happen:

```
Running on http://localhost:5000/
[INFO] 09:12:44 Restarting: /Users/czantany/projects/React-Design-Patterns-and-Best-Practices-Third-Edition/Chapter05/graphql/backend/src/index.ts has been modified
Executing (default): DROP TABLE IF EXISTS "Users" CASCADE;
Executing (default): DROP TABLE IF EXISTS "Users" CASCADE;
Executing (default): CREATE TABLE IF NOT EXISTS "Users" ("id" UUID NOT NULL , "username2" VARCHAR(255) NOT NULL UNIQUE, "password" VARCHAR(255) NOT NULL, "email" VARCHAR(255) NOT NULL UNI
QUE, "privilege" VARCHAR(255) NOT NULL DEFAULT 'user', "active" BOOLEAN NOT NULL DEFAULT false, "createdAt" TIMESTAMP WITH TIME ZONE NOT NULL, "updatedAt" TIMESTAMP WITH TIME ZONE NOT NUL
L, PRIMARY KEY ("id"));
```

As you can see, if `force` is `true`, it will execute `DROP TABLE IF EXISTS "Users"` `CASCADE;`. This will completely remove your table and values and then recreate your table from scratch. That's why you need to be careful when you use the `force` option.

At this point, if you open `http://localhost:5000`, you should be able to see your GraphQL Playground:

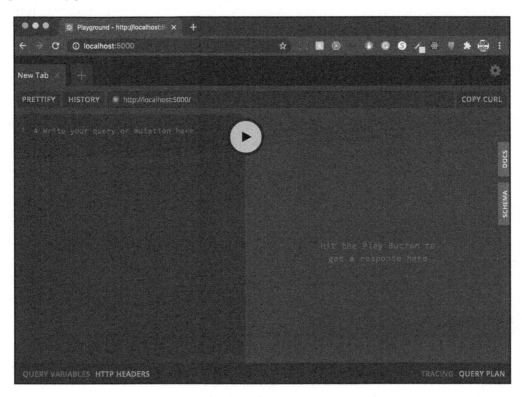

Now, we are ready to test our queries and mutations.

Testing our GraphQL queries and mutations

Great! At this point, you're very close to executing your first GraphQL query and mutation. The first query we will execute is going to be `getUsers`. The following is the correct syntax for running a query:

```
query {
  getUsers {
    id
```

```
        username
        email
        privilege
    }
}
```

When you don't have any attribute to pass to the query, you just need to specify the name of the query under the `query {...}` block and then specify the fields you want to retrieve once you've executed your query. In this case, we want to fetch the `id`, `username`, `email`, and `privilege` fields.

If you run this query, you will probably get an empty array of data. This is because we don't have any users registered yet:

This means we need to execute our `createUser` mutation in order to register our first user. One thing I like about GraphQL Playground is that you have all the schema documentation in the **DOCS** tab on the right-hand side. If you click on the **DOCS** tab, you will see all your queries and mutations listed. Let's click there and select our `createUser` mutation to see what needs to be called and what data may be returned:

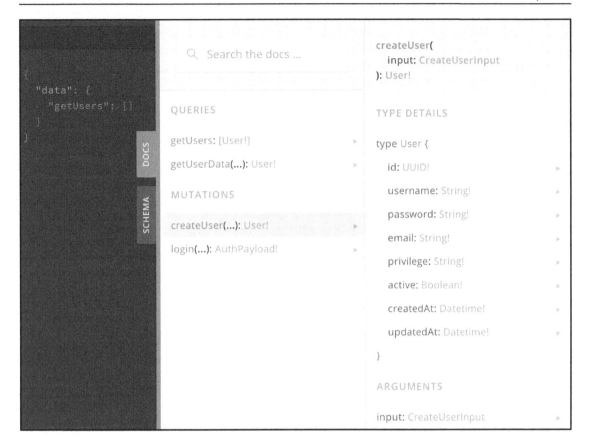

As you can see, the `createUser` mutation needs an input argument, which is `CreateUserInput`. Let's click on that input:

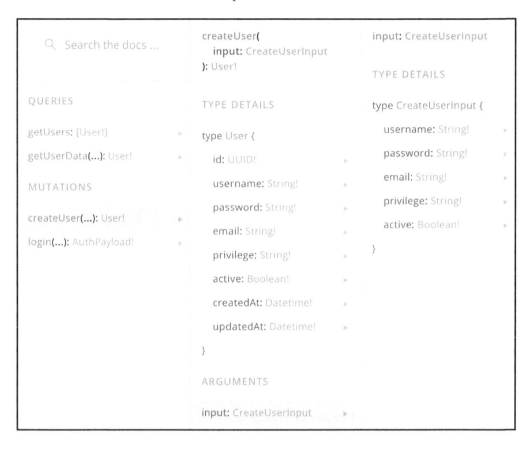

Awesome! Now, we know that we need to pass the `username`, `password`, `email`, `privilege`, and `active` fields in order to create a new user and that we will receive the same fields, plus the generated ID, for the user. Let's do this!

Create a new tab so that you don't lose the code of your first query and then write the mutation:

```
mutation {
  createUser(
    input: {
      username: "admin",
      email: "admin@js.education",
      password: "123456",
      privilege: "god",
```

```
      active: true
    }
  ) {
    id
    username
    email
    password
    privilege
  }
}
```

As you can see, your mutation needs to be written under the mutation {...} block, and you must pass the input argument as an object. Finally, you must specify the fields you want to retrieve once the mutation has been executed correctly. If everything is OK, you should see something like this:

If you're curious and wish to take a look at the terminal where you're running your Apollo Server, you will see the SQL query that was performed for this user:

```
Executing (default): INSERT INTO "Users"
("id","username","password","email","privilege","active","createdAt","updat
edAt") VALUES ($1,$2,$3,$4,$5,$6,$7,$8) RETURNING
"id","username","password","email","privilege","active","createdAt","update
dAt";
```

The VALUES variables are handled by Apollo Server, so you won't see the actual values in there, but you can find out which operation is being executed in the database.

Now, go back to your first query (getUsers) and run it again!

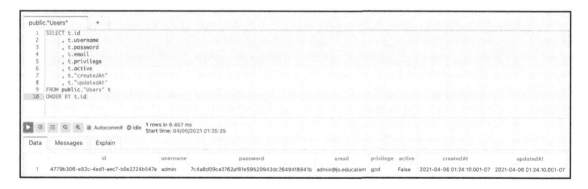

Nice – this is your first query and mutation that have been executed correctly in GraphQL. If you want to see this data in your database, you can use OmniDB to view your Users table in your PostgreSQL database:

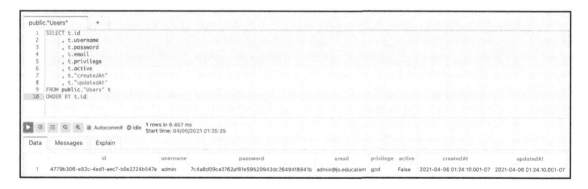

As you can see, our first record has its own id field (UUID) and also has an encrypted password field (do you remember our beforeCreate Hook in the user model?). By default, Sequelize will create the createdAt and updatedAt fields.

Validations

As you may recall, regarding our user model, you will want to make sure all the validations we did are working fine, such as whether the user is unique or whether their email is valid and unique. You just need to execute the exact same mutation again:

```
"errors": [
  {
    "message": "Validation error",
    "locations": [
      {
        "line": 2,
        "column": 3
      }
    ],
    "path": [
      "createUser"
    ],
    "extensions": {
      "code": "INTERNAL_SERVER_ERROR",
      "exception": {
        "name": "SequelizeUniqueConstraintError",
        "errors": [
          {
            "message": "username must be unique",
            "type": "unique violation",
            "path": "username",
            "value": "admin",
            "origin": "DB",
            "instance": {
              "id": "7011d5b9-be54-4a59-9767-3a77396fd7db",
              "username": "admin",
              "password": "7c4a8d09ca3762af61e59520943dc26494f8941b",
              "email": "admin@js.education",
              "privilege": "god",
              "active": true,
              "updatedAt": "2021-04-06T08:04:57.856Z",
              "createdAt": "2021-04-06T08:04:57.856Z"
            },
            "validatorKey": "not_unique",
            "validatorName": null,
            "validatorArgs": []
          }
```

As you can see, we will get a `"username must be unique"` error message because we've already registered the `"admin"` username. Now, let's try to change the username to `"admin2"` but leave the email as is (`admin@js.education`):

```
"errors": [
  {
    "message": "Validation error",
    "locations": [
      {
        "line": 2,
        "column": 3
      }
    ],
    "path": [
      "createUser"
    ],
    "extensions": {
      "code": "INTERNAL_SERVER_ERROR",
      "exception": {
        "name": "SequelizeUniqueConstraintError",
        "errors": [
          {
            "message": "email must be unique",
            "type": "unique violation",
            "path": "email",
            "value": "admin@js.education",
            "origin": "DB",
            "instance": {
              "id": "df8fc316-e2a8-4a16-b4a0-754908128e13",
              "username": "admin2",
              "password": "7c4a8d09ca3762af61e59520943dc26494f8941b",
              "email": "admin@js.education",
              "privilege": "god",
              "active": true,
              "updatedAt": "2021-04-06T08:09:10.308Z",
              "createdAt": "2021-04-06T09:09:10.308Z"
            },
            "validatorKey": "not_unique",
            "validatorName": null,
            "validatorArgs": []
          }
```

We will also get an `"email must be unique"` error for the email. Now, try to change the email to something invalid, such as `admin@myfakedomain`:

```
"errors": [
  {
    "message": "Validation error: Invalid email",
    "locations": [
      {
        "line": 2,
        "column": 3
      }
    ],
    "path": [
      "createUser"
    ],
    "extensions": {
      "code": "INTERNAL_SERVER_ERROR",
      "exception": {
        "name": "SequelizeValidationError",
        "errors": [
          {
            "message": "Invalid email",
            "type": "Validation error",
            "path": "email",
            "value": "admin@myfakedomain",
            "origin": "FUNCTION",
            "instance": {
              "id": "c4445ca7-cae1-442b-a777-f058674ba48d",
              "username": "admin2",
              "password": "123456",
              "email": "admin@myfakedomain",
              "privilege": "god",
              "active": true,
              "updatedAt": "2021-04-06T08:10:49.060Z",
              "createdAt": "2021-04-06T08:10:49.060Z"
            },
            "validatorKey": "isEmail",
            "validatorName": "isEmail",
            "validatorArgs": [
              {
```

Now, we're getting an "Invalid email" error message. This is just amazing, don't you think? Now, let's stop playing with the validations and add a new valid user (username: admin2, email: admin2@js.education). Once you've created your second user, run our getUsers query once more. However, this time, add the "active" field to the list of fields we want to return:

```
1 ▼ query {
2 ▼   getUsers {
3         id
4         username
5         email
6         privilege
7         active
8     }
9 }
```

```
▼ {
▼   "data": {
▼     "getUsers": [
▼       {
            "id": "b1caf356-b894-4e66-8eb3-2e233dcf51b9",
            "username": "admin2",
            "email": "admin2@js.education",
            "privilege": "god",
            "active": false
        },
▼       {
            "id": "4779b306-e82c-4ed1-aec7-b0e2224b547e",
            "username": "admin",
            "email": "admin@js.education",
            "privilege": "god",
            "active": false
        }
      ]
    }
}
```

Now, we have two registered users, and both are inactive accounts (active = false).

One thing I love about GraphQL is that when you're writing your queries or mutations and you don't remember a certain field, GraphQL will always show you the list of available fields for that query or mutation. For example, if you just write the letter p for the password, you will see something like this:

Now, we are ready to try and log in!

Performing a login

I want to congratulate you for getting to this point in this book – I know we have covered a lot, but we are almost there! Now, we are going to try and log in with GraphQL (how crazy is that?).

First, we need to write our login mutation:

```
mutation {
  login(
    input: {
      email: "fake@email.com",
      password: "123456"
    }
  ) {
    token
  }
}
```

Then, we need to log our user in by using "fake@email.com" as our email and "123456" as our password. These do not exist in our database:

Because the email does not exist in our database, an "Invalid Login" error message will be returned. Now, let's add the correct email but use a fake password:

As you can see, we are receiving the exact same error ("Invalid Login"). This is because we don't want to provide too much information about what's wrong with the login as someone may be trying to hack another user. If we say something such as "Invalid password" or "Your email does not exist in our system", we are giving the attackers extra information that they may find useful.

Now, let's try to connect with the correct user and password (`admin@js.education` / `123456`) and see what happens:

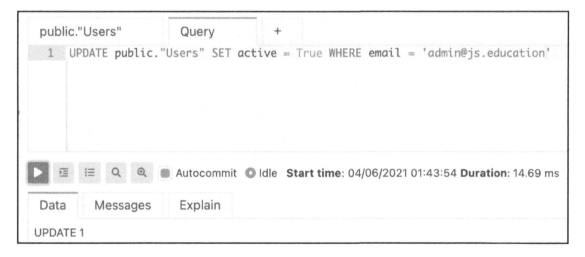

Now, we are receiving an error stating `"Your account is not activated yet"`. This is OK because our user has not been activated yet. Normally, when a user is registered in a system, you need to send a link to their email so that they can activate their account. We don't have this feature at the moment, but let's suppose we sent that email and the user has already activated their account. We can simulate this by manually changing the value in our database using OnmiDB. We can do this by performing an UPDATE SQL query:

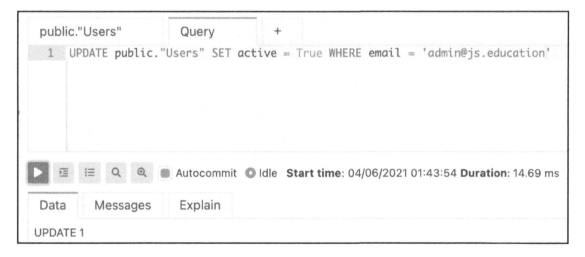

Now, let's try to log in again!

```
{
  "data": {
    "login": {
      "token":
"eyJhbGciOiJIUzI1NiIsInR5cCI6IkpXVCJ9.eyJkYXRhIjoiZXlKcFpDSTZJalEzTnpsaU16QTJMV1U0TW1NdE5HVmtNUz
FoWldNM0xXSXdaVEl5TWpSaU5UNaU0lzSW5WelpYSnVZVZVzFsSWppaVlXUnhhVzpTENKbGGJXRnBiQ0k2SW1Ga2JXbkVRR3
B6TG1Wa2RXTmhkR2x2YmlJc0luQnlhHWFpwYkdWblpTSTZJbWR2WkJNWRNJc0ltRmpkR2wyWWlNJNmRISjFaU3dppZEc5clpXNGlPaU
pOUkddjeldWUkZNMXBVWWjNwTmJWVjVVV33BWTWs1SFJtMWFiVTB6V21wTk5GBFVRWGGxhVkdSSb1RVUm9iVTFIV1ROTmJWa3dkXVl
JrYWs1SFJUUUmFSRUUxV1RKRmVrNTZXWGGxaVjFreVRWWZFZNVTlVVlhsTlJHc3dUVUVpTYWsxcVdUUQlBWRkp0VDBSck1FMVVVhTVD
BpZlE9PSIsImlhdCI6MTYxNzY5ODY4OSwiZXhwIjoxNjE4MzAzNDg5fQ.6icaBFibjEOICUt5QQ0OPAoDsb7_ohb8W10JzHn
bf7k"
    }
  }
}
```

Nice – we are in baby! **You at this point**:

We are anonymous, we are legion, we do not forgive, we do not forget, expect us!

Now that we've logged in and retrieved our JWT, let's copy that huge string and use it in our `getUserData` query to see whether we can get the user's data:

```
query {
  getUserData(at:
"eyJhbGciOiJIUzI1NiIsInR5cCI6IkpXVCJ9.eyJkYXRhIjoiZXlKcFpDSTZJalEzTnpsaU16Q
TJMV1U0TW1NdE5HVmtNUzFoWldNM0xXSXdaVEl5TWpSaU5UNaU0lzSW5WelpYSnVZVZVzFsSWppv
aVlXUnhhVzpTENKbGGJXRnBiQ0k2SW1Ga2JXbkVRR3B6TG1Wa2RXTmhkR2x2YmlJc0luQnlhHWFp
wYkdWblpTSTZJbWR2WkJNWRNJc0ltRmpkR2wyWWlNJNmRISjFaU3dppZEc5clpXNGlPaUpOUkddjeldWUk
ZNMXBVWWjNwTmJWVjVVV33BWTWs1SFJtMWFiVTB6V21wTk5GBFVRWGGxhVkdSb1RVUm9iVTFIV1lROT
mJXYTN3dXVlJrYWs1SFJUUUmFSRUUxV1RKRmVrNTZXWGGxaVjFreVRWWZFZNVTlVVlhsTlJHc3dVVEpT
```

```
YWsxcVdUQlBWRkp0VDBSck1FMVhTVDBpZlE9PSIsImlhdCI6MTYxNzY5ODY4OSwiZXhwIjoxNjE
4MzAzNDg5fQ.6icaBFibjEOICUt5QQ0OPAoDsb7_ohb8W10JzHnbf7k") {
    id
    email
    privilege
    active
  }
}
```

If everything went well, then you should get the user's data:

```
{
  "data": {
    "getUserData": {
      "id": "4779b306-e82c-4ed1-aec7-b0e2224b547e",
      "email": "admin@js.education",
      "privilege": "god",
      "active": true
    }
  }
}
```

If you change or remove any letter from the string (meaning the token is invalid), then you should get empty user data:

```
{
  "data": {
    "getUserData": {
      "id": "",
      "email": "",
      "privilege": "",
      "active": false
    }
  }
}
```

Now that our login system works perfectly in the backend, it is time to implement this in the frontend application. We'll do this in the next section.

Building a frontend login system with Apollo Client

In the previous section, we learned how to build the backend for a login system using Apollo Server to create our GraphQL queries and mutations. You are probably thinking, *Great, I have the backend working, but how can I use this on the frontend?* And you're right – I always like to explain things with full examples and not just show basic things, even if this will take longer to do, so let's get started!

You can find the code for the example in this section at `https://github.com/ PacktPublishing/React-17-Design-Patterns-and-Best-Practices-Third-Edition/tree/ main/Chapter05/graphql/frontend`.

Configuring Webpack 5

Instead of using a `create-react-app` project, we will configure a React project from scratch using Webpack 5 and Node.

The first thing we need to do is install all the packages we are going to use:

```
npm init --yes

npm install @apollo/client @contentpi/lib cookie-parser cors express
express-session jsonwebtoken react react-dom react-cookie react-router-dom
styled-components

npm install --save-dev @babel/core @babel/preset-env @babel/preset-react
buffer cross-env crypto-browserify dotenv prettier stream-browserify ts-
loader ts-node ts-node-dev typescript webpack webpack-cli webpack-dev-
server html-webpack-plugin
```

The buffer, `crypto-browserify`, and `stream-browserify` are polyfills that were included by default in Webpack <= 4. However, in the latest version (Webpack 5), these are not included anymore, so you will get the following error:

```
ERROR in ./node_modules/@contentpi/lib/dist/security/index.js 8:33-50
Module not found: Error: Can't resolve 'crypto' in '/Users/czantany/projects/React-Design-Patterns-and-Best-Practices-Third-Edition/Chapter05/graph
ql/frontend/node_modules/@contentpi/lib/dist/security'

BREAKING CHANGE: webpack < 5 used to include polyfills for node.js core modules by default.
This is no longer the case. Verify if you need this module and configure a polyfill for it.

If you want to include a polyfill, you need to:
        - add a fallback 'resolve.fallback: { "crypto": require.resolve("crypto-browserify") }'
        - install 'crypto-browserify'
If you don't want to include a polyfill, you can use an empty module like this:
        resolve.fallback: { "crypto": false }
```

You need to have those scripts in your `package.json`:

```
"scripts": {
    "start": "ts-node src/server",
    "dev": "ts-node-dev src/server",
    "webpack": "cross-env NODE_ENV=development webpack serve --mode
development",
    "build": "cross-env NODE_ENV=production webpack --mode production",
    "clean": "rimraf dist/ && rimraf public/app",
    "lint": "eslint . --ext .js,.tsx,.ts",
    "lint:fix": "eslint . --fix --ext .js,.tsx,.ts",
    "test": "jest src",
    "test:coverage": "jest src --coverage"
}
```

Let's check our Webpack 5 configuration file (`/frontend/webpack.config.ts`):

```
// Dependencies
import path from 'path'
import webpack, { Configuration } from 'webpack'
import HtmlWebPackPlugin from 'html-webpack-plugin'

// Environment
const isProduction = process.env.NODE_ENV === 'production'

const webpackConfig: Configuration = {
  devtool: !isProduction ? 'source-map' : false,
  target: 'web',
  mode: isProduction ? 'production' : 'development',
  entry: './src/index.tsx',
  output: {
    path: path.join(__dirname, 'dist'),
    filename: '[name].js',
    publicPath: '/'
  },
  resolve: {
    extensions: ['.ts', '.tsx', '.js', '.json'],
    fallback: { // This is to fix the polifylls errors
      buffer: require.resolve('buffer'),
      crypto: require.resolve("crypto-browserify"),
      stream: require.resolve("stream-browserify")
    }
  },
  module: {
    rules: [
      {
        test: /\.(ts|tsx)$/,
        use: {
```

```
              loader: 'ts-loader',
              options: {
                transpileOnly: true
              }
          },
          exclude: /node_modules/
      }
    ]
  },
  optimization: {
    splitChunks: { // This will split our bundles into vendor.js and
    // main.js
      cacheGroups: {
        default: false,
        commons: {
          test: /node_modules/,
          name: 'vendor',
          chunks: 'all'
        }
      }
    }
  },
  plugins: [
    new webpack.HotModuleReplacementPlugin(),
    new HtmlWebPackPlugin({
      template: './src/index.html',
      filename: './index.html',
      publicPath: !isProduction ? 'http://localhost:8080/' : '' // For dev
      // we will read the bundle from localhost:8080 (webpack-dev-server)
    })
  ]
}

export default webpackConfig
```

At this point, you need to create the index.html file, which should be
at /frontend/src/index.html:

```html
<!DOCTYPE html>
<html>
  <head>
    <meta charset="UTF-8" />
    <meta name="viewport" content="width=device-width, initial-scale=1,
      maximum-scale=1" />
    <meta http-equiv="X-UA-Compatible" content="ie=edge" />
    <title>Login System</title>
  </head>
```

```
<body>
  <div id="root"></div>
</body>
</html>
```

In the next section, we will configure our TypeScript.

Configuring our TypeScript

Our tsconfig.json file should look like this:

```
{
  "compilerOptions": {
    "sourceMap": true,
    "target": "es5",
    "lib": ["dom", "dom.iterable", "esnext"],
    "allowJs": true,
    "skipLibCheck": true,
    "esModuleInterop": true,
    "allowSyntheticDefaultImports": true,
    "strict": true,
    "forceConsistentCasingInFileNames": true,
    "noFallthroughCasesInSwitch": true,
    "module": "commonjs",
    "moduleResolution": "node",
    "resolveJsonModule": true,
    "isolatedModules": true,
    "noEmit": true,
    "jsx": "react-jsx",
    "noImplicitAny": false,
    "types": ["node", "express"]
  },
  "include": ["src"]
}
```

Now, let's learn how to configure the Express server.

Configuring the Express server

Our application requires the Express server so that we can perform validations. These will help us find out whether the user is connected (using a custom middleware, which I'll explain later) and can also configure our Express sessions. We have four main routes on our site:

- `/`: Our home page **(handled by React)**.
- `/dashboard`: Our dashboard, which is protected. Only connected users with god or admin permissions are allowed **(handled by Express first then by React)**.
- `/login`: Our login page **(handled by React)**.
- `/logout`: This will delete our existing session **(handled by Express)**.

Let's look at our server code. The following file should exist at `/frontend/src/server.ts`:

```typescript
// Dependencies
import express, { Request, Response, NextFunction } from 'express'
import path from 'path'
import cookieParser from 'cookie-parser'
import cors from 'cors'
import session from 'express-session'

// Middleware
import { isConnected } from './lib/middlewares/user'

// Config
import config from './config'

// Express app
const app = express();
const port = process.env.NODE_PORT || 3000
const DIST_DIR = path.join(__dirname, '../dist')
const HTML_FILE = path.join(DIST_DIR, 'index.html')

// Making the dist directory static
app.use(express.static(DIST_DIR));

// Middlewares
app.use(
  session({
    resave: false,
    saveUninitialized: true,
    secret: config.security.secretKey
  })
```

```
  )
  app.use(express.json());
  app.use(express.urlencoded({ extended: true }));
  app.use(cookieParser(config.security.secretKey))
  app.use(cors({ credentials: true, origin: true }))

  // Routes
  app.get('/dashboard',
    isConnected(
      true,
      ['god', 'admin'], // Those are the allowed permissions
      `/login?redirectTo=/dashboard` // If the user is not allowed will be
      // redirect to this path
    ),
    (req: Request, res: Response, next: NextFunction) => {
      // If the user isConnected then we allow the access to the dashboard
      // page otherwise will be redirect to /login
      next()
    }
  )

  // Forcing only No connected users to access to /login, if a connected user
  // try to access will be redirect to the homepage
  app.get('/login', isConnected(false), (req: Request, res: Response, next:
  NextFunction) => {
    next()
  })

  app.get(`/logout`, (req: Request, res: Response) => {
    // This will cler our "at" cookie and redirect to home
    res.clearCookie('at')
    res.redirect('/')
  })

  app.get('*', (req: Request, res: Response) => {
    // We render our React application
    res.sendFile(HTML_FILE)
  })

  // Listening
  app.listen(port, () => console.log(`Running at http://localhost:${port}`))
```

As you can see, we are protecting our dashboard route with the isConnected middleware. Here, we are validating that we only accept users that are not connected in the login route.

Creating our frontend configuration

Now, we need to create our frontend configuration. So, let's create the `common.json` configuration at `/frontend/src/config/common.json`:

```json
{
  "server": {
    "port": 3000
  },
  "security": {
    "secretKey": "C0nt3ntP1", // This needs to be the same as the backend
      // secretKey
    "expiresIn": "7d"
  }
}
```

Now, let's create our `local.json` file:

```json
{
  "baseUrl": "http://localhost:3000",
  "apiUrl": "http://localhost:5000/graphql"
}
```

Now, we need to create our `production.json` file; for now since we don't have an actual production environment we will use the same localhost URL, but once you put this project in a production environment then you will need to change it for the actual domain name:

```json
{
  "baseUrl": "http://localhost:3000",
  "apiUrl": "http://localhost:5000/graphql"
}
```

Now that we've defined our configuration files, we need to create an `index.ts` file so that we can merge and export our configuration as an object:

```typescript
// Configuration
import common from './common.json'
import local from './local.json'
import production from './production.json'

// Interface
interface IConfig {
 baseUrl: string
 apiUrl: string
 server: {
 port: number
 }
```

```
  security: {
  secretKey: string
  expiresIn: string
   }
}

const { NODE_ENV = 'development' } = process.env

// development => local
let environment = 'local'

if (NODE_ENV !== 'development') {
 environment = NODE_ENV
}

// Configurations by environment
const config: IConfig = {
 ...common,
 ...(environment === 'local' ? local : production)
}

// Environments validations
export const isLocal = () => environment === 'local'
export const isProduction = () => environment === 'production'

export default config
```

Now, we need to create a user called `middleware` and the `jwt` functions to validate whether the user is connected and has the correct privileges.

Creating the user middleware

A middleware is a function that has access to the request object (**req**), the response object (**res**), and the next function in the application's request-response cycle. The **next** function is a function in the Express router that, when invoked, executes the middleware succeeding the current middleware. The following diagram describes the middleware flow:

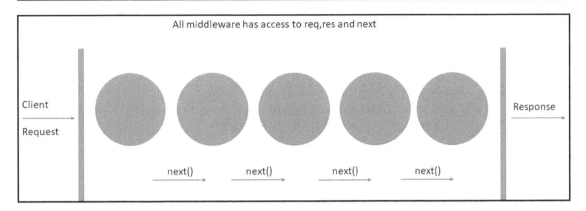

In our case, we will create the `isConnected` middleware to validate if a user is connected and has the correct privileges. If not, then we will break the flow and redirect them to the login page. If the user is valid, we will execute the next piece of middleware, which will render our React application.

The following diagram describes this process:

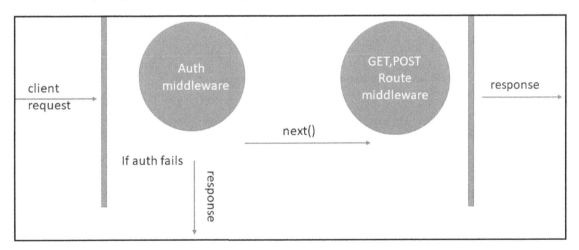

Let's apply the theoretical part to our code. The required file should exist at /frontend/src/lib/middlewares/user.ts:

```ts
// Dependencies
import { Request, Response, NextFunction } from 'express'

// Lib
import { getUserData } from '../jwt'
```

```
export const isConnected = (isLogged = true, privileges = ['user'],
redirectTo = '/') => async (
  req: Request,
  res: Response,
  next: NextFunction
): Promise<void> => {
  // Getting the user information by passing our 'at' cookie
  const user = await getUserData(req.cookies.at)

  if (!user && !isLogged) {
    // This is to allow No connected users
    return next()
  }

  // Allowing just connected users and validating privileges...
  if (user && isLogged) {
    // If the user is connected and is god...
    if (privileges.includes('god') && user.privilege === 'god') {
      return next()
    }

    // If the user is conencted and is admin...
    if (privileges.includes('admin') && user.privilege === 'admin') {
      return next()
    }

    // If the user is connected but is not god or admin.
    res.redirect(redirectTo)
  } else {
    // If the user is not connected
    res.redirect(redirectTo)
  }
}
```

Basically, with this middleware, we can control whether we want to validate whether the user is connected (isLogged = true). Then, we can validate specific privileges (privileges = ['god', 'admin']) and redirect the user if they are not connected or do not have the correct privileges (redirectTo = '/').

As you can see, we are using the getUserData function from jwt. We'll create our jwt functions in the next section.

Creating JWT functions

In the previous section, when I explained the backend code, I talked about JWTs. In the frontend, we need those functions to validate our token and get the user's data. Let's create a file containing the following code at `/frontend/src/lib/jwt.ts`:

```
// Dependencies
import jwt from 'jsonwebtoken'
import { getBase64 } from '@contentpi/lib'

// Configuration
import config from '../config'

// Getting our secretKey
const {
  security: { secretKey }
} = config

export function jwtVerify(accessToken: any, cb: any): void {
  // Validating our accessToken
  jwt.verify(accessToken, secretKey, (error: any, accessTokenData: any =
  {}) => {
    const { data: user } = accessTokenData

    // If we got an error or the user is not connected we return false
    if (error || !user) {
      return cb(false)
    }

    // Getting the user data
    const userData = getBase64(user)

    return cb(userData)
  })
}

export async function getUserData(accessToken: any): Promise<any> {
  // This is an async function to retrieve the user data from the
  // jwtVerify function
  const UserPromise = new Promise(resolve => jwtVerify(accessToken, (user:
  any) => resolve(user)))

  const user = await UserPromise

  return user
}
```

As you can see, our `getUserData` function will retrieve the user data using `accessToken`, which we grabbed from the cookies. It is important that the JWT is valid.

Creating our GraphQL queries and mutations

We've already created the required queries and mutations in our backend project. At this point, we need to create some files that will execute them in our frontend project. For now, we just need to define our `getUserData` query and our login mutation.

Let's create our `getUserData` query at `/frontend/src/graphql/user/getUserData.query.ts`:

```
// Dependencies
import { gql } from '@apollo/client'

export default gql`
  query getUserData($at: String!) {
    getUserData(at: $at) {
      id
      email
      username
      privilege
      active
    }
  }
`
```

Our login mutation should be at `/frontend/src/graphql/user/login.mutation.ts`:

```
// Dependencies
import { gql } from '@apollo/client'

export default gql`
  mutation login($email: String!, $password: String!) {
    login(input: { email: $email, password: $password }) {
      token
    }
  }
`
```

Now that we have defined our query and mutation, let's create the user context so that we can use them.

Creating our user context to handle the login and the connected user

In our user context, we are going to have a login method that will execute our mutation and validate whether the email and password are correct. We are also going to export the user data.

Let's create this context at /frontend/src/contexts/user.tsx:

```
// Dependencies
import { FC, createContext, ReactElement, useState, useEffect } from
'react'
import { useCookies } from 'react-cookie'
import { getGraphQlError, redirectTo, getDebug } from '@contentpi/lib'
import { useQuery, useMutation } from '@apollo/client'

// Mutations
import LOGIN_MUTATION from '../graphql/user/login.mutation'

// Queries
import GET_USER_DATA_QUERY from '../graphql/user/getUserData.query'

// Interfaces
interface IUserContext {
  login(input: any): any
  connectedUser: any
}

interface IProps {
  page?: string
  children: ReactElement
}

// Creating context
export const UserContext = createContext<IUserContext>({
  login: () => null,
  connectedUser: null
})

const UserProvider: FC<IProps> = ({ page = '', children }): ReactElement =>
{
  const [cookies, setCookie] = useCookies()
```

```
const [connectedUser, setConnectedUser] = useState(null)

// Mutations
const [loginMutation] = useMutation(LOGIN_MUTATION)

// Queries
const { data: dataUser } = useQuery(GET_USER_DATA_QUERY, {
  variables: {
    at: cookies.at || ''
  }
})

// Effects
useEffect(() => {
  if (dataUser) {
    if (!dataUser.getUserData.id && page !== 'login') {
      // If the user session is invalid and is on a different page than
      // login
      // we redirect them to login
      redirectTo('/login?redirectTo=/dashboard')
    } else {
      // If we have the user data available we save it in our
      // connectedUser state
      setConnectedUser(dataUser.getUserData)
    }
  }
}, [dataUser, page])

async function login(input: { email: string; password: string }):
 Promise<any> {
  try {
    // Executing our loginMutation passing the email and password
    const { data: dataLogin } = await loginMutation({
      variables: {
        email: input.email,
        password: input.password
      }
    })

    if (dataLogin) {
      // If the login was success, we save the token in our "at" cookie
      setCookie('at', dataLogin.login.token, { path: '/' })

      return dataLogin.login.token
    }
  } catch (err) {
    // If there is an error we return it
    return getGraphQlError(err)
```

```
    }
  }

  // Exporting our context
  const context = {
    login,
    connectedUser
  }

  return <UserContext.Provider
value={context}>{children}</UserContext.Provider>
}

export default UserProvider
```

As you can see, we are handling the login and got the `connectedUser` data in our context. Here, we are executing `GET_USER_DATA_QUERY` all the time to verify whether the user is connected (validating against the database and not just with the cookies).

Configuring our Apollo Client

So far, we have created a lot of code, but none of it is going to work if we don't configure our Apollo Client. To configure it, we need to add it to our index file at `/frontend/src/index.tsx`:

```
// Dependencies
import { render } from 'react-dom'

// Apollo
import { ApolloProvider, ApolloClient, InMemoryCache } from
'@apollo/client';

// Components
import AppRoutes from './AppRoutes'

// Config
import config from './config'

// Apollo Client configuration
const client = new ApolloClient({
  uri: config.apiUrl,
  cache: new InMemoryCache()
});

render(
  <ApolloProvider client={client}>
```

```
    <AppRoutes />
  </ApolloProvider>
, document.querySelector('#root'))
```

Basically, we are passing `config.apiUrl`, which is where GraphQL Playground is running (`http://localhost:5000/graphql`), and then wrapping our `AppRoutes` component with the `ApolloProvider` component.

Creating our app routes

We are going to use `react-router-dom` to create our application routes. Let's create the required code at `/frontend/src/AppRoutes.tsx`:

```
// Dependencies
import { BrowserRouter as Router, Route, Switch } from 'react-router-dom'

// Components
import HomePage from './pages/home'
import DashboardPage from './pages/dashboard'
import LoginPage from './pages/login'
import Error404 from './pages/error404'

const AppRoutes = () => (
  <Router>
    <Switch>
      <Route path="/" component={HomePage} exact />
      <Route path="/dashboard" component={DashboardPage} exact />
      <Route path="/login" component={LoginPage} exact />
      <Route component={Error404} />
    </Switch>
  </Router>
)pag

export default AppRoutes
```

As you can see, we are adding some pages to our routes, such as `HomePage`, `DashboardPage` (protected), and `LoginPage`. If the user tries to access a different URL, then we will display an `Error404` component. We'll create these pages in the next section.

Creating our pages

The **Home** page should be at `/frontend/src/pages/home.tsx`:

```tsx
const Page = () => (
  <div className="home">
    <h1>Home</h1>

    <ul>
      <li><a href="/dashboard">Go to Dashboard</a></li>
    </ul>
  </div>
)

export default Page
```

The **Dashboard** page should be at `/frontend/src/pages/dashboard.tsx`:

```tsx
// Components
import DashboardLayout from '../components/dashboard/DashboardLayout'

// Contexts
import UserProvider from '../contexts/user'

const Page = () => (
  <UserProvider>
    <DashboardLayout />
  </UserProvider>
)

export default Page
```

The **Login** page should be at `/frontend/src/pages/login.tsx`:

```tsx
// Dependencies
import { FC, ReactElement } from 'react'
import { isBrowser } from '@contentpi/lib'

// Contexts
import UserProvider from '../contexts/user'

// Components
import LoginLayout from '../components/users/LoginLayout'

interface IProps {
  currentUrl: string
}
```

```
const Page: FC<IProps> = ({
  currentUrl = isBrowser() ? window.location.search.replace
    ('?redirectTo=', '') :''}): ReactElement => (
  <UserProvider page="login">
    <LoginLayout currentUrl={currentUrl} />
  </UserProvider>
)

export default Page
```

Finally, we need to create our `Error404` page (`/frontend/src/pages/error404.tsx`):

```
const Page = () => (
  <div className="error404">
    <h1>Error404</h1>
  </div>
)

export default Page
```

We are almost done. The last piece of this puzzle is to create the `Login` and `Dashboard` components. We'll do that in the next section.

Creating our Login components

I created some basic components for our login and our dashboard. Of course, their styles can be improved, but let's see how they work and how our login system is going to look.

The first file you need to create is called `LoginLayout.tsx` at `/frontend/src/components/users/LoginLayout.tsx`:

```
// Dependencies
import { redirectTo } from '@contentpi/lib'
import { FC, ReactElement, useContext, useEffect } from 'react'

// Contexts
import { UserContext } from '../../contexts/user'

// Components
import Login from './Login'

// Interfaces
interface IProps {
  currentUrl: string
}
```

```
const Layout: FC<IProps> = ({ currentUrl }): ReactElement => {
  const { login } = useContext(UserContext)

  return (
    <Login login={login} currentUrl={currentUrl} />
  )
}


export default Layout
```

The layout file is good when we want to add a specific layout to our components. It is also good for consuming data from a context and passing the data or functions as props.

Our Login component should look like this (/frontend/src/components/users/Login.tsx):

```
// Dependencies
import { FC, ReactElement, useState, ChangeEvent } from 'react'
import { redirectTo } from '@contentpi/lib'

// Interfaces
import { IUser } from '../../types'

// Styles
import { StyledLogin } from './Login.styled'

interface IProps {
  login(input: any): any
  currentUrl: string
}

const Login: FC<IProps> = ({ login, currentUrl }) => {
  // States
  const [values, setValues] = useState({
    email: '',
    password: ''
  })
  const [errorMessage, setErrorMessage] = useState('')
  const [invalidLogin, setInvalidLogin] = useState(false)

  // Methods
  const onChange = (e: ChangeEvent<HTMLInputElement>): void => {
    const {
      target: { name, value }
    } = e

    if (name) {
      setValues((prevValues: any) => ({
```

```
          ...prevValues,
          [name]: value
        }))
      }
    }

    const handleSubmit = async (user: IUser): Promise<void> => {
      // Here we execute the login mutation
      const response = await login(user)

      if (response.error) {
        // If the login is invalid...
        setInvalidLogin(true)
        setErrorMessage(response.message)
      } else {
        // If the login is correct...
        redirectTo(currentUrl || '/')
      }
    }

    return (
      <>
        <StyledLogin>
          <div className="wrapper">
            {invalidLogin && <div className="alert">{errorMessage}</div>}
            <div className="form">
              <p>
                <input
                  autoComplete="off"
                  type="email"
                  className="email"
                  name="email"
                  placeholder="Email"
                  onChange={onChange}
                  value={values.email}
                />
              </p>

              <p>
                <input
                  autoComplete="off"
                  type="password"
                  className="password"
                  name="password"
                  placeholder="Password"
                  onChange={onChange}
                  value={values.password}
                />
```

```
          </p>

          <div className="actions">
            <button name="login" onClick={(): Promise<void> =>
              handleSubmit(values)}>
              Login
            </button>
          </div>
        </div>
      </div>
    </StyledLogin>
  </>
  )
}

export default Login
```

We'll create the `Dashboard` components in the next section.

Creating our Dashboard components

Now, let's create our `Dashboard` components. The first one should be
the `DashboardLayout.tsx` file
at `/frontend/src/components/dashboard/DashboardLayout.tsx`:

```
// Dependencies
import { FC, ReactElement, useContext } from 'react'

// Contexts
import { UserContext } from '../../contexts/user'

// Components
import Dashboard from './Dashboard'

const Layout: FC = () => {
  const { connectedUser } = useContext(UserContext)
  // We only render the Dashboard if the user is connected
  if (connectedUser) {
    return (
      <Dashboard connectedUser={connectedUser} />
    )
  }

  return <div />
}
```

```
export default Layout
```

This is how we protect our **Dashboard** page to allow only connected users. Now, let's create our Dashboard component at
/frontend/src/components/dashboard/Dashboard.tsx:

```
interface IProps {
  connectedUser: any
}

const Dashboard = ({ connectedUser }) => (
  <div className="dashboard">
    <h1>Welcome, {connectedUser.username}!</h1>

    <ul>
      <li><a href="/logout">Logout</a></li>
    </ul>
  </div>
)

export default Dashboard
```

And with that, we're done! We'll test the login system in the next section.

Testing our login system

If you followed the previous sections correctly, then you should be able to run the login system successfully. To do this, we need to open three terminals:

- In the first one, you need to run your backend project (npm run dev).
- In the second one in your frontend project, you need to build your project (npm run build).
- In the last one, you need to run the node server in the frontend project (npm run dev).

When you open `http://localhost:3000` for the first time, you should be able to see the **Home** page:

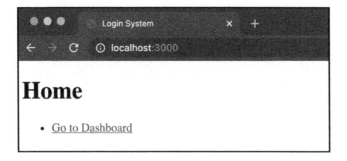

Then, if you click on the **Go to Dashboard** (`http://localhost:3000/dashboard`) link, you will be redirected to `http://localhost:3000/login?redirectTo=/dashboard`, as shown in the following screenshot:

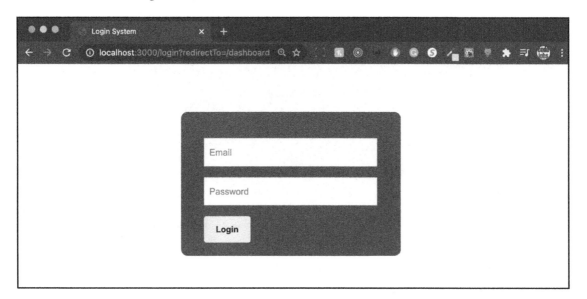

This is our login form. If you try to log in with some fake credentials, you should get an error:

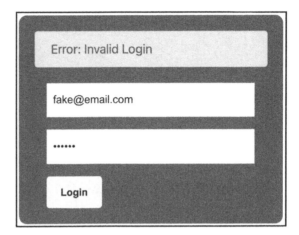

If you want to see the GraphQL request, you can do so on the **Chrome Network** tab:

Here, you can see the query you're executing and the variables you're sending (email and password). You can see the response on the **Preview** tab:

```
Name              × Headers  Preview  Response  Initiator  Timing
graphql     ▼{errors: [{message: "Invalid Login", locations: [{line: 2, column: 3}], path: ["login"],…}],…}
               data: null
            ▼errors: [{message: "Invalid Login", locations: [{line: 2, column: 3}], path: ["login"],…}]
              ▼0: {message: "Invalid Login", locations: [{line: 2, column: 3}], path: ["login"],…}
                ▼extensions: {code: "UNAUTHENTICATED", exception: {stacktrace: ["AuthenticationError: Invalid Login",…]}}
                   code: "UNAUTHENTICATED"
                  ▼exception: {stacktrace: ["AuthenticationError: Invalid Login",…]}
                    ▶stacktrace: ["AuthenticationError: Invalid Login",…]
                ▶locations: [{line: 2, column: 3}]
                   message: "Invalid Login"
                ▶path: ["login"]
```

As you can see, we are getting an `"Invalid Login"` error message, and that's why we are rendering it in our `Login` component. Now, let's try to connect with the correct account (`admin@js.education` / `123456`).

If your login is correct, then you should be redirected to the dashboard, where you will see the following page:

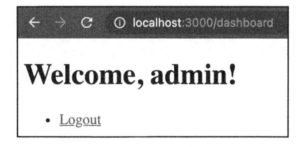

Also, you can take a look at the query that is being executed to retrieve the user data (`getUserData`):

```
▼Request Payload      view source
  ▼{operationName: "getUserData", variables: {,…},…}
     operationName: "getUserData"
     query: "query getUserData($at: String!) {… getUserData(at: $at) {… id… email… username… privilege… active… __typename…
  ▼variables: {,…}
     at: "eyJhbGci0iJIUzI1NiIsInR5cCI6IkpXVCJ9.eyJkYXRhIjoiZXlKcFpDSTZJalEzTnpsaU16Q1JMV1U0TW1NdE5HVmtNUzFoWldN0xXSXdaVE5TWpSaU5UUTUTNaU01zS
```

Here, you will see that the payload is being returned:

We are getting the user information from the access token (`at`). Now, if you refresh the page, you should remain connected to the page. This is because we saved a cookie containing our token:

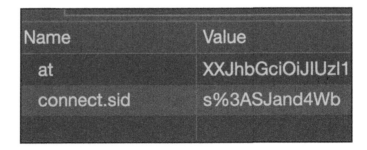

Now, let's try to modify the cookie by changing any letter of the token. For example, let's change the first two letters (`ey`) to `XX`:

Name	Value
at	XXJhbGciOiJIUzI1
connect.sid	s%3ASJand4Wb

Here, you will receive empty data for the user. This is going to invalidate the session and redirect you to the login page again:

```
×   Headers   Preview   Response   Initiator   Timing
▼{,…}
  ▼data: {getUserData: {id: "", email: "", username: "", privilege: "", active: false, __typename: "User"}}
    ▼getUserData: {id: "", email: "", username: "", privilege: "", active: false, __typename: "User"}
       active: false
       email: ""
       id: ""
       privilege: ""
       username: ""
       __typename: "User"
```

At this point, you have learned how to implement GraphQL in a backend and how to consume queries and mutations in the frontend.

This login system is part of a course I'm doing on YouTube where I'm teaching viewers how to develop a headless CMS from scratch, so if you're eager to learn more, you can check out the course at https://www.youtube.com/watch?v=4n1AfD6aV4M.

Summary

I really hope you enjoyed reading this chapter, which contained a lot of information about GraphQL and how to create JWTs, perform a login, and create models with Sequelize.

It is now time to talk about data fetching and one-way data flow, which is what we will look at in the next chapter.

6
Managing Data

Proper data fetching goes through some of the most common patterns to make a child and parent communicate using callbacks. We'll learn how we can use a common parent to share data across components that are not directly connected. We will then start learning about the new React Context API and React Suspense.

We will cover the following topics in this chapter:

- React Context API
- How to consume a context with useContext
- How to use React Suspense with SWR

Technical requirements

To complete this chapter, you will need the following:

- Node.js 12+
- Visual Studio Code

You can find the code for this chapter in the book's GitHub repository: https://github.com/PacktPublishing/React-17-Design-Patterns-and-Best-Practices-Third-Edition/tree/main/Chapter06.

Introducing the React Context API

The React Context API has been officially added since version 16.3.0; before it was just experimental. The new Context API is a game-changer. A lot of people are moving away from Redux in order to use the new Context API. Context provides a way to share data between components without passing a prop to all the child components.

Let's see a basic example where we can use the new Context API. We will do the same example we did in *Chapter 3, React Hooks,* where we fetched some GitHub issues, but now using the Context API.

Creating our first context

The first thing you need to do is to create the issue context. For this, you can create a folder called `contexts` inside your `src` folder and then inside that, add the `Issue.tsx` file.

Then, you need to import some functions from React and `axios`:

```
import { FC, createContext, useState, useEffect, ReactElement, useCallback
} from 'react'
import axios from 'axios'
```

At this point, it is clear that you should install `axios`. If you still don't have it, just do the following:

```
npm install axios
npm install --save-dev @types/axios
```

Then we need to declare our interfaces:

```
export type Issue = {
  number: number
  title: string
  url: string
  state: string
}

interface Issue_Context {
  issues: Issue[]
  url: string
}

interface Props {
  url: string
}
```

The first thing we need to do after this is to create our context by using the `createContext` function and define the value we want to export:

```
export const IssueContext = createContext<Issue_Context>({
  issues: [],
  url: ''
})
```

Once we have `IssueContext`, we need to create a component where we can receive props, set some states, and perform the fetch by using `useEffect`, and then we render `IssueContext.Provider` where we specify the context (value) we will export:

```
const IssueProvider: FC<Props> = ({ children, url }) => {
  // State
  const [issues, setIssues] = useState<Issue[]>([])

  const fetchIssues = useCallback(async () => {
    const response = await axios(url)

    if (response) {
      setIssues(response.data)
    }
  }, [url])

  // Effects
  useEffect(() => {
    fetchIssues()
  }, [fetchIssues])

  const context = {
    issues,
    url
  }

  return <IssueContext.Provider
value={context}>{children}</IssueContext.Provider>
}

export default IssueProvider
```

As you know, every time you want to use a function inside the `useEffect` Hook, you need to wrap your function with the `useCallback` Hook. A good practice if you want to use `async/await` is to have it in a separate function and not directly in `useEffect`.

Once we perform the fetch and get the data in our `issues` state, then we add all the values we want to export as context, then when we render `IssueContext.Provider`, we pass the context on the `value` prop, and finally, we render the children of the component.

Wrapping our components with the provider

The way you consume a context is divided into two parts. The first one is where you wrap your app with your context provider, so this code can be added to App.tsx (normally all the providers are defined in parent components).

Notice that here we are importing the IssueProvider component:

```
// Providers
import IssueProvider from '../contexts/Issue'

// Components
import Issues from './Issues'

const App = () => {
  return (
    <IssueProvider url=
      "https://api.github.com/repos/ContentPI/ContentPI/issues">
      <Issues />
    </IssueProvider>
  )
}

export default App;
```

As you can see we are wrapping the Issues component with IssueProvider, which means inside the Issues component we can consume our context and get the issues value.

 Many people get confused with this sometimes. If you forget to wrap your components with the provider, then you can't consume your context inside your components, and the hard part is that you probably won't get any error; you will just get some undefined data, which makes this hard to identify.

Consuming context with useContext

If you've already placed `IssueProvider` in `App.tsx`, now you can consume your context in your `Issues` component by using the `useContext` Hook.

Notice that here we are importing the `IssueContext` context (between { }):

```
// Dependencies
import { FC, useContext } from 'react'

// Contexts
import { IssueContext, Issue } from '../contexts/Issue'

const Issues: FC = () => {
  // Here you consume your Context, and you can grab the issues value.
  const { issues, url } = useContext(IssueContext)

  return (
    <>
      <h1>ContentPI Issues from Context</h1>

      {issues.map((issue: Issue) => (
        <p key={`issue-${issue.number}`}>
          <strong>#{issue.number}</strong> {' '}
          <a href={`${url}/${issue.number}`}>{issue.title}</a> {' '}
          {issue.state}
        </p>
      ))}
    </>
  )
}

export default Issues
```

If you did everything correctly, you should be able to see the issues list:

```
ContentPI Issues from Context

#112 Creating new backend using tinyhttp open

#111 Evalute if we need to get rid of Next open

#110 Remove and evaluate if a component actually needs React.memo open

#109 Options when you create a new app open

#99 Fix Playground open

#97 CPI-35 - Added Drag-n-Drop Functionality to sort fields open

#81 Edit Reference Field open

#80 Edit Dropdown Field open

#75 Page for empty Content (when you don't have any model) open

#74 Page for empty Schema (create your first model) open

#73 Remove all any on ContentPI open

#71 Remove all any in @contentpi/ui open

#69 Create a Toast Alert open

#62 Removing a reference field should also remove the reference and its values open

#61 When a user removes a field we need to make sure we are removing all the related values first open

#60 Validate that a model does not have content before delete it open
```

The Context API is super useful when you want to separate your application from your data and do all the fetching in there. Of course, there are multiple uses for the Context API, which can also be used for theming or to pass functions; it all depends on your application.

In the next section, we are going to learn how to implement React Suspense using the SWR library.

Introducing React Suspense with SWR

React Suspense was introduced in React 16.6. Right now (April 2021) this feature is still experimental and you should not use it in your production applications. Suspense lets you suspend component rendering until a condition is met. You can render a loading component or anything you want as a fallback of Suspense. Right now there are only two use cases for this:

- **Code splitting**: When you split your application and you're waiting to download a chunk of your app when a user wants to access it
- **Data fetching**: When you're fetching data

In both scenarios, you can render a fallback, which can normally be a loading spinner, some loading text, or even better, a placeholder skeleton.

 WARNING: The new React Suspense feature is still experimental so I recommend you do not use it on production because it is not yet available in a stable release.

Introducing SWR

Stale-While-Revalidate (SWR) is a React Hook for data fetching; it is an HTTP cache invalidation strategy. SWR is a strategy to first return the data from cache (stale), then send the fetch request (revalidate), and finally, return with up-to-date data, and was developed by Vercel, the company that created Next.js.

Building a Pokedex!

I could not find a better example to explain React Suspense and SWR than building a Pokedex. We will use a public Pokemon API (`https://pokeapi.co`); *gotta catch 'em all*!

The first thing you need to do is to install some packages:

```
npm install swr react-loading-skeleton styled-components
```

For this example, you will need to create the Pokemon directory at `src/components/Pokemon`. The first thing we need to do to work with SWR is to create a fetcher file where we will perform our requests.

This file should be created at `src/components/Pokemon/fetcher.ts`:

```
const fetcher = (url: string) => {
  return fetch(url).then((response) => {
    if (response.ok) {
      return response.json()
    }

    return {
      error: true
    }
  })
}


export default fetcher
```

If you notice, we are returning an object with an error if the response is not successful. This is because sometimes we can get a 404 error from the API that can cause the app to break.

Once you have created your fetcher, let's modify `App.tsx` to configure `SWRConfig` and enable Suspense:

```
// Dependencies
import { SWRConfig } from 'swr'

// Components
import PokeContainer from './Pokemon/PokeContainer'
import fetcher from './Pokemon/fetcher'

// Styles
import { StyledPokedex, StyledTitle } from './Pokemon/Pokemon.styled'

const App = () => {
  return (
    <>
      <StyledTitle>Pokedex</StyledTitle>

      <SWRConfig
        value={{
          fetcher,
          suspense: true,
        }}
      >
        <StyledPokedex>
          <PokeContainer />
        </StyledPokedex>
      </SWRConfig>
    </>
```

```
      )
  }

  export default App
```

As you can see, we need to wrap our `PokeContainer` component inside `SWRConfig` to be able to fetch the data. The `PokeContainer` component will be our parent component where we will add our first Suspense. This file exists at `src/components/Pokemon/PokeContainer.tsx`:

```
import { FC, Suspense } from 'react'

import Pokedex from './Pokedex'

const PokeContainer: FC = () => {
  return (
    <Suspense fallback={<h2>Loading Pokedex...</h2>}>
      <Pokedex />
    </Suspense>
  )
}

export default PokeContainer
```

As you can see, we are defining a fallback for our first Suspense, which is just `Loading Pokedex...` text. You can render whatever you want in there, React components or plain text. Then, we have our `Pokedex` component inside Suspense.

Now let's take a look at our `Pokedex` component where we are going to fetch data for the first time by using the `useSWR` Hook:

```
// Dependencies
import { FC, Suspense } from 'react'
import useSWR from 'swr'

// Components
import LoadingSkeleton from './LoadingSkeleton'
import Pokemon from './Pokemon'

import { StyledGrid } from './Pokemon.styled'

const Pokedex: FC = () => {
  const { data: { results } } =
    useSWR('https://pokeapi.co/api/v2/pokemon?limit=150')
  return (
    <>
      {results.map((pokemon: { name: string }) => (
```

```
            <Suspense fallback={<StyledGrid><LoadingSkeleton /></StyledGrid>}>
              <Pokemon key={pokemon.name} pokemonName={pokemon.name} />
            </Suspense>
          ))}
        </>
      )
    }

    export default Pokedex
```

As you can see, we are fetching the first 150 Pokemon because I'm old school and those were the first generation. Right now I don't know how many Pokemon exist. Also, if you notice, we are grabbing the `results` variable that comes from the data (this is the actual response from the API). Then we map our results to render each Pokemon but we add a Suspense component to each one with a `<LoadingSkeleton />` fallback (`<StyledGrid />` has some CSS styles to make it look nicer), and finally, we pass `pokemonName` to our `<Pokemon>` component, and this is because the first fetch just brings us the name of the Pokemon but we need to do another fetch to bring the actual Pokemon data (name, types, power, and so on).

Then, finally, our Pokemon component will perform a specific fetch by the Pokemon name and will render the data:

```
// Dependencies
import { FC } from 'react'
import useSWR from 'swr'

// Styles
import { StyledCard, StyledTypes, StyledType, StyledHeader } from
'./Pokemon.styled'

type Props = {
  pokemonName: string
}

const Pokemon: FC<Props> = ({ pokemonName }) => {
  const { data, error } =
    useSWR(`https://pokeapi.co/api/v2/pokemon/${pokemonName}`)

  // Do you remember the error we set on the fetcher?
  if (error || data.error) {
    return <div />
  }

  if (!data) {
    return <div>Loading...</div>
```

```
  }

  const { id, name, sprites, types } = data
  const pokemonTypes = types.map((pokemonType: any) =>
    pokemonType.type.name)

  return (
    <StyledCard pokemonType={pokemonTypes[0]}>
      <StyledHeader>
        <h2>{name}</h2>
        <div>#{id}</div>
      </StyledHeader>
      <img alt={name} src={sprites.front_default} />

      <StyledTypes>
        {pokemonTypes.map((pokemonType: string) => (
          <StyledType key={pokemonType}>{pokemonType}</StyledType>
        ))}
      </StyledTypes>
    </StyledCard>
  )
}

export default Pokemon
```

Basically, in this component, we put together all the Pokemon data (`id`, `name`, `sprites`, and `types`) and we render the information. As you have seen, I'm using `styled` components, which are amazing, so if you want to know the styles I'm using for `Pokedex`, here is the `Pokemon.styled.ts` file:

```
import styled from 'styled-components'

// Type colors
const type: any = {
  bug: '#2ADAB1',
  dark: '#636363',
  dragon: '#E9B057',
  electric: '#ffeb5b',
  fairy: '#ffdbdb',
  fighting: '#90a4b5',
  fire: '#F7786B',
  flying: '#E8DCB3',
  ghost: '#755097',
  grass: '#2ADAB1',
  ground: '#dbd3a2',
  ice: '#C8DDEA',
  normal: '#ccc',
```

```
    poison: '#cc89ff',
    psychic: '#705548',
    rock: '#b7b7b7',
    steel: '#999',
    water: '#58ABF6'
}

export const StyledPokedex = styled.div`
  display: flex;
  flex-wrap: wrap;
  flex-flow: row wrap;
  margin: 0 auto;
  width: 90%;

  &::after {
    content: '';
    flex: auto;
  }
`

type Props = {
  pokemonType: string
}

export const StyledCard = styled.div<Props>`
  position: relative;
  ${({ pokemonType }) => `
    background: ${type[pokemonType]} url(./pokeball.png) no-repeat;
    background-size: 65%;
    background-position: center;
  `}
  color: #000;
  font-size: 13px;
  border-radius: 20px;
  margin: 5px;
  width: 200px;

  img {
    margin-left: auto;
    margin-right: auto;
    display: block;
  }
`

export const StyledTypes = styled.div`
  display: flex;
  margin-left: 6px;
  margin-bottom: 8px;
```

```
export const StyledType = styled.span`
  display: inline-block;
  background-color: black;
  border-radius: 20px;
  font-weight: bold;
  padding: 6px;
  color: white;
  margin-right: 3px;
  opacity: 0.4;
  text-transform: capitalize;
`

export const StyledHeader = styled.div`
  display: flex;
  justify-content: space-between;
  width: 90%;

  h2 {
    margin-left: 10px;
    margin-top: 5px;
    color: white;
    text-transform: capitalize;
  }

  div {
    color: white;
    font-size: 20px;
    font-weight: bold;
    margin-top: 5px;
  }
`

export const StyledTitle = styled.h1`
  text-align: center;
`

export const StyledGrid = styled.div`
  display: flex;
  flex-wrap: wrap;
  flex-flow: row wrap;
  div {
    margin-right: 5px;
    margin-bottom: 5px;
  }
`
```

Finally, our `LoadingSkeleton` component should be like this:

```
import { FC } from 'react'
import Skeleton from 'react-loading-skeleton'

const LoadingSkeleton: FC = () => (
  <div>
    <Skeleton height={200} width={200} />
  </div>
)

export default LoadingSkeleton
```

This library is amazing. It lets you create skeleton placeholders to wait for the data. Of course, you can build as many forms as you want. You have probably seen this effect on sites such as LinkedIn or YouTube.

Testing our React Suspense

Once you have all the pieces of the code working, there is a trick you can do in order to see all the Suspense fallbacks. Normally, if you have a high-speed connection, it is hard to see it, but you can slow down your connection to see how everything is being rendered. You can do this by selecting **Slow 3G** connection in your **Network** tab on your Chrome inspector:

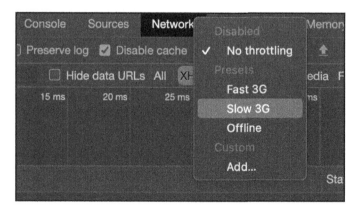

Once you set the **Slow 3G** preset and you run your project, the first fallback you will see is **Loading Pokedex...**:

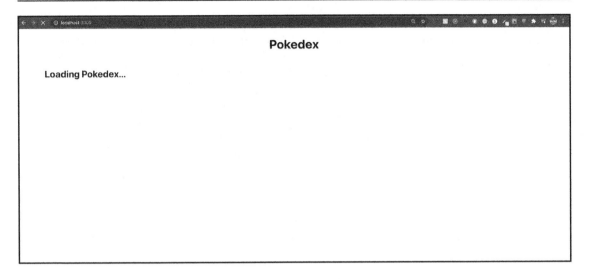

Then, you will see the Pokemon fallbacks that are rendering `SkeletonLoading` for each Pokemon that is being loaded:

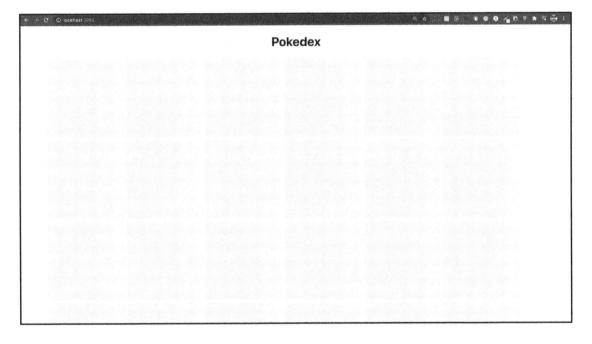

Normally those loaders have animation but you won't see that in this book, of course! And then you will start seeing how the data is rendering and some images start appearing:

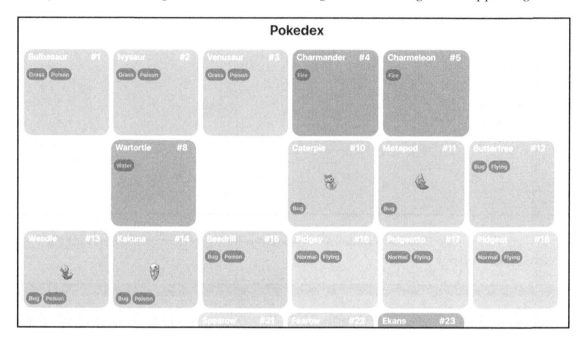

If you wait until all the data has downloaded correctly, you should now see the Pokedex with all the Pokemon:

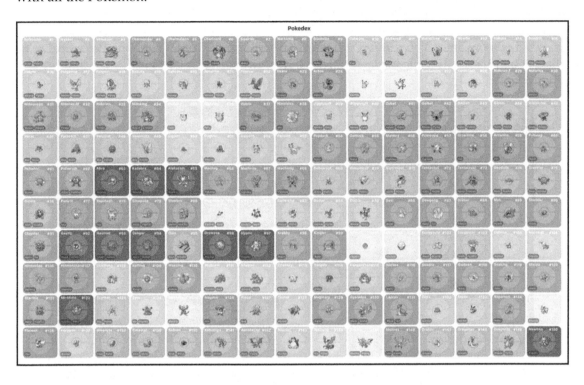

Pretty nice, huh? But there is something else to mention; as I mentioned before, SWR will bring the data from the cache first and then will revalidate the data all the time to see whether there are new updates. This means that any time the data changes, SWR will perform another fetch to re-validate whether the old data is still valid or needs to be replaced by new ones. You can see this effect even if you move out from the **Pokedex** tab to another and then you come back. You'll see that your **Network** terminal for the first time should look like this:

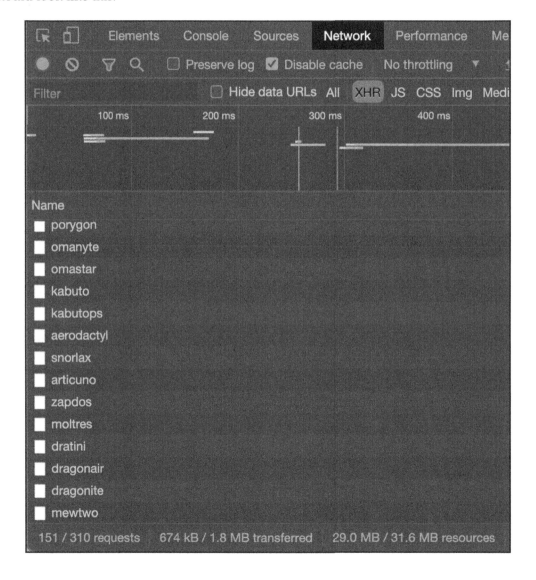

As you can see, we performed **151** initial requests (1 for the Pokemon lists and 150 others, 1 for each Pokemon), but if you change the tab and you come back, you will see how SWR is fetching again:

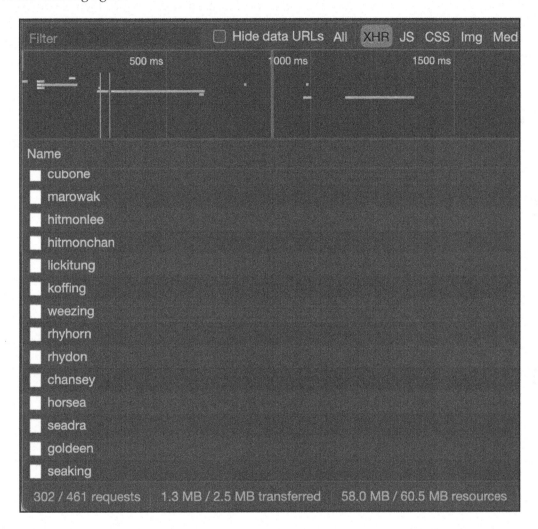

Now you can see that it is performing **302** requests (another 151). This is very useful when you have real-time data that you want to fetch every second or every minute.

Right now, React Suspense does not have a defined pattern of use, which means you can find different ways to use it and there are not yet some good practices defined for this. I found SWR is the easiest and most understandable way of playing with React Suspense and I think it is a very powerful library that can be used even without Suspense.

Summary

I really hope you enjoyed reading this chapter, which contains a lot of information about the React Context API and how to implement React Suspense with SWR.

In the next chapter, we will learn how to handle forms and animations.

Writing Code for the Browser 7

There are some specific operations we can do when we work with React and the browser. For example, we can ask our users to enter some information using forms, and in this chapter, we will look at how we can apply different techniques to deal with forms. We can implement **uncontrolled components** and let the fields keep their internal states, or we can use controlled ones, where we have full control over the state of the fields.

In this chapter, we will also look at how events in React work and how the library implements some advanced techniques to give us a consistent interface across different browsers. We will look at some interesting solutions that the React team has implemented to make the event system very performant.

After events, we will jump into refs to look at how we can access the underlying DOM nodes in our React components. This represents a powerful feature, but it should be used carefully because it breaks some of the conventions that make React easy to work with.

After refs, we will look at how we can implement animations easily with the React add-ons and third-party libraries such as `react-motion`. Finally, we will learn how easy it is to work with **Scalable Vector Graphics (SVG)** in React, and how we can create dynamically configurable icons for our applications.

In this chapter, we will go through the following topics:

- Using different techniques to create forms with React
- Listening to DOM events and implementing custom handlers
- A way of performing imperative operations on DOM nodes using refs
- Creating simple animations that work across different browsers
- The React way of generating SVG

Technical requirements

To complete this chapter, you will need the following:

- Node.js 12+
- Visual Studio Code

You can find the code for this chapter in the book's GitHub repository: https://github.com/PacktPublishing/React-17-Design-Patterns-and-Best-Practices-Third-Edition/tree/main/Chapter07.

Understanding and implementing forms

In this chapter, we are going to learn how to implement forms with React. As soon as we start building a real application with React, we need to interact with the users. If we want to ask for information from our users within the browser, forms are the most common solution. Due to the way the library works and its declarative nature, dealing with input fields and other form elements is non-trivial with React, but as soon as we understand its logic, it will become clear. In the next sections, we are going to learn how to use uncontrolled and controlled components.

Uncontrolled components

Uncontrolled components are like regular HTML form inputs for which you will not be able to manage the value yourself but instead, the DOM will take care of handling the value and you can get this value by using a React ref. Let's start with a basic example—displaying a form with an input field and a **Submit** button.

The code is pretty straightforward:

```
import { useState, ChangeEvent, MouseEvent } from 'react'

const Uncontrolled = () => {
  const [value, setValue] = useState('')

  return (
    <form>
      <input type="text" />
      <button>Submit</button>
    </form>
  )
}
```

```
}

export default Uncontrolled
```

If we run the preceding snippet in the browser, we will see exactly what we expect—an input field in which we can write something and a clickable button. This is an example of an uncontrolled component, where we do not set the value of the input field, but we let the component manage its own internal state.

Most likely, we want to do something with the value of the element when the **Submit** button is clicked. For example, we may want to send the data to an API endpoint.

We can do this easily by adding an onChange listener (we will talk more about event listeners later in this chapter). Let's look at what it means to add a listener.

We need to create the handleChange function:

```
const handleChange = (e: ChangeEvent<HTMLInputElement>) => {
  console.log(e.target.value)
}
```

The event listener is receiving an event object, where the target represents the field that generated the event, and we are interested in its value. We start by just logging it because it is important to proceed with small steps, but we will store the value into the state soon.

Finally, we render the form:

```
return (
  <form>
    <input type="text" onChange={handleChange} />
    <button>Submit</button>
  </form>
)
```

If we render the component inside the browser and type the word React into the form field, we will see something like the following inside the console:

```
R
Re
Rea
Reac
React
```

The handleChange listener is fired every time the value of the input changes. Therefore, our function is called once for each typed character. The next step is to store the value that's entered by the user and make it available when the user clicks the **Submit** button.

We just have to change the implementation of the handler to store it in the state instead of logging it, as follows:

```
const handleChange = (e: ChangeEvent<HTMLInputElement>) => {
  setValue(e.target.value)
}
```

Getting notified of when the form is submitted is very similar to listening to the change event of the input field; they are both events that are called by the browser when something happens.

Let's define the handleSubmit function, where we just log the value. In a real-world scenario, you could send the data to an API endpoint or pass it to another component:

```
const handleSubmit = (e: MouseEvent<HTMLButtonElement>) => {
  e.preventDefault()
  console.log(value)
}
```

This handler is pretty straightforward; we just log the value currently stored in the state. We also want to overcome the default behavior of the browser when the form is submitted, to perform a custom action. This seems reasonable, and it works very well for a single field. The question now is, what if we have multiple fields? Suppose we have tens of different fields?

Let's start with a basic example, where we create each field and handler manually and look at how we can improve it by applying different levels of optimization.

Let's create a new form with first and last name fields. We can reuse the Uncontrolled component and add some new states:

```
const [firstName, setFirstName] = useState('')
const [lastName, setLastName] = useState('')
```

We initialize the two fields inside the state and we define an event handler for each one of the fields as well. As you may have noticed, this does not scale very well when there are lots of fields, but it is important to understand the problem clearly before moving to a more flexible solution.

Now, we implement the new handlers:

```
const handleChangeFirstName = ({ target: { value } }) => {
  setFirstName(value)
}
const handleChangeLastName = ({ target: { value } }) => {
  setLastName(value)
```

```
}
```

We also have to change the submit handler a little bit so that it displays the first and the last name when it gets clicked:

```
const handleSubmit = (e: MouseEvent<HTMLButtonElement>) => {
  e.preventDefault()
  console.log(`${firstName} ${lastName}`)
}
```

Finally, we render the form:

```
return (
  <form onSubmit={handleSubmit}>
    <input type="text" onChange={handleChangeFirstName} />
    <input type="text" onChange={handleChangeLastName} />
    <button>Submit</button>
  </form>
)
```

We are ready to go: if we run the preceding component in the browser, we will see two fields, and if we type Carlos into the first one and Santana into the second one, we will see the full name displayed in the browser console when the form is submitted.

Again, this works fine, and we can do some interesting things this way, but it does not handle complex scenarios without requiring us to write a lot of boilerplate code.

Let's look at how we can optimize it a little bit. Our goal is to use a single change handler so that we can add an arbitrary number of fields without creating new listeners.

Let's go back to the component and let's change our states:

```
const [values, setValues] = useState({ firstName: '', lastName: '' })
```

We may still want to initialize the values, and later in this section, we will look at how to provide prefilled values for the form.

Now, the interesting bit is the way in which we can modify the onChange handler implementation to make it work in different fields:

```
const handleChange = ({ target: { name, value } }) => {
  setValues({
    ...values,
    [name]: value
  })
}
```

As we have seen previously, the `target` property of the event we receive represents the input field that has fired the event, so we can use the name of the field and its value as variables.

We then have to set the name for each field:

```
return (
  <form onSubmit={handleSubmit}>
    <input
      type="text"
      name="firstName"
      onChange={handleChange}
    />
    <input
      type="text"
      name="lastName"
      onChange={handleChange}
    />
    <button>Submit</button>
  </form>
)
```

That's it! We can now add as many fields as we want without creating additional handlers.

Controlled components

A controlled component is a React component that controls the values of input elements in a form by using the component state.

Here we are going to look at how we can prefill the form fields with some values, which we may receive from the server or as props from the parent. To understand this concept fully, we will start again from a very simple stateless function component, and we will improve it step by step.

The first example shows a predefined value inside the input field:

```
const Controlled = () => (
  <form>
    <input type="text" value="Hello React" />
    <button>Submit</button>
  </form>
)
```

If we run this component inside the browser, we realize that it shows the default value as expected, but it does not let us change the value or type anything else inside it.

The reason it does this is that in React, we declare what we want to see on the screen, and setting a fixed-value attribute always results in rendering that value, no matter what other actions are taken. This is unlikely to be a behavior we want in a real-world application.

If we open the console, we get the following error message. React itself is telling us that we are doing something wrong:

```
You provided a `value` prop to a form field without an `onChange` handler.
This will render a read-only field.
```

Now, if we just want the input field to have a default value and we want to be able to change it by typing, we can use the `defaultValue` property:

```
import { useState } from 'react'

const Controlled = () => {
  return (
    <form>
      <input type="text" defaultValue="Hello React" />
      <button>Submit</button>
    </form>
  )
}

export default Controlled
```

In this way, the field is going to show `Hello React` when it is rendered, but then the user can type anything inside it and change its value. Now let's add some states:

```
const [values, setValues] = useState({ firstName: 'Carlos', lastName:
'Santana' })
```

The handlers are the same as the previous ones:

```
const handleChange = ({ target: { name, value } }) => {
  setValues({
    [name]: value
  })
}
const handleSubmit = (e) => {
  e.preventDefault()
  console.log(`${values.firstName} ${values.lastName}`)
}
```

In fact, we will use the `value` attributes of the input fields to set their initial values, as well as the updated one:

```
return (
  <form onSubmit={handleSubmit}>
    <input
      type="text"
      name="firstName"
      value={values.firstName}
      onChange={handleChange}
    />
    <input
      type="text"
      name="lastName"
      value={values.lastName}
      onChange={handleChange}
    />
    <button>Submit</button>
  </form>
)
```

The first time the form is rendered, React uses the initial values from the state as the value of the input fields. When the user types something into the field, the `handleChange` function is called and the new value for the field is stored in the state.

When the state changes, React re-renders the component and uses it again to reflect the current values of the input fields. We now have full control over the values of the fields, and we call this pattern **controlled components**.

In the next section, we are going to work with events, which are a fundamental part of React to handle data coming from forms.

Handling events

Events work in a slightly different way across various browsers. React tries to abstract the way events work and give developers a consistent interface to deal with. This is a great feature of React because we can forget about the browsers we are targeting and write event handlers and functions that are vendor-agnostic.

To offer this feature, React introduced the concept of the **synthetic event**. A synthetic event is an object that wraps the original event object provided by the browser, and it has the same properties, no matter where it is created.

To attach an event listener to a node and get the event object when the event is fired, we can use a simple convention that recalls the way events are attached to the DOM nodes. In fact, we can use the word on plus the camelCased event name (for example, onKeyDown) to define the callback to be fired when the events happen. A popular convention is to name the event handler functions after the event name and prefix them using handle (for example, handleKeyDown).

We have seen this pattern in action in the previous examples, where we were listening to the onChange event of the form fields. Let's reiterate a basic event listener example to see how we can organize multiple events inside the same component in a nicer way. We are going to implement a simple button, and we start, as usual, by creating a component:

```
const Button = () => {

}
export default Button
```

Then we define the event handler:

```
const handleClick = (syntheticEvent) => {
  console.log(syntheticEvent instanceof MouseEvent)
  console.log(syntheticEvent.nativeEvent instanceof MouseEvent)
}
```

As you can see here, we are doing a very simple thing: we just check the type of the event object we receive from React and the type of native event attached to it. We expect the first to return false and the second to return true.

You should never need to access the original native event, but it is good to know you can do it if you need to. Finally, we define the button with the onClick attribute to which we attach our event listener:

```
return (
  <button onClick={handleClick}>Click me!</button>
)
```

Now, suppose we want to attach a second handler to the button that listens to the double-click event. One solution would be to create a new separate handler and attach it to the button using the onDoubleClick attribute, as follows:

```
<button
  onClick={handleClick}
  onDoubleClick={handleDoubleClick}
>
  Click me!
</button>
```

Remember that we always aim to write less boilerplate and avoid duplicating code. For that reason, a common practice is to write a **single event handler** for each component, which can trigger different actions according to the event type.

 This technique is described in a collection of patterns by Michael Chan: http://reactpatterns.com/#event-switch.

Let's implement the generic event handler:

```
const handleEvent = (event) => {
  switch (event.type) {
    case 'click':
      console.log('clicked')
      break
    case 'dblclick':
      console.log('double clicked')
      break
    default:
      console.log('unhandled', event.type)
  }
}
```

The generic event handler receives the event object and switches on the event type to fire the right action. This is particularly useful if we want to call a function on each event (for example, analytics) or if some events share the same logic.

Finally, we attach the new event listener to the onClick and onDoubleClick attributes:

```
return (
  <button
    onClick={handleEvent}
    onDoubleClick={handleEvent}
  >
    Click me!
  </button>
)
```

From this point on, whenever we need to create a new event handler for the same component, instead of creating a new method and binding it, we can just add a new case to the switch.

A couple more interesting things to know about events in React are that synthetic events are reused and that there is a **single global handler**. The first concept means that we cannot store a synthetic event and reuse it later because it becomes null right after the action. This technique is very good in terms of performance, but it can be problematic if we want to store the event inside the state of the component for some reason. To solve this problem, React gives us a `persist` method on the synthetic events, which we can call to make the event persistent so that we can store it and retrieve it later.

The second very interesting implementation detail is again about performance, and it is to do with the way React attaches the event handlers to the DOM.

Whenever we use the `on` attribute, we are describing to React the behavior we want to achieve, but the library does not attach the actual event handler to the underlying DOM nodes.

What it does instead attaches a single event handler to the root element, which listens to all the events, thanks to **event bubbling**. When an event we are interested in is fired by the browser, React calls the handler on the specific components on its behalf. This technique is called **event delegation** and is used for memory and speed optimization.

In our next section, we are going to explore React refs and see how we can take advantage of them.

Exploring refs

One of the reasons people love React is that it is declarative. Being declarative means that you just describe what you want to be displayed on the screen at any point in time and React takes care of the communications with the browser. This feature makes React very easy to reason about and very powerful at the same time.

However, there might be some cases where you need to access the underlying DOM nodes to perform some imperative operations. This should be avoided because, in most cases, there is a more React-compliant solution to achieve the same result, but it is important to know that we have the option to do it and to know how it works so that we can make the right decision.

Suppose we want to create a simple form with an input element and a button, and we want it to behave in such a way that when the button is clicked, the input field gets focused. What we want to do is call the `focus` method on the input node, the actual DOM instance of the input, inside the browser's window.

Let's create a component called `Focus`; you need to import `useRef` and create an `inputRef` constant:

```
import { useRef } from 'react'

const Focus = () => {
  const inputRef = useRef(null)
}

export default Focus
```

Then, we implement the `handleClick` method:

```
const handleClick = () => {
  inputRef.current.focus()
}
```

As you can see, we are referencing the `current` attribute of `inputRef` and calling the `focus` method on it.

To understand where it comes from, you just have to check the implementation of `render`:

```
return (
  <>
    <input
      type="text"
      ref={inputRef}
    />
    <button onClick={handleClick}>Set Focus</button>
  </>
)
```

Here comes the core of the logic. We create a form with an input element inside it and we define a function on its `ref` attribute.

The callback we defined is called when the component gets mounted, and the element parameter represents the DOM instance of the input. It is important to know that, when the component gets unmounted, the same callback is called with a `null` parameter to free the memory.

What we are doing in the callback is storing the reference of the element to be able to use it in the future (for example, when the `handleClick` method is fired). Then, we have the button with its event handler. Running the preceding code in a browser will show the form with the field and the button, and clicking on the button will focus the input field, as expected.

As we mentioned previously, in general, we should try to avoid using refs because they force the code to be more imperative, and they become harder to read and maintain.

Implementing animations

When we think about UIs and the browser, we must surely think about animations as well. Animated UIs are more pleasant for users, and they are a very important tool to show users that something has happened or is about to occur.

This section does not aim to be an exhaustive guide to creating animations and beautiful UIs; the goal here is to provide you with some basic information about the common solutions we can put in place to animate our React components.

For a UI library such as React, it is crucial to provide an easy way for developers to create and manage animations. React comes with an add-on, called `react-addons-css-transition-group`, which is a component that helps us build animations in a declarative way. Again, being able to perform operations declaratively is incredibly powerful, and it makes the code much easier to reason about and share with the team.

Let's look at how to apply a simple fade-in effect to text with the React add-on, and then we will perform the same operation using `react-motion`, a third-party library that makes creating complex animations even easier.

The first thing we need to do to start building an animated component is to install the add-on:

```
npm install --save react-addons-css-transition-group @types/react-addons-css-transition-group
```

Once we have done that, we can import the component:

```
import CSSTransitionGroup from 'react-addons-css-transition-group'
```

Then, we just wrap the component to which we want to apply the animation:

```
const Transition = () => (
  <CSSTransitionGroup
    transitionName="fade"
    transitionAppear
    transitionAppearTimeout={500}
  >
    <h1>Hello React</h1>
```

```
    </CSSTransitionGroup>
  )
```

As you can see, there are some props that need explaining.

First, we are declaring the `transitionName` prop. `ReactCSSTransitionGroup` applies a class with the name of that property to the child element so that we can then use CSS transitions to create our animations.

With a single class, we cannot easily create a proper animation, and that is why the transition group applies multiple classes according to the state of the animation. In this case, with the `transitionAppear` prop, we are telling the component that we want to animate the children when they appear on the screen.

So, what the library does is apply the `fade-appear` class (where `fade` is the value of the `transitionName` prop) to the component as soon as it gets rendered. On the next tick, the `fade-appear-active` class is applied so that we can fire our animation from the initial state to the new one, using CSS.

We also have to set the `transitionAppearTimeout` property to tell React the length of the animation so that it doesn't remove elements from the DOM before animations are completed.

The CSS to make an element fade-in is as follows.

First, we define the opacity of the element in the initial state:

```
.fade-appear {
  opacity: 0.01;
}
```

Then, we define our transition using the second class, which starts as soon as it gets applied to the element:

```
.fade-appear.fade-appear-active {
  opacity: 1;
  transition: opacity .5s ease-in;
}
```

We are transitioning the opacity from `0.01` to `1` in `500ms` using the `ease-in` function. This is pretty easy, but we can create more complex animations, and we can also animate different states of the component. For example, the `*-enter` and `*-enter-active` classes are applied when a new element is added as a child of the transition group. A similar thing applies to remove elements.

In our next section, we are going to check out the most popular library to create animations in React: `react-motion`, which is maintained by Cheng Lou. It provides a very clean and easy-to-use API that gives us a very powerful tool to create any animations.

React Motion

React Motion is an animation library for React applications that make it easy to create and implement realistic animations. As soon as the complexity of the animations grows, or when we need animations that depend on other animations, or when we need to apply some physics-based behavior to our components (which is a bit more advanced), we will realize that the transition group is not helping us enough, so we may consider using a third-party library.

To use it, we first have to install it:

```
npm install --save react-motion @types/react-motion
```

Once the installation is successfully completed, we need to import the `Motion` component and the `spring` function. `Motion` is the component we will use to wrap the elements we want to animate, while the function is a utility that can interpolate a value from its initial state to the final one:

```
import { Motion, spring } from 'react-motion'
```

Let's look at the code:

```
const Transition = () => (
  <Motion
    defaultStyle={{ opacity: 0.01 }}
    style={{ opacity: spring(1) }}
  >
    {interpolatingStyle => (
      <h1 style={interpolatingStyle}>Hello React</h1>
    )}
  </Motion>
)
```

There are a lot of interesting things here. First, you may have noticed that this component uses the function as a child pattern (see *Chapter 4, Exploring Popular Composition Patterns*), which is a pretty powerful technique to define children that receive values at runtime.

Then, we can see that the `Motion` component has two attributes: the first one is `defaultStyle`, which represents the initial `style` attribute. Again, we set the opacity to `0.0.1` to hide the element and start the fade.

The `style` attribute represents the final style instead, but we do not set the value directly; instead, we use the `spring` function so that the value is interpolated from the initial state to the final one.

On each iteration of the `spring` function, the child function receives the interpolated style for the given point in time and, just by applying the received object to the `style` attribute of the component, we can see the transition of the opacity.

This library can do some more cool stuff, but the first things to learn about are the basic concepts, and this example should clarify them.

It is also interesting to compare the two different approaches of the transition group and `react-motion` to be able to choose the right one for the project you are working on.

Finally, in our next section, we are going to see how we can work with SVG in React.

Exploring SVG

Last but not least, one of the most interesting techniques we can apply in the browser to draw icons and graphs is **Scalable Vector Graphics (SVG)**.

SVG is great because it is a declarative way of describing vectors and it fits perfectly with the purposes of React. We used to use icon fonts to create icons, but they have well-known problems, with the first being that they are not accessible. It is also pretty hard to position icon fonts with CSS, and they do not always look beautiful in all browsers. These are the reasons we should prefer SVG for our web applications.

From a React point of view, it does not make any difference if we output a `div` or an SVG element from the `render` method, and this is what makes it so powerful. We also tend to choose SVG because we can easily modify them at runtime using CSS and JavaScript, which makes them an excellent candidate for the functional approach of React.

So, if we think about our components as a function of their props, we can easily imagine how we can create self-contained SVG icons that we can manipulate by passing different props to them. A common way to create SVG in a web app with React is to wrap our vectors into a React component and use the props to define their dynamic values.

Let's look at a simple example where we draw a blue circle, thus creating a React component that wraps an SVG element:

```
const Circle = ({ x, y, radius, fill }) => (
  <svg>
```

```
        <circle cx={x} cy={y} r={radius} fill={fill} />
    </svg>
)
```

As you can see, we can easily use a stateless functional component that wraps the SVG markup, and it accepts the same props as SVG does.

An example usage is as follows:

```
<Circle x={20} y={20} radius={20} fill="blue" />
```

We can obviously use the full power of React and set some default parameters so that, if the circle icon is rendered without props, we still show something.

For example, we can define the default color:

```
const Circle = ({ x, y, radius, fill = 'red' }) => (...)
```

This is pretty powerful when we build UIs, especially in a team where we share our icon set and we want to have some default values in it, but we also want to let other teams decide their settings without having to recreate the same SVG shapes.

However, in some cases, we prefer to be more strict and fix some values to keep consistency. With React, this is a super simple task.

For example, we can wrap the base circle component into `RedCircle`, as follows:

```
const RedCircle = ({ x, y, radius }) => (
    <Circle x={x} y={y} radius={radius} fill="red" />
)
```

Here, the color is set by default and it cannot be changed, while the other props are transparently passed to the original circle.

The following screenshot shows two circles, blue and red, that are generated by React using SVG:

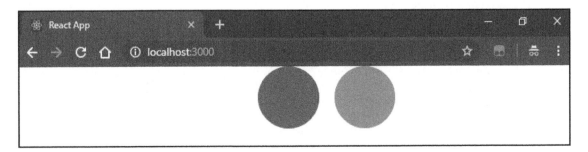

We can apply this technique and create different variations of the circle, such as `SmallCircle` and `RightCircle`, and everything else we need to build our UIs.

Summary

In this chapter, we looked at the different things we can do when we target the browser with React, from form creation to events, and animations to SVG. Also, we learned how to use the new `useRef` Hook. React gives us a declarative way to manage all the aspects we need to deal with when we create a web application.

In case we need it, React gives us access to the actual DOM nodes in a way that means we can perform imperative operations with them, which is useful if we need to integrate React with an existing imperative library.

The next chapter will be about CSS and inline styles, and it will clarify what it means to write CSS in JavaScript.

3
Performance, Improvements, and Production!

This section explains how to improve the performance of your React applications, how to handle styles with CSS modules and `styled-components`, and finally how to deploy your applications to production.

We will cover the following chapters in this section:

Making Your Components Look Beautiful

8

Our journey into React best practices and design patterns has now reached the point where we want to make our components look beautiful. To do that, we will go through all the reasons why regular CSS may not be the best approach for styling components, and we will check out various alternative solutions.

Starting with inline styles, then Radium, CSS modules, and `styled-components`, this chapter will guide you through the magical world of CSS in JavaScript.

In this chapter, we will cover the following topics:

- Common problems with regular CSS at scale
- What it means to use inline styles in React and the downsides
- How the Radium library can help fix issues of inline styles
- How to set up a project from scratch using Webpack and CSS modules
- Features of CSS modules and why they represent a great solution to avoid global CSS
- `styled-components`, a new library that offers a modern approach to styling React components

Technical requirements

To complete this chapter, you will need the following:

- Node.js 12+
- Visual Studio Code

You can find the code for this chapter in the book's GitHub repository: `https://github.`
`com/PacktPublishing/React-17-Design-Patterns-and-Best-Practices-Third-Edition/`
`tree/main/Chapter08`.

CSS in JavaScript

In the community, everyone agrees that a revolution took place in the styling of React components in November 2014, when Christopher Chedeau gave a talk at the NationJS conference.

Also known as **vjeux** on the internet, Christopher works at Facebook and contributes to React. In his talk, he went through all the problems related to CSS on the scale that they were facing at Facebook. It is worth understanding all of them because some are pretty common and they will help us introduce concepts such as inline styles and locally scoped class names.

The following is a list of the issues with CSS, basically problems with CSS at scale:

- Global namespace
- Dependencies
- Dead code elimination
- Minification
- Sharing constants
- Non-deterministic resolution
- Isolation

The first well-known problem of CSS is that all the selectors are global. No matter how we organize our styles, using namespaces or a procedure such as the **Block, Element, Modifier (BEM)** methodology, in the end, we are always polluting the global namespace, which we all know is wrong. It is not only wrong in principle, but it also leads to many errors in big code bases, and it makes maintainability very hard in the long term. Working with big teams, it is non-trivial to know whether a particular class or element has already been styled, and most of the time, we tend to add more classes instead of reusing existing ones.

The second problem with CSS regards the definition of the dependencies. It is very hard, in fact, to state clearly that a particular component depends on a specific CSS and that the CSS has to be loaded for the style to be applied. Since styles are global, any style from any file can be applied to any element, and losing control is very easy.

The third is that frontend developers tend to use preprocessors to be able to split their CSS into submodules, but in the end, a big, global CSS bundle is generated for the browser. Since CSS code bases tend to become huge quickly, we lose control over them, and the third problem is to do with **dead code elimination**. It is not easy to identify quickly which styles belong to which component, and this makes deleting code incredibly hard. In fact, due to the cascading nature of CSS, removing a selector or a rule can result in an unintended result within the browser.

Another pain of working with CSS concerns the minification of the selectors and the class names, both in the CSS and in the JavaScript application. It might seem an easy task but it is not, especially when classes are applied on the fly or concatenated in the client; this is the fourth problem.

Not being able to minify and optimize class names is pretty bad for performance, and it can make a huge difference to the size of the CSS. Another pretty common operation that is non-trivial with regular CSS is sharing constants between the styles and the client application. We often need to know the height of a header, for example, to recalculate the position of other elements that depend on it.

Usually, we read the value in the client using the JavaScript APIs, but the optimal solution would be to share constants and avoid doing expensive calculations at runtime. This represents the fifth problem that vjeux and the other developers at Facebook tried to solve.

The sixth issue concerns the non-deterministic resolution of CSS. In fact, in CSS, the order matters, and if the CSS is loaded on demand, the order is not guaranteed, which leads to the wrong styles being applied to the elements.

Suppose, for example, that we want to optimize the way we request CSS, loading the CSS related to a particular page only when the users navigate to it. If the CSS related to this last page has some rules that also apply to the elements of different pages, the fact that it has been loaded last could affect the styling of the rest of the app. For example, if the user goes back to the previous page, they might see a page with a UI that is slightly different than the first time they visited it.

It is incredibly hard to control all the various combinations of styles, rules, and navigation paths, but again, being able to load the CSS when needed could have a critical impact on the performance of a web application.

Last but not least, the seventh problem of CSS, according to Christopher Chedeau, is related to isolation. In CSS, it is almost impossible to achieve proper isolation between files or components. Selectors are global, and they can easily be overwritten. It is tricky to predict the final style of an element just by knowing the class names applied to it because styles are not isolated and other rules in other parts of the application can affect unrelated elements. This can be solved by using inline styles.

In the following section, we will look at what it means to use inline styles with React and the benefits and downsides of it.

Understanding and implementing inline styles

The official React documentation suggests developers use inline styles to style their React components. This seems odd because we all learned in past years that separating the concerns is important and we should not mix markup and CSS.

React tries to change the concept of separation of concerns by moving it from the separation of technologies to the separation of components. Separating markup, styling, and logic into different files when they are tightly coupled and where one cannot work without the other is just an illusion. Even if it helps keep the project structure cleaner, it does not give any real benefit.

In React, we compose components to create applications where components are a fundamental unit of our structure. We should be able to move components across the application, and they should provide the same result regarding both logic and UI, no matter where they get rendered.

This is one of the reasons why collocating the styles within our components and applying them using inline styles on the elements could make sense in React.

First, let's look at an example of what it means to use the style attribute of the nodes to apply the styling to our components in React. We are going to create a button with the text `Click me!` and we are going to apply color and background color to it:

```
const style = {
  color: 'palevioletred',
  backgroundColor: 'papayawhip'
};
const Button = () => <button style={style}>Click me!</button>;
```

As you can see, it is pretty easy to style elements with inline styles in React. We just have to create an object where the attributes are the CSS rules, and the values are the values we would use in a regular CSS file.

The only differences are that the hyphenated CSS rules must be camelCased to be JavaScript-compliant, and the values are strings, so they have to be wrapped in quote marks.

There are some exceptions regarding the vendor prefixes. For example, if we want to define a transition on `webkit`, we should use the `WebkitTransition` attribute, where the `webkit` prefix begins with a capital letter. This rule applies to all the vendor prefixes, except for `ms`, which is lowercase.

Other use cases are numbers – they can be written without quotes or units of measurement and, by default, they are treated as pixels.

The following rule applies a height of `100` pixels:

```
const style = {
  height: 100
}
```

By using inline styles, we can also do things that are hard to implement with regular CSS. For example, we can recalculate some CSS values on the client at runtime, which is a very powerful concept, as you will see in the following example.

Suppose you want to create a form field in which the font size changes according to its value. So, if the value of the field is `24`, the font size is going to be 24 pixels. With normal CSS, this behavior is almost impossible to reproduce without putting in a huge effort and duplicated code.

Let's look at how easy it is to use inline styles instead, by creating a `FontSize` component first and then declare a value state:

```
import { useState, ChangeEvent } from 'react'

const FontSize = () => {
  const [value, setValue] = useState<number>(16)
}

export default FontSize
```

We implement a simple change handler, where we use the target attribute of the event to retrieve the current value of the field:

```
const handleChange = (e: ChangeEvent<HTMLInputElement>) => {
  setValue(Number(e.target.value))
}
```

Finally, we render the input file of the `number` type, which is a controlled component because we keep its value updated by using the state. It also has an event handler, which is fired every time the value of the field changes.

Last but not least, we use the style attribute of the field to set its `font-size` value. As you can see, we are using the camelCased version of the CSS rule to follow the React convention:

```
return (
  <input
    type="number"
    value={value}
    onChange={handleChange}
    style={{ fontSize: value }}
  />
)
```

Rendering the preceding component, we can see an input field, which changes its font size according to its value. The way it works is that when the value changes, we store the new value of the field inside the state. Modifying the state forces the component to re-render, and we use the new state value to set the display value of the field and its font size; it's easy and powerful.

Every solution in computer science has its downsides, and it always represents a trade-off. In the case of inline styles, unfortunately, the problems are many.

For example, with inline styles, it is not possible to use pseudo-selectors (for example, `:hover`) and pseudo-elements, which is a pretty significant limitation if you are creating a UI with interactions and animations.

There are some workarounds and, for example, you can always create real elements instead of pseudo ones, but for the pseudo-classes, it is necessary to use JavaScript to simulate the CSS behavior, which is not optimal.

The same applies to **media queries**, which cannot be defined using inline styles, and it makes it harder to create responsive web applications. Since styles are declared using JavaScript objects, it is also not possible to use style fallbacks:

```
display: -webkit-flex;
display: flex;
```

JavaScript objects cannot have two attributes with the same name. Style fallbacks should be avoided, but it is always good to have the ability to use them if needed.

Another feature of CSS that it is not possible to emulate using inline styles is **animations**. The workaround here is to define animations globally and use them inside the style attribute of the elements. With inline styles, whenever we need to override a style with regular CSS, we are always forced to use the !important keyword, which is bad practice because it prevents any other style from being applied to the element.

The most difficult thing that happens to work with inline styles is debugging. We tend to use class names to find elements in the browser DevTools to debug and check which styles have been applied. With inline styles, all the styles of the items are listed in their style attribute, which makes it very hard to check and debug the result.

For example, the button that we created earlier in this section is rendered in the following way:

```
<button style="color:palevioletred;background-color:papayawhip;">Click
me!</button>
```

By itself, it does not seem very hard to read, but if you imagine you have hundreds of elements and hundreds of styles, you realize that the problem becomes very complicated.

Also, if you are debugging a list where every single item has the same style attribute, and if you modify one on the fly to check the result in the browser, you will see that you are applying the styles only to it and not to all the other siblings, even if they share the same style.

Last but not least, if we render our application on the server-side (we will cover this topic in *Chapter 9*, *Server-Side Rendering for Fun and Profit*), the size of the page is bigger when using inline styles.

With inline styles, we are putting all the content of the CSS into the markup, which adds an extra number of bytes to the file that we send to the clients and makes the web application appear slower. Compression algorithms can help with that because they can easily compress similar patterns, and, in some cases, loading the critical path CSS is a good solution; but in general, we should try to avoid it.

It turns out that inline styles give more problems than the problems they try to solve. For this reason, the community created different tools to solve the problems of inline styles but keeping the styles inside the components, or local to the components, to get the best of both worlds.

After Christopher Chedeau's talk, a lot of developers started talking about inline styles, and many solutions and experiments have been made to find new ways of writing CSS in JavaScript. In the beginning, there were two or three solutions, while today there are more than 40.

In the following sections, we will go through the most popular solutions.

Exploring the Radium library

One of the first libraries that were created to solve the problems of inline styles that we encountered in the previous section is **Radium**. It is maintained by the great developers at Formidable Labs, and it is still one of the most popular solutions.

In this section, we will look at how Radium works, which problems it solves, and why it is a great library to use in conjunction with React for styling components. We are going to create a very simple button, similar to the one we built in the example earlier in this chapter.

We will start with a basic button without styling, and we will add some basic styling, as well as pseudo-classes and media queries, so that we can learn about the main features of the library.

The button we will start with is created as follows:

```
const Button = () => <button>Click me!</button>
```

First, we have to install Radium using npm:

```
npm install --save radium @types/radium
```

Once the installation is complete, we can import the library and wrap the button in it:

```
import Radium from 'radium'
const Button = () => <button>Click me!</button>
export default Radium(Button)
```

The `Radium` function is a **Higher-Order Component (HOC)** (see *Chapter 4, Exploring All Composition Patterns*), which extends the functionalities of `Button`, returning a new enhanced component. If we render the button inside the browser, we will not see anything in particular at the moment, because we are not applying any styles to it.

Let's start with a simple style object, where we set the background color, the padding, the size, and a couple of other CSS properties. As we saw in the previous section, inline styles in React are defined using JavaScript objects with camelCased CSS properties:

```
const styles = {
  backgroundColor: '#ff0000',
  width: 320,
  padding: 20,
  borderRadius: 5,
  border: 'none',
  outline: 'none'
}
```

The preceding snippet is no different from plain inline styles with React, and if we pass it to our button as follows, we can see all the styles applied to the button inside the browser:

```
const Button = () => <button style={styles}>Click me!</button>
```

The result is the following markup:

```
<button data-radium="true" style="background-color: rgb(255, 0, 0); width: 320px; padding: 20px; border-radius: 5px; border: none; outline: none;">Click me!</button>
```

The only difference you can see here is that there is a `data-radium` attribute set to `true` attached to the element.

Now, we have seen that inline styles do not let us define any pseudo-classes; let's take a look at how to solve the problem using Radium.

Using pseudo-classes, such as `:hover`, with Radium is pretty straightforward. We have to create a `:hover` property inside our style object, and Radium will do the rest:

```
const styles = {
  backgroundColor: '#ff0000',
  width: 320,
  padding: 20,
  borderRadius: 5,
  border: 'none',
  outline: 'none',
  ':hover': {
    color: '#fff'
```

```
    }
  }
```

If you apply this style object to your button and render it on the screen, you can see that passing the mouse over the button results in a button with white text, as opposed to the default black one. That is great! We can use pseudo-classes and inline styles together.

However, if you open your DevTools and try to force the :hover status in the Styles panel, you will see that nothing happens. The reason you can see the hover effect but you cannot simulate it with CSS is that Radium uses JavaScript to apply and remove the hover state defined in the style object.

If you hover over the element with the DevTools open, you can see that the style string changes and the color gets added to it dynamically:

```
<button data-radium="true" style="background-color: rgb(255, 0, 0); width:
320px; padding: 20px; border-radius: 5px; border: none; outline: none;
color: rgb(255, 255, 255);">Click me!</button>
```

The way Radium works is by adding an event handler for each one of the events that can trigger the behavior of pseudo-classes and listening to them.

As soon as one of the events gets fired, Radium changes the state of the component, which re-renders with the right style for the state. This might seem weird in the beginning, but there are no real downsides to this approach, and the difference regarding performance is not perceivable.

We can add new pseudo-classes, for example, :active, and they will work as well:

```
const styles = {
  backgroundColor: '#ff0000',
  width: 320,
  padding: 20,
  borderRadius: 5,
  border: 'none',
  outline: 'none',
  ':hover': {
    color: '#fff'
  },
  ':active': {
    position: 'relative',
    top: 2
  }
}
```

Another critical feature that Radium enables is media queries. Media queries are crucial for creating responsive applications, and Radium again uses JavaScript to enable that CSS feature in our application.

Let's look at how it works – the API is pretty similar; we have to create a new attribute on our style object and nest the styles that must be applied when the media query matches inside it:

```
const styles = {
  backgroundColor: '#ff0000',
  width: 320,
  padding: 20,
  borderRadius: 5,
  border: 'none',
  outline: 'none',
  ':hover': {
    color: '#fff'
  },
  ':active': {
    position: 'relative',
    top: 2
  },
  '@media (max-width: 480px)': {
    width: 160
  }
}
```

There is one thing we must do to make media queries work, and that is wrapping our application in the StyleRoot component provided by Radium.

For the media queries to work properly, especially with server-side rendering, Radium will inject the rules related to the media query in a style element inside the **Document Object Model (DOM)**, with all the properties set as !important.

This is to avoid flickering between the different styles that are applied to the document before the library figures out which is the matching query. Implementing the styles inside a style element prevents this by letting the browser do its regular job.

So, the idea is to import the Radium.StyleRoot component:

```
import Radium from 'radium'
```

Then, we can wrap our entire application inside it:

```
const App = () => {
  return (
    <Radium.StyleRoot>
```

```
      . . .
    </Radium.StyleRoot>
  )
}
```

As a result of this, if you open the DevTools, you can see that Radium injected the following style into the DOM:

```
<style>@media (max-width: 480px) { .rmq-1d8d7428{width: 160px
!important;}}</style>
```

The `rmq-1d8d7428` class has been applied to the button automatically as well:

```
<button class="rmq-1d8d7428" data-radium="true" style="background-color:
rgb(255, 0, 0); width: 320px; padding: 20px; border-radius: 5px; border:
none; outline: none;">Click me!</button>
```

If you now resize the browser window, you can see that the button becomes smaller for small screens, as expected.

In the next section, we are going to learn how to use the CSS modules.

Using CSS modules

If you feel that inline styles are not a suitable solution for your project and your team, but you still want to keep the styles as close as possible to your components, there is a solution for you, called **CSS modules**. The CSS modules are CSS files in which all class names and animation names are scoped locally by default. Let's see how we can use them in our projects; but first, we need to configure Webpack.

Webpack 5

Before diving into CSS modules and learning how they work, it is important to understand how they were created and the tools that support it.

In *Chapter 2, Cleaning Up Your Code*, we looked at how we can write ES6 code and transpile it using Babel and its presets. As soon as the application grows, you may want to split your code base into modules as well.

You can use Webpack or Browserify to divide the application into small modules that you can import whenever you need them, while still creating a big bundle for the browser. These tools are called **module bundlers**, and what they do is load all the dependencies of your application into a single bundle that can be executed in the browser, which does not have any concept of modules (yet).

In the React world, Webpack is especially popular because it offers many interesting and useful features, with the first one being the concept of loaders. With Webpack, you can potentially load any dependencies other than JavaScript, if there is a loader for it. For example, you can load JSON files, as well as images and other assets, inside the bundle.

In May 2015, Mark Dalgleish, one of the creators of CSS modules, figured out that you could import CSS inside a Webpack bundle as well, and he pushed the concept forward. He thought that, since the CSS could be imported locally into a component, all the imported class names could be locally scoped as well, this is great because this will isolate the styles.

Setting up a project

In this section, we will look at how to set up a very simple Webpack application, using Babel to transpile the JavaScript and the CSS modules to load our locally scoped CSS into the bundle. We will also go through all the features of CSS modules and look at the problems they can solve. The first thing to do is move to an empty folder and run the following command:

```
npm init
```

This will create a package.json file with some defaults.

Now, it is time to install the dependencies, with the first one being webpack and the second being webpack-dev-server, which we will use to run the application locally and to create the bundle on the fly:

```
npm install --save-dev webpack webpack-dev-server webpack-cli
```

Once Webpack is installed, it is time to install Babel and its loader. Since we are using Webpack to create the bundle, we will use the Babel loader to transpile our ES6 code within Webpack itself:

```
npm install --save-dev @babel/core @babel/preset-env @babel/preset-react
ts-loader
```

Finally, we install `style-loader` and the CSS loader, which are the two loaders we need to enable the CSS modules:

```
npm install --save-dev style-loader css-loader
```

There is one more thing to do to make things easier, and that is to install `html-webpack-plugin`, which is a plugin that can create an HTML page to host our JavaScript application on the fly, just by looking into the Webpack configuration and without us needing to create a regular file. Also, we need to install the `fork-ts-checker-webpack-plugin` package to make TypeScript work with Webpack:

```
npm install --save-dev html-webpack-plugin fork-ts-checker-webpack-plugin
typescript
```

Last but not least, we install `react` and `react-dom` to use them in our simple example:

```
npm install react react-dom
```

Now that all the dependencies are installed, it is time to configure everything to make it work.

First, you need to create a `.babelrc` file in your root path:

```
{
  "presets": ["@babel/preset-env", "@babel/preset-react"]
}
```

The first thing to do is add an `npm` script in `package.json` to run the `webpack-dev-server`, which will serve the application in development:

```
"scripts": {
  "dev": "webpack serve --mode development --port 3000"
}
```

 In Webpack 5, you need to use this way to call `webpack` instead of `webpack-dev-server` but you still need to have this package installed.

Webpack needs a configuration file to know how to handle the different types of dependencies we are using in our application, and to do so, we must create a file called `webpack.config.js`, which exports an object:

```
module.exports = {}
```

The object we export represents the configuration object used by Webpack to create the bundle, and it can have different properties depending on the size and the features of the project.

We want to keep our example very simple, so we are going to add three attributes. The first one is `entry`, which tells Webpack where the main file of our application is:

```
entry: './src/index.tsx'
```

The second one is `module`, which is where we tell Webpack how to load the external dependencies. It has an attribute called `rules`, where we set a specific loader for each one of the file types:

```
module: {
  rules: [
    {
      test: /\.(tsx|ts)$/,
      exclude: /node_modules/,
      use: {
        loader: 'ts-loader',
        options: {
          transpileOnly: true
        }
      }
    },
    {
      test: /\.css/,
      use: [
        'style-loader',
        'css-loader?modules=true'
      ]
    }
  ]
}
```

We are saying that the files that match the `.ts` or `.tsx` regular expression are loaded using `ts-loader` so that they get transpiled and loaded into the bundle.

You may also have noticed that we added our presets in the `.babelrc` file. As we saw in *Chapter 2, Cleaning Up Your Code*, the presets are sets of configuration options that instruct Babel on how to deal with the different types of syntax (for example, TSX).

The second entry in the `rules` array tells Webpack what to do when a CSS file is imported, and it uses `css-loader` with the `modules` flag enabled to activate CSS modules. The result of the transformation is then passed to `style-loader`, which injects the styles into the header of the page.

Finally, we enable the HTML plugin to generate the page for us, adding the `script` tag automatically using the entry path we specified earlier:

```
const HtmlWebpackPlugin = require('html-webpack-plugin')
const ForkTsCheckerWebpackPlugin = require('fork-ts-checker-webpack-
plugin')

plugins: [
  new ForkTsCheckerWebpackPlugin(),
  new HtmlWebpackPlugin({
    title: 'Your project name',
    template: './src/index.html',
    filename: './index.html'
  })
]
```

The complete `webpack.config.js` should be as shown in the following code block:

```
const HtmlWebpackPlugin = require('html-webpack-plugin')
const path = require('path')
const ForkTsCheckerWebpackPlugin = require('fork-ts-checker-webpack-
plugin')

const isProduction = process.env.NODE_ENV === 'production'

module.exports = {
  devtool: !isProduction ? 'source-map' : false, // We generate source maps
  // only for development
  entry: './src/index.tsx',
  output: { // The path where we want to output our bundles
    path: path.resolve(__dirname, 'dist'),
    filename: '[name].[hash:8].js',
    sourceMapFilename: '[name].[hash:8].map',
    chunkFilename: '[id].[hash:8].js',
    publicPath: '/'
  },
  resolve: {
    extensions: ['.ts', '.tsx', '.js', '.json', '.css'] // Here we add the
    // extensions we want to support
  },
  target: 'web',
  mode: isProduction ? 'production' : 'development', // production mode
  // minifies the code
  module: {
    rules: [
      {
        test: /\.(tsx|ts)$/,
        exclude: /node_modules/,
```

```
      use: {
        loader: 'ts-loader',
        options: {
          transpileOnly: true
        }
      }
    },
    {
      test: /\.css/,
      use: [
        'style-loader',
        'css-loader?modules=true'
      ]
    }
  ]
},
plugins: [
  new ForkTsCheckerWebpackPlugin(),
  new HtmlWebpackPlugin({
    title: 'Your project name',
    template: './src/index.html',
    filename: './index.html'
  })
],
optimization: { // This is to split our bundles into vendor and main
  splitChunks: {
    cacheGroups: {
      default: false,
      commons: {
        test: /node_modules/,
        name: 'vendor',
        chunks: 'all'
      }
    }
  }
}
}
```

Then, to configure TypeScript, you need this `tsconfig.json` file:

```
{
  "compilerOptions": {
    "allowJs": true,
    "allowSyntheticDefaultImports": true,
    "baseUrl": "src",
    "esModuleInterop": true,
    "forceConsistentCasingInFileNames": true,
    "isolatedModules": true,
```

```
        "jsx": "react-jsx",
        "lib": ["dom", "dom.iterable", "esnext"],
        "module": "esnext",
        "moduleResolution": "node",
        "noEmit": true,
        "noFallthroughCasesInSwitch": true,
        "noImplicitAny": false,
        "resolveJsonModule": true,
        "skipLibCheck": true,
        "sourceMap": true,
        "strict": true,
        "target": "es6"
    },
    "include": ["src/**/*.ts", "src/**/*.tsx"],
    "exclude": ["node_modules"]
}
```

In order to import css files using TypeScript, you need to create a declarations file at src/declarations.d.ts:

```
declare module '*.css' {
  const content: Record<string, string>
  export default content
}
```

Then, you need to create the main file at src/index.tsx:

```
import { render } from 'react-dom'

const App = () => {
  return <div>Hello World</div>
}

render(<App />, document.querySelector('#root'))
```

Finally, you need to create the initial HTML file at src/index.html:

```
<!DOCTYPE html>
<html>
  <head>
    <meta charset="UTF-8" />
    <meta name="viewport" content="width=device-width, initial-scale=1.0"
      />
    <meta http-equiv="X-UA-Compatible" content="ie=edge" />
    <title><%= htmlWebpackPlugin.options.title %></title>
  </head>
  <body>
    <div id="root"></div>
```

```
  </body>
</html>
```

We are done, and if we run the `npm run dev` command in the terminal and point the browser to `http://localhost:8080`, we should be able to see the following markup being served:

```html
<!DOCTYPE html>
<html>
  <head>
    <meta charset="UTF-8">
    <title>Your project name</title>
    <script defer src="/vendor.12472959.js"></script>
    <script defer src="/main.12472959.js"></script>
  </head>
  <body>
    <div id="root"></div>
  </body>
</html>
```

Perfect – our React application is working! Let's see now how we can add some CSS to our project.

Locally scoped CSS

Now, it is time to create our app, which will consist of a simple button, of the same sort we used in previous examples. We will use it to show all the features of the CSS modules.

Let's update the `src/index.tsx` file, which is the entry we specified in the Webpack configuration:

```tsx
import { render } from 'react-dom'
```

We can then create a simple button. As usual, we are going to start with a non-styled button, and we will add the styles step by step:

```tsx
const Button = () => <button>Click me!</button>
```

Finally, we can render the button into the DOM:

```tsx
render(<Button />, document.querySelector('#root'))
```

Now, suppose we want to apply some styles to the button – a background color, the size, and so on. We create a regular CSS file, called `index.css`, and we put the following class into it:

```
.button {
  background-color: #ff0000;
  width: 320px;
  padding: 20px;
  border-radius: 5px;
  border: none;
  outline: none;
}
```

Now, we said that with CSS modules we could import the CSS files into the JavaScript; let's look at how it works.

Inside our `index.js` file where we defined the button component, we can add the following line:

```
import styles from './index.css'
```

The result of this `import` statement is a `styles` object, where all the attributes are the classes defined in `index.css`.

If we run `console.log(styles)`, we can see the following object in the DevTools:

```
{
  button: "_2wpxM3yizfwbWee6k0UlD4"
}
```

So, we have an object where the attributes are the class names and the values are (apparently) random strings. We will see later that they are non-random, but let's check what we can do with that object first.

We can use the object to set the class name attribute of our button, as follows:

```
const Button = () => (
  <button className={styles.button}>Click me!</button>
);
```

If we go back to the browser, we can now see that the styles we defined in `index.css` have been applied to the button. This is not magic, because if we check in DevTools, the class that has been applied to the element is the same string that's attached to the `style` object we imported inside our code:

```
<button class="_2wpxM3yizfwbWee6k0UlD4">Click me!</button>
```

If we look at the header section of the page, we can now see that the same class name has also been injected into the page:

```
<style type="text/css">
  ._2wpxM3yizfwbWee6k0UlD4 {
    background-color: #ff0000;
    width: 320px;
    padding: 20px;
    border-radius: 5px;
    border: none;
    outline: none;
  }
</style>
```

This is how the CSS and the style loaders work.

The CSS loader lets you import the CSS files into your JavaScript modules and, when the module flag is activated, all the class names are locally scoped to the module they are imported into. As we mentioned previously, the string we imported was non-random, but it is generated using the hash of the file and some other parameters in a way that is unique within the code base.

Finally, `style-loader` takes the result of the CSS module's transformation and injects the styles inside the header section of the page. This is very powerful because we have the full power and expressiveness of the CSS, combined with the advantages of having locally scoped class names and explicit dependencies.

As mentioned at the beginning of this chapter, CSS is global, and that makes it very hard to maintain in large applications. With CSS modules, class names are locally scoped and they cannot clash with other class names in different parts of the application, enforcing a deterministic result.

Moreover, explicitly importing the CSS dependencies inside our components helps us see clearly which components need which CSS. It is also very useful for eliminating dead code because when we delete a component for any reason, we can tell exactly which CSS it was using.

CSS modules are regular CSS, so we can use pseudo-classes, media queries, and animations.

For example, we can add CSS rules such as the following:

```
.button:hover {
  color: #fff;
}
.button:active {
```

```
    position: relative;
    top: 2px;
  }
@media (max-width: 480px) {
  .button {
    width: 160px
  }
}
```

This will be transformed into the following code and injected into the document:

```
._2wpxM3yizfwbWee6k0UlD4:hover {
  color: #fff;
}
._2wpxM3yizfwbWee6k0UlD4:active {
  position: relative;
  top: 2px;
}
@media (max-width: 480px) {
  ._2wpxM3yizfwbWee6k0UlD4 {
    width: 160px
  }
}
```

The class names get created and they get replaced everywhere the button is used, making it reliable and local, as expected.

As you may have noticed, those class names are great, but they make debugging pretty hard because we cannot easily tell which classes generated the hash. What we can do in development mode is add a special configuration parameter, with which we can choose the pattern that's used to produce the scoped class names.

For example, we can change the value of the loader as follows:

```
{
  test: /\.css/,
  use: [
    {
      loader: 'style-loader'
    },
    {
      loader: "css-loader",
      options: {
        modules: {
          localIdentName: "[local]--[hash:base64:5]"
        }
      }
    }
```

```
    ]
  }
```

Here, `localIdentName` is the parameter, and `[local]` and `[hash:base64:5]` are placeholders for the original class name value and a five-character hash. Other available placeholders are `[path]`, which represents the path of the CSS file, and `[name]`, which is the name of the source CSS file.

Activating the previous configuration option, the result we have in the browser is as follows:

```
<button class="button--2wpxM">Click me!</button>
```

This is way more readable and easier to debug.

In production, we do not need class names like this, and we are more interested in performance, so we may want shorter class names and hashes.

With Webpack, it is pretty straightforward because we can have multiple configuration files that can be used in the different stages of our application life cycle. Also, in production, we may want to extract the CSS file instead of injecting it into the browser from the bundle so that we can have a lighter bundle and cache the CSS on a Content Delivery Network for better performance.

To do that, you need to install another Webpack plugin, called `mini-css-extract-plugin`, which can write an actual CSS file, putting in all the scoped classes that were generated from CSS modules.

There are a couple of features of CSS modules that are worth mentioning.

The first one is the `global` keyword. Prefixing any class with `:global`, in fact, means asking CSS modules not to scope the current selector locally.

For example, let's say we change our CSS as follows:

```
:global .button {
   ...
}
```

The output will be as follows:

```
.button {
   ...
}
```

This is good if you want to apply styles that cannot be scoped locally, such as third-party widgets.

My favorite feature of CSS modules is **composition**. With composition, we can extract classes from the same file or external dependencies and get all the styles applied to the element.

For example, extract the rule to set the background to red from the rules for the button into a separate block, as follows:

```
.background-red {
  background-color: #ff0000;
}
```

We can then compose it inside our button in the following way:

```
.button {
  composes: background-red;
  width: 320px;
  padding: 20px;
  border-radius: 5px;
  border: none;
  outline: none;
}
```

The result is that all the rules of the button and all the rules of the `composes` declaration are applied to the element.

This is a very powerful feature and it works in a fascinating way. You might expect that all the composed classes are duplicated inside the classes where they are referenced as SASS `@extend` does, but that is not the case. Simply put, all the composed class names are applied one after the other on the component in the DOM.

In our specific case, we would have the following:

```
<button class="_2wpxM3yizfwbWee6k0UlD4 Sf8w9cFdQXdRV_i9dgcOq">Click
me!</button>
```

Here, the CSS that is injected into the page is as follows:

```
.Sf8w9cFdQXdRV_i9dgcOq {
  background-color: #ff0000;
}
._2wpxM3yizfwbWee6k0UlD4 {
  width: 320px;
  padding: 20px;
  border-radius: 5px;
```

```
  border: none;
  outline: none;
}
```

As you can see, our CSS class names have unique names, which is good to isolate our styles. Now, let's take a look at the Atomic CSS modules.

Atomic CSS modules

It should be clear how composition works and why it is a very powerful feature of CSS modules. At YPlan, the company where I worked when I started writing this book, we tried to push it a step further, combining the power of `composes` with the flexibility of **Atomic CSS** (also known as **Functional CSS**).

Atomic CSS is a way to use CSS where every class has a single rule.

For example, we can create a class to set `margin-bottom` to 0:

```
.mb0 {
  margin-bottom: 0;
}
```

We can use another one to set `font-weight` to 600:

```
.fw6 {
  font-weight: 600;
}
```

Then, we can apply all those atomic classes to the elements:

```
<h2 class="mb0 fw6">Hello React</h2>
```

This technique is controversial and particularly efficient at the same time. It is hard to start using it because you end up having too many classes in your markup, which makes it hard to predict the final result. If you think about it, it is pretty similar to inline styles, because you apply one class per rule, apart from the fact that you are using a shorter class name as a proxy.

The biggest argument against Atomic CSS is usually that you are moving the styling logic from the CSS to the markup, which is wrong. Classes are defined in CSS files, but they are composed in the views, and every time you have to modify the style of an element, you end up editing the markup.

On the other hand, we tried using Atomic CSS for a bit and we found that it makes prototyping incredibly fast.

In fact, when all the base rules have been generated, applying those classes to the elements and creating new styles is a very quick process, which is good. Second, using Atomic CSS, we can control the size of the CSS file, because as soon as we create new components with their styles, we are using existing classes and we do not need to create new ones, which is great for performance.

So, we tried to solve the problems of Atomic CSS using CSS modules and we called the technique **Atomic CSS modules**.

In essence, you start creating your base CSS classes (for example, `mb0`), and then, instead of applying the class names one by one in the markup, you compose them into placeholder classes using CSS modules.

Let's look at an example:

```
.title {
  composes: mb0 fw6;
}
```

Here's another example:

```
<h2 className={styles.title}>Hello React</h2>
```

This is great because you still keep the styling logic inside the CSS, and the CSS module's `composes` does the job for you by applying all the single classes in the markup.

The result of the preceding code is as follows:

```
<h2 class="title--3JCJR mb0--21SyP fw6--1JRhZ">Hello React</h2>
```

Here, `title`, `mb0`, and `fw6` are all applied automatically to the element. They are scoped locally as well, so we have all the advantages of CSS modules.

React CSS modules

Last but not least, there is a great library that can help us work with CSS modules. You may have noticed how we were using a `style` object to load all the classes of the CSS, and because JavaScript does not support hyphenated attributes, we are forced to use a camelCased class name.

Also, if we are referencing a class name that does not exist in the CSS file, there is no way to know it, and `undefined` is added to the list of classes. For these and other useful features, we may want to try a package that makes working with CSS modules even smoother.

Let's look at what this means by going back to the index.tsx file we were using previously in this section with plain CSS modules, and changing it to use React CSS modules instead.

The package is called react-css-modules, and the first thing we must do is install it:

```
npm install react-css-modules
```

Once the package is installed, we import it inside our index.tsx file:

```
import cssModules from 'react-css-modules'
```

We use it as an HOC, passing to it the Button component we want to enhance and the styles object we imported from the CSS:

```
const EnhancedButton = cssModules(Button, styles)
```

Now, we have to change the implementation of the button to avoid using the styles object. With React CSS modules, we use the styleName property, which is transformed into a regular class.

The great thing about this is that we can use the class name as a string (for example, "button"):

```
const Button = () => <button styleName="button">Click me!</button>;
```

If we now render EnhancedButton into the DOM, we will see that nothing has really changed from before, which means that the library works.

Let's say we try to change the styleName property to reference a non-existing class name, as follows:

```
import { render } from 'react-dom'
import styles from './index.css'
import cssModules from 'react-css-modules'

const Button = () => <button styleName="button1">Click me!</button>

const EnhancedButton = cssModules(Button, styles)

render(<EnhancedButton />, document.querySelector('#root'))
```

We will see the following error in the console of the browser by doing so:

```
Uncaught Error: "button1" CSS module is undefined.
```

This is particularly helpful when the code base grows and we have multiple developers working on different components and styles.

Implementing styled-components

There is a library that is very promising because it takes into account all the problems other libraries have encountered in styling components. Different paths have been followed for writing CSS in JavaScript, and many solutions have been tried, so now the time is ripe for a library that takes all the learning and then builds something on top of it.

The library is conceived and maintained by two popular developers in the JavaScript community: *Glenn Maddern* and *Max Stoiberg*. It represents a very modern approach to the problem, and it uses edge features of ES2015 and some advanced techniques that have been applied to React to provide a complete solution for styling.

Let's look at how it is possible to create the same button we saw in the previous sections, and check whether all the CSS features we are interested in (for example, pseudo-classes and media queries) work with `styled-components`.

First, we have to install the library by running the following command:

```
npm install styled-components
```

Once the library is installed, we have to import it inside our component's file:

```
import styled from 'styled-components'
```

At that point, we can use the `styled` function to create any element by using `styled.elementName`, where `elementName` can be a `div`, a button, or any other valid DOM element.

The second thing to do is to define the style of the element we are creating and to do so, we use an ES6 feature called **tagged template literals**, which is a way of passing template strings to a function without them being interpolated beforehand.

This means that the function receives the actual template with all the JavaScript expressions, and this makes the library able to use the full power of JavaScript to apply the styles to the elements.

Let's start by creating a simple button with a basic styling:

```
const Button = styled.button`
  backgroundColor: #ff0000;
  width: 320px;
```

```
  padding: 20px;
  borderRadius: 5px;
  border: none;
  outline: none;
`;
```

This *kind-of-weird* syntax returns a proper React component called `Button`, which renders a button element and applies to it all the styles defined in the template. The way the styles are applied is by creating a unique class name, adding it to the element, and then injecting the corresponding style in the head of the document.

The following is the component that gets rendered:

```
<button class="kYvFOg">Click me!</button>
```

The style that gets added to the page is as follows:

```
.kYvFOg {
  background-color: #ff0000;
  width: 320px;
  padding: 20px;
  border-radius: 5px;
  border: none;
  outline: none;
}
```

The good thing about `styled-components` is that it supports almost all the features of CSS, which makes it a good candidate to be used in a real-world application.

For example, it supports pseudo-classes using a SASS-like syntax:

```
const Button = styled.button`
  background-color: #ff0000;
  width: 320px;
  padding: 20px;
  border-radius: 5px;
  border: none;
  outline: none;
  &:hover {
    color: #fff;
  }
  &:active {
    position: relative;
    top: 2px;
  }
```

It also supports media queries:

```
const Button = styled.button`
  background-color: #ff0000;
  width: 320px;
  padding: 20px;
  border-radius: 5px;
  border: none;
  outline: none;
  &:hover {
    color: #fff;
  }
  &:active {
    position: relative;
    top: 2px;
  }
  @media (max-width: 480px) {
    width: 160px;
  }
`;
```

There are many other features that this library can bring to your project.

For example, once you have created the button, you can easily override its styles and use it multiple times with different properties. Inside the templates, it is also possible to use the props that the component received and change the style accordingly.

Another great feature is **theming**. Wrapping your components in a `ThemeProvider` component, you can inject a theme property down to the three component's children, which makes it extremely easy to create UIs where part of the style is shared between components and some other properties depend on the currently selected theme.

No doubt `styled-components` library is a game-changer when you are taking your styles to the next level, at the beginning could seem weird because the way is implementing styles with components, but once you get used to I guarantee will be your favorite styles package.

Summary

In this chapter, we looked at a lot of interesting topics. We started by going through the problems of CSS at scale, specifically, the problems that they had at Facebook while dealing with CSS. We learned how inline styles work in React and why it is good to co-locate the styles within components. We also looked at the limitations of inline styles. Then, we moved on to Radium, which solves the main problems of inline styles, giving us a clear interface to write our CSS in JavaScript. For those who think that inline styles are a bad solution, we moved into the world of CSS modules, setting up a simple project from scratch.

Importing the CSS files into our components makes the dependencies clear, and scoping the class names locally avoids clashes. We looked at how CSS module's `composes` is a great feature, and how we can use it in conjunction with Atomic CSS to create a framework for quick prototyping.

Finally, we had a quick look at `styled-components`, which is a very promising library and is meant to change the way we approach the styling of components completely.

So far, you have learned about a lot of ways to work with CSS styles with React from inline styles to CSS modules or using a library such as `styled-components`. In the next chapter, we are going to learn how to implement and get the benefits from server-side rendering.

Server-Side Rendering for Fun and Profit

9

The next step in building React applications is learning how server-side rendering works and what benefits it can give us. The **universal applications** are better for SEO, and they enable knowledge-sharing between the frontend and the backend. They can also improve the perceived speed of a web application, which usually leads to increased conversions. However, applying server-side rendering to a React application comes at a cost, and we should think carefully about whether we need it or not.

In this chapter, you will see how to set up a server-side rendered application, and by the end of the relevant sections, you will be able to build a universal application and understand the pros and the cons of the technique.

In this chapter, we will cover the following topics:

- Understanding what a universal application is
- Figuring out the reasons why we may want to enable server-side rendering
- Creating a simple static server-side rendered application with React
- Adding data fetching to server-side rendering and understanding concepts such as dehydration/hydration
- Using **Next.js** by Zeith to easily create a React application that runs on both the server and the client

Technical requirements

To complete this chapter, you will require the following:

- Node.js 12+
- Visual Studio Code

You can find the code for this chapter in the book's GitHub repository at `https://github.com/PacktPublishing/React-17-Design-Patterns-and-Best-Practices-Third-Edition/tree/main/Chapter09`.

Understanding universal applications

A universal application is an application that can run both on the server side and client side with the same code. In this section, we will look at the reasons why we should consider making our applications universal, and we will learn how React components can be easily rendered on the server side.

When we talk about JavaScript web applications, we usually think of client-side code that lives in the browser. The way they usually work is that the server returns an empty HTML page with a `script` tag to load the application. When the application is ready, it manipulates the DOM inside the browser to show the UI and to interact with users. This has been the case for the last few years, and it is still the way to go for a huge number of applications.

In this book, we have seen how easy it is to create applications using React components and how they work within the browser. What we have not seen yet is how React can render the same components on the server, giving us a powerful feature called **Server-Side Rendering (SSR)**.

Before going into the details, let's try to understand what it means to create applications that render both on the server and the client. For years, we used to have completely different applications for the server and client: for example, a Django application to render the views on the server, and some JavaScript frameworks, such as Backbone or jQuery, on the client. Those separate apps usually had to be maintained by two teams of developers with different skill sets. If you needed to share data between the server-side rendered pages and the client-side application, you could inject some variables inside a script tag. Using two different languages and platforms, there was no way to share common information, such as models or views, between the different sides of the application.

Since Node.js was released in 2009, JavaScript has gained a lot of attention and popularity on the server side as well, thanks to web application frameworks, such as **Express**. Using the same language on both sides not only makes it easy for developers to reuse their knowledge, but also enables different ways of sharing code between the server and the client.

With React in particular, the concept of isomorphic web applications became very popular within the JavaScript community. Writing an **isomorphic application** means building an application that looks the same on the server and the client. The fact that the same language is used to write the two applications means that a big part of the logic can be shared, which opens many possibilities. This makes the code base easier to reason about and avoids unnecessary duplication.

React brings the concept a step forward, giving us a simple API to render our components on the server and transparently applying all the logic needed to make the page interactive (for example, event handlers) on the browser.

The term *isomorphic* does not fit in this scenario because, in the case of React, the applications are the same, and that is why one of the creators of React Router, Michael Jackson, proposed a more meaningful name for this pattern: **Universal**.

Reasons for implementing SSR

SSR is a great feature, but we should not jump into it just for the sake of it. We should have a real and solid reason to start using it. In this section, we will look at how SSR can help our application and what problems it can solve for us. In our next sections, we are going to learn about SEO and how to improve the performance of our application.

Implementing search engine optimization

One of the main reasons why we may want to render our applications on the server side is **Search Engine Optimization (SEO)**.

If we serve an empty HTML skeleton to the crawlers of the main search engines, they are not able to extract any meaningful information from it. Nowadays, Google seems to be able to run JavaScript, but there are some limitations, and SEO is often a critical aspect of our businesses.

For years, we used to write two applications: an SSR one for the crawlers, and another one to be used on the client side by users. We used to do that because SSR applications could not give us the level of interactivity users expect, while client-side applications did not get indexed by search engines.

Maintaining and supporting two applications is difficult, and makes the code base less flexible and less prone to changes. Luckily, with React, we can render our components on the server side and serve the content of our applications to the crawlers in such a way that it is easy for them to understand and index the content.

This is great, not only for SEO, but also for social sharing services. Platforms such as Facebook or Twitter give us a way of defining the content of the snippets that are shown when our pages are shared.

For example, using Open Graph, we can tell Facebook that, for a particular page, we want a certain image to be shown and a particular title to be used as the title of the post. It is almost impossible to do that using client-side-only applications because the engine that extracts the information from the pages uses the markup returned by the server.

If our server returns an empty HTML structure for all the URLs, the result is that when the pages are shared on the social networks, the snippets of our web application are empty as well, which affects their virality.

A common code base

We do not have many options on the client side; our applications have to be written in JavaScript. There are some languages that can be converted into JavaScript at build time, but the concept does not change. The ability to use the same language on the server represents a significant win regarding maintainability and knowledge-sharing across the company.

Being able to share the logic between the client and the server makes it easy to apply any changes on both sides without doing the work twice, which, most of the time, leads to fewer errors and fewer problems.

The effort of maintaining a single code base is less than the work required to keep two different applications up to date. Another reason why you might consider introducing JavaScript on the server side in your team is sharing knowledge between frontend and backend developers.

The ability to reuse the code on both sides makes collaboration easier, and the teams speak a common language, which helps with making faster decisions and changes.

Better performance

Last, but not least, we all love client-side applications, because they are fast and responsive, but there is a problem—the bundle has to be loaded and run before users can take any action on the application.

This might not be a problem using a modern laptop or a desktop computer on a fast internet connection. However, if we load a huge JavaScript bundle using a mobile device with a 3G connection, users have to wait for a little while before interacting with the application. This is not only bad for the UX in general, but it also affects conversions. It has been proven by the major e-commerce websites that a few milliseconds added to the page load can have an enormous impact on revenues.

For example, if we serve our application with an empty HTML page and a `script` tag on the server and we show a spinner to our users until they can click on anything, the perception of the speed of the website is significantly affected.

If we render our website on the server side instead and users start seeing some of the content as soon as they hit the page, they are more likely to stay, even if they have to wait the same amount of time before doing anything for real, because the client-side bundle has to be loaded regardless of the SSR.

This perceived performance is something we can improve greatly using SSR because we can output our components on the server and return some information to users straight away.

Don't underestimate the complexity

Even if React provides an easy API to render components on the server, creating a universal application has a cost. So, we should consider carefully before enabling it for one of the preceding reasons and check whether our team is ready to support and maintain a universal application.

As we will see in the coming sections, rendering components is not the only task that needs to be done to create server-side rendered applications. We have to set up and maintain a server with its routes and its logic, manage the server data flow, and so on. Potentially, we want to cache the content to serve the pages faster and carry out many other tasks that are required to maintain a fully functional universal application.

For this reason, my suggestion is to build the client-side version first, and only when the web application is fully working on the server should you think about improving the experience by enabling SSR. SSR should only be enabled when strictly necessary. For example, if you need SEO or if you need to customize the social sharing information, you should start thinking about it.

If you realize that your application takes a lot of time to load fully and you have already done all the optimization (refer to the following *Chapter 10, Improving the Performance of Your Applications*, for more on this topic), you can consider using SSR to offer a better experience to your users and improve the perceived speed. Now that we have learned what SSR is and the benefits of universal applications, let's jump into some basic examples of SSR in our next section.

Creating a basic example of SSR

We will now create a very simple server-side application to look at the steps that are needed to build a basic universal setup. It is going to be a minimal and simple setup on purpose because the goal here is to show how SSR works rather than providing a comprehensive solution or a boilerplate, even though you could use the example application as a starting point for a real-world application.

 This section assumes that all the concepts regarding JavaScript build tools, such as webpack and its loaders, are clear, and it requires a little bit of knowledge of Node.js. As a JavaScript developer, it should be easy for you to follow this section, even if you have never seen a Node.js application before.

The application will consist of two parts:

- On the server side, where we will use **Express** to create a basic web server and serve an HTML page with the server-side rendered React application
- On the client side, where we will render the application, as usual, using `react-dom`

Both sides of the application will be transpiled with Babel and bundled with webpack before being run, which will let us use the full power of ES6 and the modules both on Node.js and on the browser.

Let's start by creating a new project folder (you can call it `ssr-project`) and running the following command to create a new package:

```
npm init
```

Once `package.json` is created, it is time to install the dependencies. We can start with webpack:

```
npm install webpack
```

After this is done, it is time to install `ts-loader` and the presets that we need to write an ES6 application using React and TSX:

```
npm install --save-dev @babel/core @babel/preset-env @babel/preset-react ts-loader typescript
```

We also have to install a dependency, which we will need in order to create the server bundle. `webpack` lets us define a set of externals, which are dependencies that we do not want to add to the bundle. When creating a build for the server, in fact, we do not want to add to the bundle of all the node packages that we use; we just want to bundle our server code. There's a package that helps with that, and we can simply apply it to the external entry in our `webpack` configuration to exclude all the modules:

```
npm install --save-dev webpack-node-externals
```

Great. It is now time to create an entry in the npm `scripts` section of `package.json` so that we can easily run the `build` command from the terminal:

```
"scripts": {
  "build": "webpack"
}
```

Next, you need to create a `.babelrc` file in your root path:

```
{
  "presets": ["@babel/preset-env", "@babel/preset-react"]
}
```

We now have to create the configuration file, called `webpack.config.js`, to tell `webpack` how we want our files to be bundled.

Let's start importing the library we will use to set our node externals. We will also define the configuration for `ts-loader`, which we will use for both the client and the server:

```
const nodeExternals = require('webpack-node-externals')
const path = require('path')

const rules = [{
  test: /\.(tsx|ts)$/,
  use: 'ts-loader',
  exclude: /node_modules/
}]
```

In *Chapter 8, Making Your Components Look Beautiful,* we looked at how we had to export a configuration object from the configuration file. There is one cool feature in webpack that lets us export an array of configurations as well so that we can define both client and server configurations in the same place and use both in one go.

The client configuration shown in the following block should be very familiar:

```
const client = {
  entry: './src/client.tsx',
  output: {
    path: path.resolve(__dirname, './dist/public'),
    filename: 'bundle.js',
    publicPath: '/'
  },
  module: {
    rules
  }
}
```

We are telling webpack that the source code of the client application is inside the src folder, and we want the output bundle to be generated in the dist folder.

We also set the module loaders using the previous object we created with ts-loader. The server configuration is slightly different; we need to define a different entry, output, and add some new nodes, such as target, externals, and resolve:

```
const server = {
  entry: './src/server.ts',
  output: {
    path: path.resolve(__dirname, './dist'),
    filename: 'server.js',
    publicPath: '/'
  },
  module: {
    rules
  },
  target: 'node',
  externals: [nodeExternals()],
  resolve: {
    extensions: [".ts", ".tsx", ".js", ".json"],
  },
}
```

As you can see, entry, output, and module are the same, except for the filenames.

The new parameters are the `target`, where we specify the node to tell `webpack` to ignore all the built-in system packages of Node.js, such as `fs` and `externals`, where we use the library we imported earlier to tell webpack to ignore the dependencies.

Last, but not least, we have to export the configurations as an array:

```
module.exports = [client, server]
```

The configuration is done. We are now ready to write some code, and we will start with the React application, which we are more familiar with.

Let's create an `src` folder and an `app.ts` file inside it.

The `app.ts` file should have the following content:

```
const App = () => <div>Hello React</div>

export default App
```

Nothing complex here; we import React, create an `App` component, which renders the `Hello React` message, and export it.

Let's now create `client.tsx`, which is responsible for rendering the `App` component inside the DOM:

```
import { render } from 'react-dom'
import App from './app'

render(<App />, document.getElementById('root'))
```

Again, this should sound familiar, since we import React, ReactDOM, and the `App` component we created earlier, and we use `ReactDOM` to render it in a DOM element with the `app` ID.

Let's now move to the server.

The first thing to do is to create a `template.ts` file, which exports a function that we will use to return the markup of the page that our server will give back to the browser:

```
export default body => `
  <!DOCTYPE html>
  <html>
    <head>
      <meta charset="UTF-8">
    </head>
    <body>
      <div id="root">${body}</div>
```

```
      <script src="/bundle.js"></script>
    </body>
  </html>`
```

It should be pretty straightforward. The function accepts `body`, which we will later see contains the React app, and it returns the skeleton of the page.

It is worth noting that we load the bundle on the client side even if the app is rendered on the server side. SSR is only half of the job that React does to render our application. We still want our application to be a client-side application, with all the features we can use in the browser, such as event handlers, for example.

After this, you need to install `express`, `react`, and `react-dom`:

```
npm install express react react-dom @types/express @types/react
@types/react-dom
```

Now it is time to create `server.tsx`, which has more dependencies and is worth exploring in detail:

```
import React from 'react'
import express, { Request, Response } from 'express'
import { renderToString } from 'react-dom/server'
import path from 'path'
import App from './App'
import template from './template'
```

The first thing that we import is `express`, the library that allows us to create a web server with some routes easily, and which is also able to serve static files.

Secondly, we import `React` and `ReactDOM` to render `App`, which we import as well. Notice the `/server` path in the `import` statement of `ReactDOM`. The last thing we import is the template we defined earlier.

Now we create an Express application:

```
const app = express()
```

We tell the application where our static assets are stored:

```
app.use(express.static(path.resolve(__dirname, './dist/public')))
```

As you may have noticed, the path is the same that we used in the client configuration of webpack as the output destination of the client bundle.

Then, here comes the logic of SSR with React:

```
app.get('/', (req: Request, res: Response) => {
  const body = renderToString(<App />)
  const html = template(body)
  res.send(html)
})
```

We are telling Express that we want to listen to the / route, and when it gets hit by a client, we render App to a string using the ReactDOM library. Here comes the magic and simplicity of the SSR of React.

What renderToString does is return a string representation of the DOM elements generated by our App component; the same tree that it would render in the DOM if we were using the ReactDOM render method.

The value of the body variable is something like the following:

```
<div data-reactroot="" data-reactid="1" data-react-
checksum="982061917">Hello React</div>
```

As you can see, it represents what we defined in the render method of App, except for a couple of data attributes that React uses on the client to attach the client-side application to the server-side rendered string.

Now that we have the SSR representation of our app, we can use the template function to apply it to the HTML template and send it back to the browser within the Express response.

Last, but not least, we have to start the Express application:

```
app.listen(3000, () => {
  console.log('Listening on port 3000')
})
```

We are now ready to go; there are only a few operations left. The first one is to define the start script of npm and set it to run the node server:

```
"scripts": {
  "build": "webpack",
  "start": "node ./dist/server"
}
```

The scripts are ready, so we can first build the application with the following command:

```
npm run build
```

When the bundles are created, we can run the following command:

```
npm start
```

Point the browser to `http://localhost:3000` and see the result.

There are two important things to note here. First, when we use the **View Page Source** feature of the browser, we can see the source code of the application being rendered and returned from the server, which we would not see if SSR was not enabled.

Second, if we open DevTools and we have the React extension installed, we can see that the `App` component has been booted on the client as well.

The following screenshot shows the source of the page:

Great! Now that you have created your first React application using SSR, let's learn how to fetch data in the next section.

Implementing data fetching

The example in the previous section should explain clearly how to set up a universal application in React. It is pretty straightforward, and the main focus is on getting things done.

However, in a real-world application, we will likely want to load some data instead of a static React component, such as `App` in the example. Suppose we want to load Dan Abramov's `gists` on the server and return the list of items from the Express app we just created.

In the data fetching examples in *Chapter 6, Managing Data,* we looked at how we can use useEffect to fire the data loading. That wouldn't work on the server because components do not get mounted on the DOM and the life cycle Hook never gets fired.

Using Hooks that were executed earlier will not work either because the data fetching operation is async, while renderToString is not. For that reason, we have to find a way to load the data beforehand and pass it to the component as props.

Let's look at how we can take the application from the previous section and change it a bit to make it load gists during the SSR phase.

The first thing to do is to change App.tsx to accept a list of gists as prop, and loop through it in the render method to display their descriptions:

```tsx
import { FC } from 'react'

type Gist = {
  id: string
  description: string
}

type Props = {
  gists: Gist[]
}

const App: FC<Props> = ({ gists }) => (
  <ul>
    {gists.map(gist => (
      <li key={gist.id}>{gist.description}</li>
    ))}
  </ul>
)
export default App
```

Applying the concept that we learned in the previous chapter, we define a stateless functional component, which receives gists as a prop and loops through the elements to render a list of items. Now, we have to change the server to retrieve gists and pass them to the component.

To use the **fetch** API on the server side, we have to install a library called isomorphic-fetch, which implements the fetch standards. It can be used in Node.js and the browser:

```
npm install isomorphic-fetch @types/isomorphic-fetch
```

We first import the library into `server.tsx`:

```
import fetch from 'isomorphic-fetch'
```

The API call that we want to make looks as follows:

```
fetch('https://api.github.com/users/gaearon/gists')
  .then(response => response.json())
  .then(gists => {})
```

Here, `gists` are available to be used inside the last `then` function. In our case, we want to pass them down to `App`.

Therefore, we can change the / route as follows:

```
app.get('/', (req, res) => {
  fetch('https://api.github.com/users/gaearon/gists')
    .then(response => response.json())
    .then(gists => {
      const body = renderToString(<App gists={gists} />)
      const html = template(body)
      res.send(html)
    })
})
```

Here, we first fetch `gists`, and then we render `App` to a string, passing the property.

Once `App` is rendered, and we have its markup, we use the template we used in the previous section and return it to the browser.

Run the following command in the console and point the browser to `http://localhost:3000`. You should be able to see a server-side render list of `gists`:

```
npm run build && npm start
```

To make sure that the list is rendered from the Express app, you can navigate to `view-source:http://localhost:3000` and you will see the markup and the descriptions of `gists`.

That is great, and it looks easy, but if we check the DevTools console, we can see the **Cannot read property 'map' of undefined** error. The reason we see the error is that, on the client, we are rendering `App` again, but without passing `gists` to it.

This could sound counter-intuitive in the beginning because we might think that React is smart enough to use gists rendered within the server-side string on the client. But that is not what happens, so we have to find a way to make gists available on the client side as well.

You may consider that you can execute the fetch again on the client. That would work, but it is not optimal because you would end up firing two HTTP calls, one on the Express server and one in the browser. If we think about it, we already made the call on the server, and we have all the data we need. A typical solution to sharing data between the server and the client is dehydrating the data in the HTML markup and hydrating it back in the browser.

This seems like a complex concept, but it is not. We will now look at how easy it is to implement. The first thing we must do is to inject gists in the template after we have fetched them on the client.

To do this, we have to change the template slightly as follows:

```
export default (body, gists) => `
  <!DOCTYPE html>
  <html>
    <head>
      <meta charset="UTF-8">
    </head>
    <body>
      <div id="root">${body}</div>
      <script>window.gists = ${JSON.stringify(gists)}</script>
      <script src="/bundle.js"></script>
    </body>
  </html>
```

The template function now accepts two parameters—body of the app and the collection of gists. The first one is inserted inside the app element, while the second is used to define a global gists variable attached to the window object so that we can use it in the client.

Inside the Express route (server.js), we just have to change the line where we generate the template passing the body, as follows:

```
const html = template(body, gists)
```

Last, but not least, we have to use gists attached to a window inside client.tsx, which is pretty easy:

```
ReactDOM.hydrate(
  <App gists={window.gists} />,
```

```
    document.getElementById('app')
  )
```

Hydrate was introduced in React 16 and works similar to render on the client side, irrespective of whether the HTML has server-rendered markup or not. If there is no markup previously using SSR, then the `hydrate` method will fire a warning that you can silence it by using the new `suppressHydrationWarning` attribute.

We read `gists` directly, and we pass them to the `App` component that gets rendered on the client.

Now, run the following command again:

```
npm run build && npm start
```

If we point the browser window to `http://localhost:3000`, the error is gone, and if we inspect the `App` component using React DevTools, we can see how the client-side `App` component receives the collection of `gists`.

As we have created our first SSR application, let's now see how we can do this more easily by using an SSR framework called Next.js in the next section.

Using Next.js to create a React application

You have looked at the basics of SSR with React, and you can use the project we created as a starting point for a real app. However, you may think that there is too much boilerplate and that you are required to know too many different tools to run a simple universal application with React. This is a common feeling called **JavaScript fatigue**, as described in the introduction to this book.

Luckily, Facebook developers and other companies in the React community are working very hard to improve the DX and make the life of developers easier. You might have used `create-react-app` at this point to try out the examples in the previous chapters, and you should understand how it makes it very simple to create React applications without requiring developers to learn many technologies and tools.

Now, `create-react-app` does not support SSR yet, but there's a company called **Vercel** that has created a tool called **Next.js**, which makes it incredibly easy to generate universal applications without worrying about configuration files. It also reduces the boilerplate a lot.

It is important to say that using abstractions is always very good for building applications quickly. However, it is crucial to know how the internals work before adding too many layers, and that is why we started with the manual process before learning Next.js. We have looked at how SSR works and how we can pass the state from the server to the client. Now that the base concepts are clear, we can move to a tool that hides a little bit of complexity and makes us write less code to achieve the same results.

We will create the same app where all `gists` from Dan Abramov are loaded, and you will see how clean and simple the code is, thanks to Next.js.

First of all, create a new project folder (you can call it `next-project`) and run the following command:

```
npm init
```

When this is done, we can install the Next.js library and React:

```
npm install next react react-dom typescript @types/react @types/node
```

Now that the project is created, we have to add an npm script to run the binary:

```
"scripts": {
  "dev": "next"
}
```

Perfect! It is now time to generate our App component.

Next.js is based on conventions, with the most important one being that you can create pages to match the browser URLs. The default page is `index`, so we can create a folder called `pages` and put an `index.js` file inside it.

We start importing the dependencies:

```
import fetch from 'isomorphic-fetch'
```

Again, we import `isomorphic-fetch` because we want to be able to use the `fetch` function on the server side.

We then define a component called App:

```
const App = () => {

}

export default App
```

Then we define a `static async` function, called `getInitialProps`, which is where we tell Next.js which data we want to load, both on the server side and on the client side. The library will make the object returned from the function available as props inside the component.

The `static` and `async` keywords applied to a class method mean that the function can be accessed outside the instance of the class and that the function yields the execution of the `wait` instructions inside its body.

These concepts are pretty advanced, and they are not part of the scope of this chapter, but if you are interested in them, you should check out the ECMAScript proposals (`https://github.com/tc39/proposals`).

The implementation of the method we just described is as follows:

```
App.getInitialProps = async () => {
  const url = 'https://api.github.com/users/gaearon/gists'
  const response = await fetch(url)
  const gists = await response.json()
  return {
    gists
  }
}
```

We are telling the function to fire the fetch and wait for the response; then we are transforming the response into JSON, which returns a promise. When the promise is resolved, we can return the `props` object with `gists`.

`render` of the component looks pretty similar to the preceding one:

```
return (
  <ul>
    {props.gists.map(gist => (
      <li key={gist.id}>{gist.description}</li>
    ))}
  </ul>
)
```

Before you run the project, you need to configure `tsconfig.json`:

```
{
  "compilerOptions": {
    "baseUrl": "src",
    "esModuleInterop": true,
    "module": "esnext",
    "noImplicitAny": true,
```

```
    "outDir": "dist",
    "resolveJsonModule": true,
    "sourceMap": false,
    "target": "es6",
    "lib": ["dom", "dom.iterable", "esnext"],
    "allowJs": true,
    "skipLibCheck": true,
    "strict": true,
    "forceConsistentCasingInFileNames": true,
    "noEmit": true,
    "moduleResolution": "node",
    "isolatedModules": true,
    "jsx": "preserve"
  },
  "include": ["src/**/*.ts", "src/**/*.tsx"],
  "exclude": ["node_modules"]
}
```

Now, open the console and run the following command:

```
npm run dev
```

We will see the following output:

```
> Ready on http://localhost:3000
```

If we point the browser to that URL, we can see the universal application in action. It is really impressive how easy it is to set up a universal application with a few lines of code and zero-configuration, thanks to Next.js.

You may also notice that if you edit the application inside your editor, you will be able to see the results within the browser instantly without needing to refresh the page. That is another feature of Next.js, which enables hot module replacement. It is incredibly useful in development mode.

If you liked this chapter, go and give a star on GitHub: https://github.com/zeit/next.js.

Summary

The journey through SSR has come to an end. You are now able to create a server-side rendered application with React, and it should be clear why it can be useful for you. SEO is certainly one of the main reasons, but social sharing and performance are important factors as well. You learned how it is possible to load the data on the server and dehydrate it in the HTML template to make it available for the client-side application when it boots on the browser.

Finally, you have looked at how tools such as Next.js can help you reduce the boilerplate and hide some of the complexity that setting up a server-side render React application usually brings to the code base.

In the next chapter, we will talk about how to improve the performance of our React applications.

10
Improving the Performance of Your Applications

The effective performance of a web application is critical to providing a good user experience and improving conversions. The React library implements different techniques to render our components fast and to touch the **Document Object Model (DOM)** as little as possible. Applying changes to the DOM is usually expensive, and so minimizing the number of operations is crucial.

However, there are some particular scenarios where React cannot optimize the process, and it's up to the developer to implement specific solutions to make the application run smoothly.

In this chapter, we will go through the basic concepts of React and we will learn how to use some APIs to help the library find the optimal path to update the DOM without degrading the user experience. We will also see some common mistakes that can harm our applications and make them slower.

We should avoid optimizing our components for the sake of it, and it is important to apply the techniques that we will see in the following sections only when they are needed.

In this chapter, we will cover the following topics:

- How reconciliation works and how we can help React do a better job using the keys
- Common optimization techniques and common performance-related mistakes
- What it means to use immutable data and how to do it
- Useful tools and libraries to make our applications run faster

Technical requirements

To complete this chapter, you will require the following:

- Node.js 12+
- Visual Studio Code

You can find the code for this chapter in the book's GitHub Repository at `https://github.com/PacktPublishing/React-17-Design-Patterns-and-Best-Practices-Third-Edition/tree/main/Chapter10`.

Reconciliation

Most of the time, React is fast enough by default, and you do not need to do anything more to improve the performance of your application. React utilizes different techniques to optimize the rendering of the components on the screen.

When React has to display a component, it calls its `render` method and the `render` methods of its children recursively. The `render` method of a component returns a tree of React elements, which React uses to decide which DOM operations have to be done to update the UI.

Whenever the component state changes, React calls the `render` method on the nodes again, and it compares the result with the previous tree of React elements. The library is smart enough to figure out the minimum set of operations required to apply the expected changes on the screen. This process is called **reconciliation,** and it is managed transparently by React. Thanks to that, we can easily describe how our components have to look at a given point in time in a declarative way and let the library do the rest.

React tries to apply the smallest possible number of operations on the DOM because touching the DOM is an expensive operation.

However, comparing two trees of elements is not free either, and React makes two assumptions to reduce its complexity:

- If two elements have a different type, they render a different tree.
- Developers can use keys to mark children as stable across different render calls.

The second point is interesting from a developer's perspective because it gives us a tool to help React render our views faster.

By default, when coming back to the children of a DOM node, both lists of children are iterated by React at the same time, and whenever there is a difference, it creates a mutation.

Let's look at some examples. Converting between the following two trees will work well when adding an element at the end of the children:

```
<ul>
    <li>Carlos</li>
    <li>Javier</li>
</ul>

<ul>
    <li>Carlos</li>
    <li>Javier</li>
    <li>Emmanuel</li>
</ul>
```

The two `<li>Carlos</li>` trees match the two `<li>Javier</li>` trees by React and then it will insert the `<li>Emmanuel</li>` tree.

Inserting an element at the beginning produces an inferior performance if implemented naively. If we look at the example, it works very poorly when converting between these two trees:

```
<ul>
    <li>Carlos</li>
    <li>Javier</li>
</ul>

<ul>
    <li>Emmanuel</li>
    <li>Carlos</li>
    <li>Javier</li>
</ul>
```

Every child will be mutated by React, instead of it realizing that it can keep the subtrees line, `<li>Carlos</li>` and `<li>Javier</li>`, intact. This can possibly be an issue. This problem can, of course, be solved and the way for this is the `key` attribute that is supported by React. Let's look at that next.

Keys

Children possess keys and these keys are used by React to match children between the subsequent tree and the original tree. The tree conversion can be made efficient by adding a key to our previous example:

```
<ul>
  <li key="2018">Carlos</li>
  <li key="2019">Javier</li>
</ul>

<ul>
  <li key="2017">Emmanuel</li>
  <li key="2018">Carlos</li>
  <li key="2019">Javier</li>
</ul>
```

React now knows that the 2017 key is the new one and that the 2018 and 2019 keys have just moved.

Finding a key is not hard. The element that you will be displaying might already have a unique ID. So the key can just come from your data:

```
<li key={element.id}>{element.title}</li>
```

A new ID can be added to your model by you, or the key can be generated by some parts of the content. The key has to only be unique among its siblings; it does not have to be unique globally. An item index in the array can be passed as a key, but it is now considered a bad practice. However, if the items are never recorded, this can work well. The reorders will seriously affect performance.

If you are rendering multiple items using a map function and you don't specify the key property, you will get this message: **Warning: Each child in an array or iterator should have a unique "key" prop**.

Let's learn some optimization techniques in our next section.

Optimization techniques

It is important to notice that, in all the examples in this book, we are using apps that have either been created with create-react-app or have been created from scratch, but always with the development version of React.

Using the development version of React is very useful for coding and debugging as it gives you all the necessary information to fix the various issues. However, all the checks and warnings come with a cost, which we want to avoid in production.

So, the very first optimization that we should do to our applications is to build the bundle, setting the NODE_ENV environment variable to production. This is pretty easy with webpack, and it is just a matter of using DefinePlugin in the following way:

```
new webpack.DefinePlugin({
  'process.env': {
    NODE_ENV: JSON.stringify('production')
  }
})
```

To achieve the best performance, we not only want to create the bundle with the production flag activated, but we also want to split our bundles, one for our application and one for node_modules.

To do so, you need to use the new optimization node in webpack:

```
optimization: {
  splitChunks: {
    cacheGroups: {
      default: false,
      commons: {
        test: /node_modules/,
        name: 'vendor',
        chunks: 'all'
      }
    }
  }
}
```

Since webpack 4 has two modes, *development* and *production*, by default, production mode is enabled, meaning the code will be minified and compressed when you compile your bundles using the production mode; you can specify it with the following code block:

```
{
  mode: process.env.NODE_ENV === 'production' ? 'production' :
    'development',
}
```

Your webpack.config.ts file should look like this:

```
module.exports = {
  entry: './index.ts',
  optimization: {
```

```
     splitChunks: {
       cacheGroups: {
         default: false,
         commons: {
           test: /node_modules/,
           name: 'vendor',
           chunks: 'all'
         }
       }
     }
   },
   plugins: [
     new webpack.DefinePlugin({
       'process.env': {
         NODE_ENV: JSON.stringify('production')
       }
     })
   ],
   mode: process.env.NODE_ENV === 'production' ? 'production' :
     'development'
}
```

With this webpack configuration, we are going to get very optimized bundles, one for our vendors and one for the actual application.

Tools and libraries

In the next section, we will go through a number of techniques, tools, and libraries that we can apply to our code base to monitor and improve performance.

Immutability

The new React Hooks, such as `React.memo`, use a shallow comparison method against the props, which means that if we pass an object as a prop and we mutate one of its values, we do not get the expected behavior.

In fact, a shallow comparison cannot find mutation on the properties and the components never get re-rendered, except when the object itself changes. One way to solve this issue is by using **immutable data**, data that, once it gets created, cannot be mutated.

For example, we can set the state in the following mode:

```
const [state, setState] = useState({})

const obj = state.obj

obj.foo = 'bar'

setState({ obj })
```

Even if the value of the `foo` attribute of the object is changed, the reference to the object is still the same and the shallow comparison does not recognize it.

What we can do instead is create a new instance every time we mutate the object, as follows:

```
const obj = Object.assign({}, state.obj, { foo: 'bar' })

setState({ obj })
```

In this case, we get a new object with the `foo` property set to `bar`, and the shallow comparison will be able to find the difference. With ES6 and Babel, there is another way to express the same concept in a more elegant way, and it is by using the object spread operator:

```
const obj = {
  ...state.obj,
  foo: 'bar'
}
setState({ obj })
```

This structure is more concise than the previous one, and it produces the same result, but, at the time of writing, it requires the code to be transpiled in order to be executed inside the browser.

React provides some immutability helpers to make it easy to work with immutable objects, and there is also a popular library called `immutable.js`, which has more powerful features, but it requires you to learn new APIs.

Babel plugins

There are also a couple of interesting **Babel** plugins that we can install and use to improve the performance of our React applications. They make the applications faster, optimizing parts of the code at build time.

The first one is the React constant elements transformer, which finds all the static elements that do not change depending on the props and extracts them from render (or the functional components) to avoid calling _jsx unnecessarily.

Using a Babel plugin is pretty straightforward. We first install it with npm:

```
npm install --save-dev @babel/plugin-transform-react-constant-elements
```

You need to create the .babelrc file and add a plugins key with an array that has a value of the list of plugins that we want to activate:

```
{
   "plugins": ["@babel/plugin-transform-react-constant-elements"]
}
```

The second Babel plugin that we can choose to use to improve performance is the React inline elements transform, which replaces all the JSX declarations (or the _jsx calls) with a more optimized version of them to make execution faster.

Install the plugin using the following command:

```
npm install --save-dev @babel/plugin-transform-react-inline-elements
```

Next, you can easily add the plugin to the array of plugins in the .babelrc file, as follows:

```
{
   "plugins": ["@babel/plugin-transform-react-inline-elements"]
}
```

Both plugins should be used only in production because they make debugging harder in development mode. So far, we have learned a lot of optimization techniques and how to configure some plugins using webpack.

Summary

Our journey through performance is finished, and we can now optimize our applications to give users a better UX.

In this chapter, we learned how the reconciliation algorithm works and how React always tries to take the shortest path to apply changes to the DOM. We can also help the library to optimize its job by using the keys. Once you've found your bottlenecks, you can apply one of the techniques we have seen in this chapter to fix the issue.

We have learned how refactoring and designing the structure of your components in the proper way could provide a performance boost. Our goal is to have small components that do one single thing in the best possible way. At the end of the chapter, we talked about immutability, and we've seen why it's important not to mutate data to make `React.memo` and `shallowCompare` do their job. Finally, we ran through different tools and libraries that can make your applications faster.

In the next chapter, we'll look at testing and debugging using Jest, React Testing Library, and React DevTools.

11
Testing and Debugging

React, thanks to its components, makes it easy to test our applications. There are many different tools that we can use to create tests with React, and here we'll cover the most popular ones to understand the benefits they provide.

Jest is an *all-in-one* testing framework solution, maintained by Christopher Pojer from Facebook and contributors within the community, and aims to give you the best developer experience.

By the end of the chapter, you'll be able to create a test environment from scratch and write tests for your application's components.

In this chapter, we will look at the following topics:

- Why it is important to test our applications, and how they help developers move faster
- How to set up a Jest environment to test components using Enzyme
- What React Testing Library is and why it is a *must-have* for testing React applications
- How to test events
- React DevTools and some error-handling techniques

Technical requirements

To complete this chapter, you will need the following:

- Node.js 12+
- Visual Studio Code

You can find the code for this chapter in the book's GitHub Repository: https://github.com/PacktPublishing/React-17-Design-Patterns-and-Best-Practices-Third-Edition/tree/main/Chapter11.

Understanding the benefits of testing

Testing web UIs has always been a difficult job. From unit to *end-to-end* tests, the fact that the interfaces depend on browsers, user interactions, and many other variables makes it difficult to implement an effective testing strategy.

If you've ever tried to write end-to-end tests for the web, you'll know how complex it is to get consistent results and how the results are often affected by false negatives due to different factors, such as the network. Other than that, user interfaces are frequently updated to improve the experience, maximize conversions, or simply add new features.

If tests are hard to write and maintain, developers are less prone to cover their applications. On the other hand, tests are pretty important because they make developers more confident with their code, which is reflected in speed and quality. If a piece of code is well tested (and the tests are well written), developers can be sure that it works and is ready to ship. Similarly, thanks to tests, it becomes easier to refactor the code because tests guarantee that the functionalities do not change during the rewrite.

Developers tend to focus on the feature they are currently implementing, and sometimes it is hard to know if other parts of the application are affected by those changes. Tests help to avoid regressions because they can tell if the new code breaks the old tests. Greater confidence in writing new features leads to faster releases.

Testing the main functionalities of an application makes the code base more solid, and whenever a new bug is found, it can be reproduced, fixed, and covered by tests so that it does not happen again in the future.

Luckily, React (and the component era) makes testing user interfaces easy and efficient. Testing components, or trees of components, is a less arduous job because every single part of the application has its responsibilities and boundaries. If components are built in the right way, if they are pure and aim for composability and reusability, they can be tested as simple functions.

Another great power that modern tools bring us is the ability to run tests using Node.js and the console. Spinning up a browser for every single test makes tests slower and less predictable, degrading the developer experience; instead, running the tests using the console is faster.

Testing components only in the console can sometimes give unexpected behaviors when they are rendered in a real browser, but in my experience this is rare. When we test React components, we want to make sure that they work properly and that, given different sets of props, their output is always correct.

We may also want to cover all the various states that a component can have. The state might change by clicking a button, so we write tests to check if all the event handlers are doing what they are supposed to do.

When all the functionalities of the component are covered, but we want to do more, we can write tests to verify the component's behavior on **edge cases**. Edge cases are states that the component can assume when, for example, all the props are `null`, or there is an error. Once the tests are written, we can be pretty confident that the component behaves as expected.

Testing a single component is great, but it does not guarantee that multiple individually tested components will still work once they are put together. As we will see later, with React we can mount a tree of components and test the integration between them.

There are different techniques that we can use to write tests, and one of the most popular ones is **test-driven development (TDD)**. Applying TDD means writing the tests first and then writing the code to pass the tests.

Following this pattern helps us to write better code because we are forced to think more about the design before implementing the functionalities, which usually leads to higher quality.

Painless JavaScript testing with Jest

The most important way to learn how to test React components in the right way is by writing some code, and that is what we are going to do in this section.

The React documentation says that at Facebook they use Jest to test their components. However, React does not force you to use a particular test framework, and you can use your favorite one without any problems. To see Jest in action, we are going to create a project from scratch, installing all the dependencies and writing a component with some tests. It'll be fun!

The first thing to do is to move into a new folder and run the following:

```
npm init
```

Once `package.json` is created, we can start installing the dependencies, with the first one being the `jest` package itself:

```
npm install --save-dev jest
```

To tell npm that we want to use the jest command to run the tests, we have to add the following scripts to package.json:

```
"scripts": {
  "build": "webpack",
  "start": "node ./dist/server",
  "test": "jest",
  "test:coverage": "jest --coverage"
}
```

To write components and tests using ES6 and JSX, we have to install all Babel-related packages so that Jest can use them to transpile and understand the code.

The second set of dependencies is installed as follows:

```
npm install --save-dev @babel/core @babel/preset-env @babel/preset-react
ts-jest
```

As you may know, we now have to create a .babelrc file, which is used by Babel to know the presets and the plugins that we would like to use inside the project.

The .babelrc file looks like the following:

```
{
  "presets": ["@babel/preset-env", "@babel/preset-react"]
}
```

Now, it is time to install React and ReactDOM, which we need to create and render components:

```
npm install --save react react-dom
```

The setup is ready, and we can run Jest against the ES6 code and render our components into the DOM, but there is one more thing to do.

We need to install @testing-library/jest-dom and @testing-library/react:

```
npm install @testing-library/jest-dom @testing-library/react
```

After you have installed these packages, you have to create the jest.config.js file:

```
module.exports = {
  preset: 'ts-jest',
  setupFilesAfterEnv: ['<rootDir>/setUpTests.ts']
}
```

Then, let's create the setUpTests.ts file:

```
import '@testing-library/jest-dom/extend-expect'
```

Now, let's imagine we have a Hello component:

```
import React, { FC } from 'react'

type Props = {
  name: string
}

const Hello: FC<Props> = ({ name }) => <h1 className="Hello">Hello {name ||
'World'}</h1>

export default Hello
```

In order to test this component, we need to create a file with the same name but add the .test (or .spec) suffix to the new file. This will be our test file:

```
import React from 'react'
import { render, cleanup } from '@testing-library/react'

import Hello from './index'

describe('Hello Component', () => {
  it('should render Hello World', () => {
    const wrapper = render(<Hello />)
    expect(wrapper.getByText('Hello World')).toBeInTheDocument()
  })

  it('should render the name prop', () => {
    const wrapper = render(<Hello name="Carlos" />)
    expect(wrapper.getByText('Hello Carlos')).toBeInTheDocument()
  });

  it('should has .Home classname', () => {
    const wrapper = render(<Hello />)
    expect(wrapper.container.firstChild).toHaveClass('Hello')
  });

  afterAll(cleanup)
})
```

Then, in order to run the `test`, you need to execute the following command:

```
npm test
```

You should see this result:

```
→  testing git:(main) x npm test

> css-modules@1.0.0 test
> jest

 PASS  src/components/Hello/index.test.tsx
  Hello Component
    ✓ should render Hello World (21 ms)
    ✓ should render the name prop (3 ms)
    ✓ should has .Home classname (2 ms)

Test Suites: 1 passed, 1 total
Tests:       3 passed, 3 total
Snapshots:   0 total
Time:        2.652 s, estimated 3 s
Ran all test suites.
```

The `PASS` label means that all tests have been passed successfully; if you failed at least one test, you would see the `FAIL` label. Let's change one of our tests to make it fail:

```
it('should render the name prop', () => {
  const wrapper = render(<Hello name="Carlos" />)
  expect(wrapper.getByText('Hello World')).toBeInTheDocument()
});
```

This is the result:

```
→ testing git:(main) x npm test

> css-modules@1.0.0 test
> jest

 FAIL  src/components/Hello/index.test.tsx
  Hello Component
    ✓ should render Hello World (27 ms)
    ✗ should render the name prop (6 ms)
    ✓ should has .Home classname (3 ms)

  ● Hello Component › should render the name prop

    TestingLibraryElementError: Unable to find an element with the text: Hello World. This could be because the text is broken up by
multiple elements. In this case, you can provide a function for your text matcher to make your matcher more flexible.

    <body>
      <div>
        <h1
          class="Hello"
        >
          Hello
          Carlos
        </h1>
      </div>
    </body>

      11 |     it('should render the name prop', () => {
      12 |       const wrapper = render(<Hello name="Carlos" />)
    > 13 |       expect(wrapper.getByText('Hello World')).toBeInTheDocument()
      14 |     });
      15 |
      16 |     it('should has .Home classname', () => {

      at Object.getElementError (node_modules/@testing-library/dom/dist/config.js:37:19)
      at node_modules/@testing-library/dom/dist/query-helpers.js:90:38
      at node_modules/@testing-library/dom/dist/query-helpers.js:62:17
      at node_modules/@testing-library/dom/dist/query-helpers.js:111:19
      at Object.<anonymous> (src/components/Hello/index.test.tsx:13:20)

Test Suites: 1 failed, 1 total
Tests:       1 failed, 2 passed, 3 total
Snapshots:   0 total
Time:        2.817 s, estimated 3 s
Ran all test suites.
```

As you can see, the FAIL label is specified with an X. Also, the expected and received values provide useful information, and you can see which value is expected and which value is being received.

If you want to see the coverage percentage of all your unit tests, you can execute the following command:

```
npm run test:coverage
```

The result is the following:

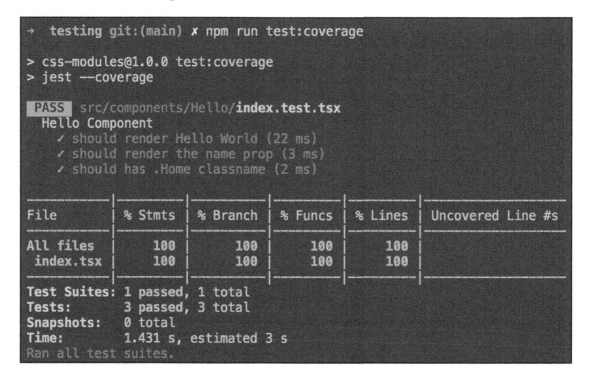

The coverage also generates an HTML version of the result; it creates a directory called `coverage` and inside another called `Icov-report`. If you open the `index.html` file in your browser, you will see the HTML version as follows:

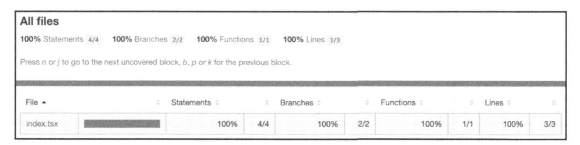

Now that you made your first tests and you know how to collect the coverage data, let's see how we can test events in the next section.

Testing events

The events are very common in any web application and we need to test them as well, so let's learn how to test events. For this, let's create a new ShowInformation component:

```
import { FC, useState, ChangeEvent } from 'react'

const ShowInformation: FC = () => {
  const [state, setState] = useState({ name: '', age: 0, show: false })

  const handleOnChange = (e: ChangeEvent<HTMLInputElement>) => {
    const { name, value } = e.target

    setState({
      ...state,
      [name]: value
    })
  }

  const handleShowInformation = () => {
    setState({
      ...state,
      show: true
    })
  }

  if (state.show) {
    return (
      <div className="ShowInformation">
        <h1>Personal Information</h1>

        <div className="personalInformation">
          <p>
            <strong>Name:</strong> {state.name}
          </p>
          <p>
            <strong>Age:</strong> {state.age}
          </p>
        </div>
      </div>
    )
  }

  return (
    <div className="ShowInformation">
      <h1>Personal Information</h1>
```

```
      <p>
        <strong>Name:</strong>
      </p>

      <p>
        <input name="name" type="text" value={state.name}
onChange={handleOnChange} />
      </p>

      <p>
        <input name="age" type="number" value={state.age}
onChange={handleOnChange} />
      </p>

      <p>
        <button onClick={handleShowInformation}>Show Information</button>
      </p>
    </div>
  )
}

export default ShowInformation
```

Now, let's create the test file at `src/components/ShowInformation/index.test.tsx`:

```
import { render, cleanup, fireEvent } from '@testing-library/react'

import ShowInformation from './index'

describe('Show Information Component', () => {
  let wrapper

  beforeEach(() => {
    wrapper = render(<ShowInformation />)
  })

  it('should modify the name', () => {
    const nameInput = wrapper.container.querySelector('input[name="name"]')
as HTMLInputElement
    const ageInput = wrapper.container.querySelector('input[name="age"]')
as HTMLInputElement

    fireEvent.change(nameInput, { target: { value: 'Carlos' } })
    fireEvent.change(ageInput, { target: { value: 33 } })

    expect(nameInput.value).toBe('Carlos')
    expect(ageInput.value).toBe('33')
  })
```

```
it('should show the personal information when user clicks on the button',
() => {
    const button = wrapper.container.querySelector('button')

    fireEvent.click(button)

    const showInformation =
wrapper.container.querySelector('.personalInformation')

    expect(showInformation).toBeInTheDocument()
  })

  afterAll(cleanup)
})
```

If you run the test and it works fine, you should see this:

```
→ events git:(main) ✗ npm test

> css-modules@1.0.0 test
> jest

 PASS  src/components/ShowInformation/index.test.tsx
  Show Information Component
    ✓ should modify the name (33 ms)
    ✓ should show the personal information when user clicks on the button (8 ms)

Test Suites: 1 passed, 1 total
Tests:       2 passed, 2 total
Snapshots:   0 total
Time:        2.499 s, estimated 3 s
Ran all test suites.
```

Using React DevTools

When testing in the console is not enough, and we want to inspect our application while it is running inside the browser, we can use React DevTools.

You can install this as a Chrome extension at the following URL: https://chrome.google.com/webstore/detail/react-developer-tools/fmkadmapgofadopljbjfkapdkoienihi?hl=en.

The installation adds a tab to the Chrome DevTools called **React**, where you can inspect the rendered tree of components and check which properties they have received and what their state is at a particular point in time.

Props and states can be read, and they can be changed in real time to trigger updates in the UI and see the results straight away. This is a must-have tool, and in the most recent versions, it has a new feature that can be enabled by ticking the **Trace React Updates** checkbox.

When this functionality is enabled, we can use our application and visually see which components get updated when we perform a particular action. The updated components are highlighted with colored rectangles, and it becomes easy to spot possible optimizations.

Using Redux DevTools

If you are using Redux in your application, you probably want to use Redux DevTools to be able to debug your Redux flow. You can install it at the following URL: `https://chrome.google.com/webstore/detail/redux-devtools/lmhkpmbekcpmknklioeibfkpmmfibljd?hl=es`.

Also, you need to install the `redux-devtools-extension` package:

```
npm install --save-dev redux-devtools-extension
```

Once you have installed React DevTools and Redux DevTools, you will need to configure them.

If you try to use Redux DevTools directly, it won't work; this is because we need to pass the `composeWithDevTools` method into the Redux store; this should be the `configureStore.ts` file:

```
// Dependencies
import { createStore, applyMiddleware } from 'redux';
import thunk from 'redux-thunk';
import { composeWithDevTools } from 'redux-devtools-extension';

// Root Reducer
import rootReducer from '@reducers';

export default function configureStore({
  initialState,
  reducer
}) {
  const middleware = [
```

```
    thunk
  ];
  return createStore(
    rootReducer,
    initialState,
    composeWithDevTools(applyMiddleware(...middleware))
  );
}
```

This is the best tool to test our Redux applications.

Summary

In this chapter, you learned about the benefits of testing, and the frameworks you can use to cover your React components with tests.

You learned how to implement and test components and events with React Testing Library, how to use the Jest coverage, and how to use React DevTools and Redux DevTools. It is important to bear in mind common solutions when it comes to testing complex components, such as higher-order components or forms with multiple nested fields.

In the next chapter, you will learn how to implement routes in your application using React Router.

12
React Router

React, unlike Angular, is a library instead of a framework, meaning specific functionalities (for example, routing or PropTypes) are not part of the React Core. Instead, routing is handled by a third-party library called **React Router**.

In this chapter, you will see how to implement React Router in your application, and by the end of the relevant sections, you will be able to add dynamic routes and understand how React Router works.

In this chapter, we will cover the following topics:

- Understanding the differences between the `react-router`, `react-router-dom`, and `react-router-native` packages
- How to install and configure React Router
- Adding the `<Switch>` component
- Adding the `exact` property
- Adding parameters to the routes

Technical requirements

To complete this chapter, you will need the following:

- Node.js 12+
- Visual Studio Code

You can find the code for this chapter in the book's GitHub Repository at `https://github.com/PacktPublishing/React-17-Design-Patterns-and-Best-Practices-Third-Edition/tree/main/Chapter12`.

Installing and configuring React Router

After you create a new React application using `create-react-app`, the first thing you need to do is to install React Router v5.x, using the following command:

```
npm install react-router-dom @types/react-router-dom
```

You probably are confused about why we are installing `react-router-dom` instead of `react-router`. React Router contains all the common components of `react-router-dom` and `react-router-native`. That means that if you are using React for the web, you should use `react-router-dom`, and if you are using React Native, you need to use `react-router-native`.

The `react-router-dom` package was created originally to contain version 4, and `react-router` uses version 3. The `react-router-dom` package has some improvements over `react-router`. They are listed here:

- The improved `<Link>` component (which renders `<a>`).
- Includes `<BrowserRouter>`, which interacts with the browser `window.history`.
- Includes `<NavLink>`, which is a `<Link>` wrapper that knows whether it's active or not.
- Includes `<HashRouter>`, which uses the hash in the URL to render the components. If you have one static page, you should use this component instead of `<BrowserRouter>`.

Creating our sections

Let's create some sections to test some basic routes. We need to create four stateless components (`About`, `Contact`, `Home`, and `Error404`) and name them as `index.tsx` in their directories.

You can add the following to the `src/components/Home.tsx` component:

```
const Home = () => (
  <div className="Home">
    <h1>Home</h1>
  </div>
)

export default Home
```

The `src/components/About.tsx` component can be created with the following:

```
const About = () => (
  <div className="About">
    <h1>About</h1>
  </div>
)

export default About
```

The following creates the `src/components/Contact.tsx` component:

```
const Contact = () => (
  <div className="Contact">
    <h1>Contact</h1>
  </div>
)

export default Contact
```

Finally, the `src/components/Error404.tsx` component is created as follows:

```
const Error404 = () => (
  <div className="Error404">
    <h1>Error404</h1>
  </div>
)

export default Error404
```

After we have created all the functional components, we need to modify our `index.tsx` file to import our route file, which we will create in the next step:

```
// Dependencies
import { render } from 'react-dom'
import { BrowserRouter as Router } from 'react-router-dom'

// Routes
import AppRoutes from './routes'

render(
  <Router>
    <AppRoutes />
  </Router>,
  document.getElementById('root')
)
```

Now, we need to create the `routes.tsx` file, where we will render our `Home` component when the user accesses the root path (`/`):

```
// Dependencies
import { Route } from 'react-router-dom'

// Components
import App from './App'
import Home from './components/Home'

const AppRoutes = () => (
  <App>
    <Route path="/" component={Home} />
  </App>
)

export default AppRoutes
```

After that, we need to modify our `App.tsx` file to render the route components as children:

```
import { FC, ReactNode } from 'react'
import './App.css'

type Props = {
  children: ReactNode
}

const App: FC<Props> = ({ children }) => (
  <div className="App">
    {children}
  </div>
)

export default App
```

If you run the application, you will see the `Home` component in the root (`/`):

Now, let's add `Error404` when the user tries to access any other route:

```
// Dependencies
import { Route } from 'react-router-dom'

// Components
import App from './App'
import Home from './components/Home'
import Error404 from './components/Error404'

const AppRoutes = () => (
  <App>
    <Route path="/" component={Home} />
    <Route component={Error404} />
  </App>
)

export default AppRoutes
```

Let's run the application again. You will see that both the `Home` and `Error404` components are rendered:

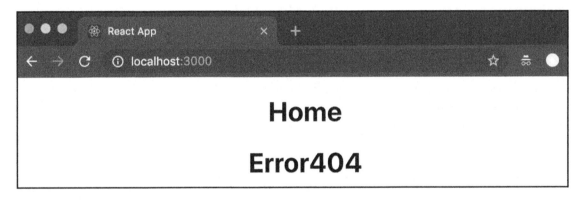

You are probably wondering why this is happening. It's because we need to use the `<Switch>` component to execute just one component if it matches the path. For this, we need to import the `Switch` component and add it as a wrapper for our routes:

```
// Dependencies
import { Route, Switch } from 'react-router-dom'

// Components
import App from './App'
import Home from './components/Home'
import Error404 from './components/Error404'
```

```
const AppRoutes = () => (
  <App>
    <Switch>
      <Route path="/" component={Home} />
      <Route component={Error404} />
    </Switch>
  </App>
)

export default AppRoutes
```

Now, if you go to the root (/), you will see that the Home component and Error404 won't be executed at the same time, but if we go to /somefakeurl, we will see that the Home component is executed as well, and this is a problem:

To fix the problem, we need to add the exact prop in the route that we want to match. The problem is that /somefakeurl will match our root path (/), but if we want to be very specific about the paths, we need to add the exact prop to our Home route:

```
const AppRoutes = () => (
  <App>
    <Switch>
      <Route path="/" component={Home} exact />
      <Route component={Error404} />
    </Switch>
  </App>
)
```

Now, if you go to `/somefakeurl` one more time, you will be able to see the **Error404** component:

Now, we can add our other components (`About` and `Contact`):

```
// Dependencies
import { Route, Switch } from 'react-router-dom'

// Components
import App from './App'
import About from './components/About'
import Contact from './components/Contact'
import Home from './components/Home'
import Error404 from './components/Error404'

const AppRoutes = () => (
  <App>
    <Switch>
      <Route path="/" component={Home} exact />
      <Route path="/about" component={About} exact />
      <Route path="/contact" component={Contact} exact />
      <Route component={Error404} />
    </Switch>
  </App>
)

export default AppRoutes
```

Now, you can visit `/about`:

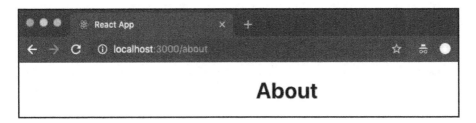

Alternatively, you can now visit /contact:

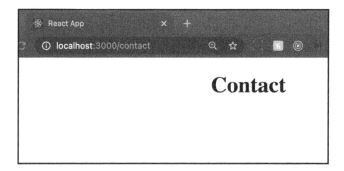

Now that you have implemented your first routes, now let's add some parameters to the routes in the next section.

Adding parameters to the routes

So far, you have learned how to use React Router for basic routes (one-level routes). Now, I will show you how to add some parameters to the routes and get them into our components.

For this example, we will create a Contacts component to display a list of contacts when we visit the /contacts route, but we will show the contact information (name, phone, and email) when the user visits /contacts/:contactId.

The first thing we need to do is to create our Contacts component. Let's use the following skeleton.

Let's use these CSS styles:

```
.Contacts ul {
  list-style: none;
  margin: 0;
  margin-bottom: 20px;
  padding: 0;
}

.Contacts ul li {
  padding: 10px;
}

.Contacts a {
```

```
  color: #555;
  text-decoration: none;
}

.Contacts a:hover {
  color: #ccc;
  text-decoration: none;
}
```

Once you have created the `Contacts` component, you need to import it into our route file:

```
// Dependencies
import { Route, Switch } from 'react-router-dom'

// Components
import App from './components/App'
import About from './components/About'
import Contact from './components/Contact'
import Home from './components/Home'
import Error404 from './components/Error404'
import Contacts from './components/Contacts'

const AppRoutes = () => (
  <App>
    <Switch>
      <Route path="/" component={Home} exact />
      <Route path="/about" component={About} exact />
      <Route path="/contact" component={Contact} exact />
      <Route path="/contacts" component={Contacts} exact />
      <Route component={Error404} />
    </Switch>
  </App>
)

export default AppRoutes
```

Now, you will be able to see the `Contacts` component if you go to the `/contacts` URL:

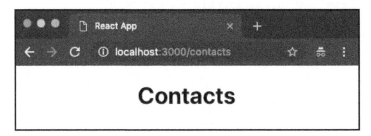

Now that the `Contacts` component is connected to React Router, let's render our contacts as a list:

```
import { FC, useState } from 'react'
import { Link } from 'react-router-dom'
import './Contacts.css'

type Contact = {
  id: number
  name: string
  email: string
  phone: string
}

const data: Contact[] = [
  {
    id: 1,
    name: 'Carlos Santana',
    email: 'carlos.santana@dev.education',
    phone: '415-307-3112'
  },
  {
    id: 2,
    name: 'John Smith',
    email: 'john.smith@dev.education',
    phone: '223-344-5122'
  },
  {
    id: 3,
    name: 'Alexis Nelson',
    email: 'alexis.nelson@dev.education',
    phone: '664-291-4477'
  }
]

const Contacts: FC = (props) => {
  // For now we are going to add our contacts to our
  // local state, but normally this should come
  // from some service.
  const [contacts, setContacts] = useState<Contact[]>(data)

  const renderContacts = () => (
    <ul>
      {contacts.map((contact: Contact, key) => (
        <li key={contact.id}>
          <Link to={`/contacts/${contact.id}`}>{contact.name}</Link>
        </li>
      ))}
```

```
      </ul>
    )

    return (
      <div className="Contacts">
        <h1>Contacts</h1>

        {renderContacts()}
      </div>
    )
  }

  export default Contacts
```

As you can see, we are using the `<Link>` component, which will generate an `<a>` tag that points to `/contacts/contact.id`, and this is because we will add a new nested route into our route file to match the ID of the contact:

```
const AppRoutes = () => (
  <App>
    <Switch>
      <Route path="/" component={Home} exact />
      <Route path="/about" component={About} exact />
      <Route path="/contact" component={Contact} exact />
      <Route path="/contacts" component={Contacts} exact />
      <Route path="/contacts/:contactId" component={Contacts} exact />
      <Route component={Error404} />
    </Switch>
  </App>
)
```

React Router has a special prop called `match`, which is an object that contains all the data related to the route, and if we have parameters, we will be able to see them in the `match` object:

```
import { FC, useState } from 'react'
import { Link } from 'react-router-dom'
import './Contacts.css'

const data = [
  {
    id: 1,
    name: 'Carlos Santana',
    email: 'carlos.santana@js.education',
    phone: '415-307-3112'
  },
  {
```

```
      id: 2,
      name: 'John Smith',
      email: 'john.smith@js.education',
      phone: '223-344-5122'
    },
    {
      id: 3,
      name: 'Alexis Nelson',
      email: 'alexis.nelson@js.education',
      phone: '664-291-4477'
    }
  ]

type Contact = {
  id: number
  name: string
  email: string
  phone: string
}

type Props = {
  match: any
}

const Contacts: FC<Props> = (props) => {
  // For now we are going to add our contacts to our
  // local state, but normally this should come
  // from some service.
  const [contacts, setContacts] = useState<Contact[]>(data)

  // Let's see what contains the match object.
  console.log(props)

  const { match: { params: { contactId } } } = props
  // By default our selectedNote is false
  let selectedContact: any = false
  if (contactId > 0) {
    // If the contact id is higher than 0 then we filter it from our
    // contacts array.
    selectedContact = contacts.filter(
      contact => contact.id === Number(contactId)
    )[0];
  }

  const renderSingleContact = ({ name, email, phone }: Contact) => (
    <>
      <h2>{name}</h2>
      <p>{email}</p>
```

```
      <p>{phone}</p>
    </>
  )

  const renderContacts = () => (
    <ul>
      {contacts.map((contact: Contact, key) => (
        <li key={key}>
          <Link to={`/contacts/${contact.id}`}>{contact.name}</Link>
        </li>
      ))}
    </ul>
  )

  return (
    <div className="Contacts">
      <h1>Contacts</h1>
      {/* We render our selectedContact or all the contacts */}
      {selectedContact
        ? renderSingleContact(selectedContact)
        : renderContacts()}
    </div>
  )
}

export default Contacts
```

The `match` prop looks like this:

```
▼ {match: {…}, location: {…}, history: {…}, staticContext: undefined} 🔢
  ▶ history: {length: 3, action: "POP", location: {…}, createHref: ƒ, push: ƒ, …}
  ▶ location: {pathname: "/contacts/2", search: "", hash: "", state: undefined, key: "3c5xbh"}
  ▼ match:
      isExact: true
    ▶ params: {contactId: "2"}
      path: "/contacts/:contactId"
      url: "/contacts/2"
    ▶ __proto__: Object
    staticContext: undefined
  ▶ __proto__: Object
```

As you can see, the `match` props contain a lot of useful information. React Router also includes the object's history and location. Also, we can get all the parameters we pass within the routes; in this case, we are receiving the `contactId` parameter.

If you run the application again, you should see your contacts like this:

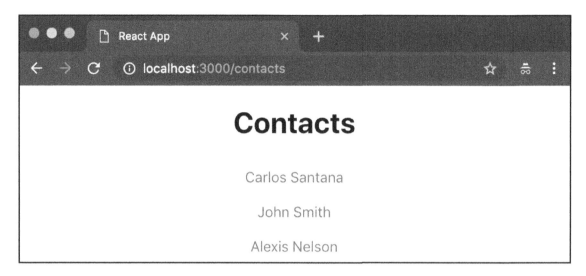

If you click on **John Smith** (whose `contactId` is 2), you will see the contact information:

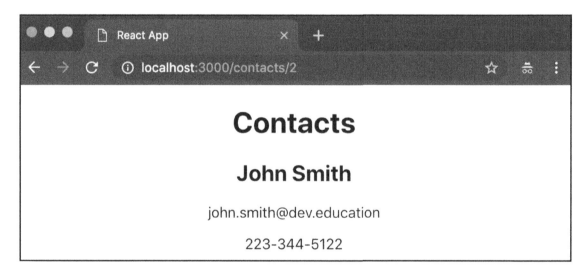

After this, you can add a navbar in the `App` component to access all the routes:

```
import { Link } from 'react-router-dom'
import './App.css'

const App = ({ children }) => (
```

```
    <div className="App">
      <ul className="menu">
        <li><Link to="/">Home</Link></li>
        <li><Link to="/about">About</Link></li>
        <li><Link to="/contacts">Contacts</Link></li>
        <li><Link to="/contact">Contact</Link></li>
      </ul>

      {children}
    </div>
  )

  export default App
```

Now, let's modify our App styles:

```
  .App {
    text-align: center;
  }

  .App ul.menu {
    margin: 50px;
    padding: 0;
    list-style: none;
  }

  .App ul.menu li {
    display: inline-block;
    padding: 0 10px;
  }

  .App ul.menu li a {
    color: #333;
    text-decoration: none;
  }

  .App ul.menu li a:hover {
    color: #ccc;
  }
```

Finally, you will see something like this:

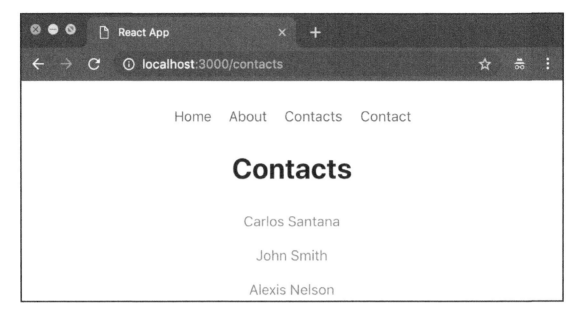

Now you know how to add routes with parameters to your application – this is amazing, right?

Summary

Our journey through React Router has come to an end, and now you know how to install and configure React Router, how to create basic routes, and how to add parameters to the nested routes.

In the next chapter, we will see how to avoid some of the most common anti-patterns in React.

Anti-Patterns to Be Avoided

13

In this book, you've learned how to apply best practices when writing a React application. In the first few chapters, we revisited the basic concepts to build a solid understanding, and then we took a leap into more advanced techniques in the following chapters.

You should now be able to build reusable components, make components communicate with each other, and optimize an application tree to get the best performance. However, developers make mistakes, and this chapter is all about the common anti-patterns we should avoid when using React.

Looking at common errors will help you to avoid them and will aid your understanding of how React works and how to build applications in the React way. For each problem, we will see an example that shows how to reproduce and solve it.

In this chapter, we will cover the following topics:

- Initializing the state using properties
- Using indexes as a key
- Spreading properties on DOM elements

Technical requirements

To complete this chapter, you will need the following:

- Node.js 12+
- Visual Studio Code

You can find the code for this chapter in the book's GitHub repository: https://github.com/PacktPublishing/React-17-Design-Patterns-and-Best-Practices-Third-Edition/tree/main/Chapter13.

Initializing the state using properties

In this section, we will see how initializing the state using properties received from the parent is usually an anti-pattern. I have used the word *usually* because, as we will see, once we have it clear in our mind what the problems with this approach are, we might still decide to use it.

One of the best ways to learn something is by looking at the code, so we will start by creating a simple component with a + button to increment a counter.

The component is implemented using a class, as shown in the following snippet of code:

```
import { FC, useState } from 'react'

type Props = {
  count: number
}

const Counter: FC<Props> = (props) => {}

export default Counter
```

Now, let's set our count state:

```
const [state, setState] = useState<any>(props.count)
```

The implementation of the click handler is pretty straightforward – we just add 1 to the current count value and store the resulting value back in state:

```
const handleClick = () => {
  setState({ count: state.count + 1 })
}
```

Finally, we render and describe the output, which is composed of the current value of the count state, and the button to increment it:

```
return (
  <div>
    {state.count}
    <button onClick={handleClick}>+</button>
  </div>
)
```

Now, let's render this component, passing 1 as the count property:

```
<Counter count={1} />
```

It works as expected – each click on the + button increments the current value. So, what's the problem?

There are two main errors, which are outlined as follows:

- We have a duplicated source of truth.
- If the `count` property passed to the component changes, the state does not get updated.

If we inspect the `Counter` element using the React DevTools, we notice that `Props` and `State` hold a similar value:

```
<Counter>
Props
   count: 1
State
   count: 1
```

This makes it unclear which is the current and trustworthy value to use inside the component and to display to the user.

Even worse, clicking + once makes the values diverge. An example of this divergence is shown in the following code:

```
<Counter>
Props
   count: 1
State
   count: 2
```

At this point, we can assume that the second value represents the current count, but this is not explicit and can lead to unexpected behaviors, or wrong values down in the tree.

The second problem centers on how the class is created and instantiated by React. The `useState` function of the component gets called only once when the component is created.

In our `Counter` component, we read the value of the `count` property and we store it in the state. If the value of that property changes during the life cycle of the application (let's say it becomes `10`), the `Counter` component will never use the new value, because it has already been initialized. This puts the component in an inconsistent state, which is not optimal and hard to debug.

What if we really want to use the prop's value to initialize the component, and we know for sure that the value does not change in the future?

In that case, it's best practice to make it explicit and give the property a name that makes your intentions clear, such as `initialCount`. For example, let's say we change the prop declaration of the `Counter` component in the following way:

```
type Props = {
  initialCount: number
}

const Counter: FC<Props> = (props) => {
  const [count, setState] = useState<any>(props.initialCount)
  ...
}
```

If we use it like so, it is clear that the parent only has a way to initialize the counter, but any future values of the `initialCount` property will be ignored:

```
<Counter initialCount={1} />
```

In our next section, we are going to learn about keys.

Using indexes as a key

In *Chapter 10, Improving the Performance of Your Applications*, which talks about performance and the reconciler, we saw how we can help React figure out the shortest path to update the DOM by using the `key` prop.

The key property uniquely identifies an element in the DOM, and React uses it to check whether the element is new or whether it has to be updated when the component properties or state change.

Using keys is always a good idea and if you don't do it, React gives a warning in the console (in development mode). However, it is not simply a matter of using a key; sometimes, the value that we decide to use as a key can make a difference. In fact, using the wrong key can give us unexpected behaviors in some instances. In this section, we will see one of those instances.

Let's again create a `List` component, as shown here:

```
import { FC, useState } from 'react'

const List: FC = () => {

}
```

```
export default List
```

Then we define our state:

```
const [items, setItems] = useState(['foo', 'bar'])
```

The implementation of the click handler is slightly different from the previous one because in this case, we need to insert a new item at the top of the list:

```
const handleClick = () => {
  const newItems = items.slice()
  newItems.unshift('baz')

  setItems(newItems)
}
```

Finally, in `render`, we show the list and the + button to add the `baz` item at the top of the list:

```
return (
  <div>
    <ul>
      {items.map((item, index) => (
        <li key={index}>{item}</li>
      ))}
    </ul>

    <button onClick={handleClick}>+</button>
  </div>
)
```

If you run the component inside the browser, you will not see any problems; clicking the + button inserts a new item at the top of the list. But let's do an experiment.

Let's change `render` in the following way, adding an input field near each item. We then use an input field because we can edit its content, making it easier to figure out the problem:

```
return (
  <div>
    <ul>
      {items.map((item, index) => (
        <li key={index}>
          {item}
          <input type="text" />
        </li>
      ))}
    </ul>
```

```
        <button onClick={handleClick}>+</button>
    </div>
)
```

If we run this component again in the browser, copy the values of the items in the input fields, and then click +, we will get unexpected behavior.

As shown in the following screenshot, the items shift down while the input elements remain in the same position, in such a way that their value does not match the value of the items anymore:

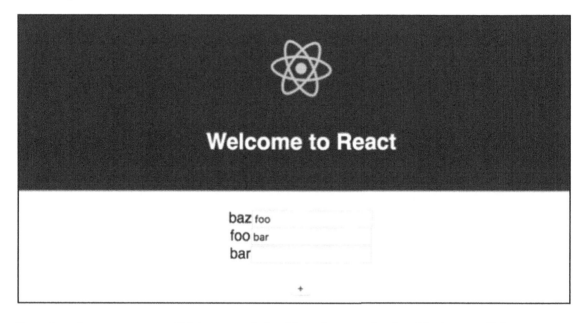

Running the component, clicking +, and checking the console should give us all the answers we need.

What we can see is that React, instead of inserting the new element on top, swaps the text of the two existing elements, and inserts the last item at the bottom as if it was new. The reason it does that is that we are using the index of the map function as the key.

In fact, the index always starts from 0, even if we push a new item to the top of the list, so React thinks that we changed the values of the existing two, and added a new element at index 2. The behavior is the same as it would have been without using the key property at all.

This is a very common pattern because we may think that providing any key is always the best solution, but it is not like that at all. The key has to be unique and stable, identifying one, and only one, item.

To solve this problem, we can, for example, use the value of the item if we expect it not to be repeated within the list, or create a unique identifier.

Spreading properties on DOM elements

There is a common practice that has recently been described as an anti-pattern by Dan Abramov; it also triggers a warning in the console when you do it in your React application.

It is a technique that is widely used in the community and I have personally seen it multiple times in real-world projects. We usually spread the properties to the elements to avoid writing every single one manually, which is shown as follows:

```
<Component {...props} />
```

This works very well and it gets transpiled into the following code by Babel:

```
_jsx(Component, props)
```

However, when we spread properties into a DOM element, we run the risk of adding unknown HTML attributes, which is bad practice.

The problem is not related only to the spread operator; passing non-standard properties one by one leads to the same issues and warnings. Since the spread operator hides the single properties we are spreading, it is even harder to figure out what we are passing to the element.

To see the warning in the console, a basic operation we can do is render the following component:

```
const Spread = () => <div foo="bar" />
```

The message we get looks like the following because the foo property is not valid for a div element:

```
Unknown prop `foo` on <div> tag. Remove this prop from the element
```

In this case, as we said, it is easy to figure out which attribute we are passing and remove it, but if we use the spread operator, as in the following example, we cannot control which properties are passed from the parent:

```
const Spread = props => <div {...props} />;
```

If we use the component in the following way, there are no issues:

```
<Spread className="foo" />
```

This, however, is not the case if we do something such as the following. React complains because we are applying a non-standard attribute to the DOM element:

```
<Spread foo="bar" className="baz" />
```

One solution we can use to solve this problem is to create a property called domProps that we can spread safely to the component because we are explicitly saying that it contains valid DOM properties.

For example, we can change the Spread component in the following way:

```
const Spread = props => <div {...props.domProps} />
```

We can then use it as follows:

```
<Spread foo="bar" domProps={{ className: 'baz' }} />
```

As we have seen many times with React, it's always good practice to be explicit.

Summary

Knowing all the best practices is always a good thing, but sometimes being aware of anti-patterns helps us avoid taking the wrong path. Most importantly, learning the reasons why some techniques are considered bad practice helps us understand how React works, and how we can use it effectively.

In this chapter, we covered four different ways of using components that can harm the performance and behavior of our web applications.

For each one of those, we used an example to reproduce the problem and supplied the changes to apply in order to fix the issue.

We learned why using properties to initialize the state can result in inconsistencies between the state and the properties. We also saw how using the wrong key attribute can produce bad effects on the reconciliation algorithm. Finally, we learned why spreading non-standard properties to DOM elements is considered an anti-pattern.

In the next chapter, we will look into deploying our React application to production.

14
Deploying to Production

Now that you have completed your first React application, it is time to learn how to deploy it to the world. For this purpose, we will use the cloud service called **DigitalOcean**.

In this chapter, you will learn how to deploy your React application using Node.js and nginx on an Ubuntu server from DigitalOcean.

In this chapter, we will cover the following topics:

- Creating a DigitalOcean Droplet and configuring it
- Configuring nginx, PM2, and a domain
- Implementing CircleCI for continuous integration

Technical requirements

To complete this chapter, you will need the following:

- Node.js 12+
- Visual Studio Code

Creating our first DigitalOcean Droplet

I have used DigitalOcean for the last six years and I can say that it is one of the best cloud services I have tried, not just because of the affordable costs, but also because it is super easy and fast to configure, and the community has a lot of updated documentation to fix most of the common issues related to server configuration.

At this point, you will need to invest some money to get this service. I will show you the cheapest way to do this, and if in the future you want to increase the power of your Droplets, you will be able to increase the capacity without redoing the configuration. The lowest price for the very basic Droplet is $5.00 per month ($0.007 per hour).

We are going to use Ubuntu 20.04 (but feel free to use the latest version 21.04); you will need to know some basic Linux commands to be able to configure your Droplet. If you're a beginner using Linux, don't worry—I'll try to show you each step in a very easy way.

Signing up to DigitalOcean

If you don't have a DigitalOcean account, you can sign up at `https://cloud.digitalocean.com/registrations/new`.

You can sign up with your Google account, or by registering manually. Once you register with Google, you will see the billing info view, as follows:

You can pay with your credit card or by using PayPal. Once you have configured your payment information, DigitalOcean will ask you for some information about your project so that it can configure your Droplet faster:

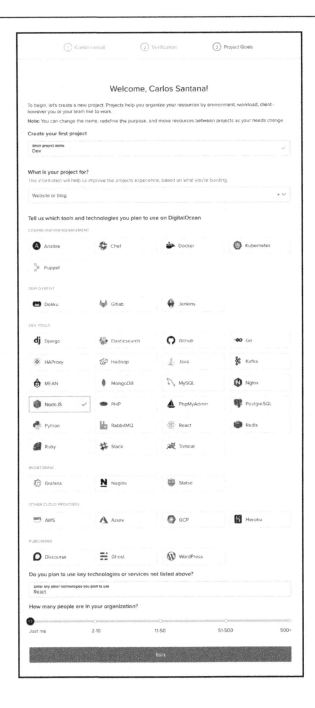

In the next section, we will create our first Droplet.

Creating our first Droplet

We will create a new Droplet from scratch. Follow these steps to do so:

1. Select the **New Droplet** option, as shown in the following screenshot:

2. Choose **Ubuntu 20.04 (LTS) x64**, as follows:

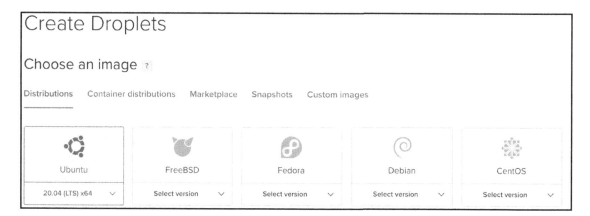

3. Then, choose the **Basic** plan, as shown here:

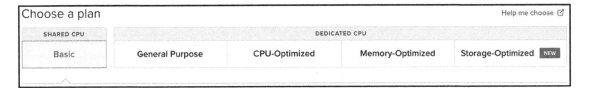

4. You can then choose **$5/mo** in the payment plan options:

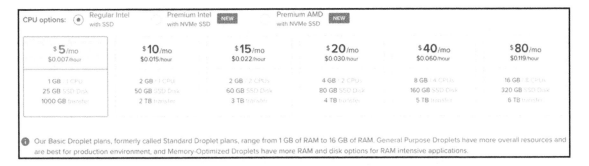

5. Select a region. In this case, we will select the **San Francisco** region:

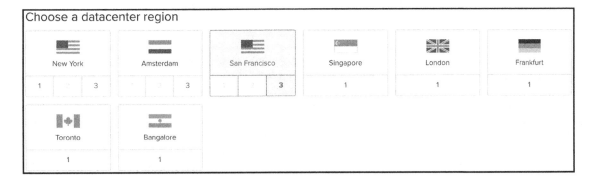

6. Create a root password, add the name of your **Droplet** and then click on the **Create Droplet** button, as follows:

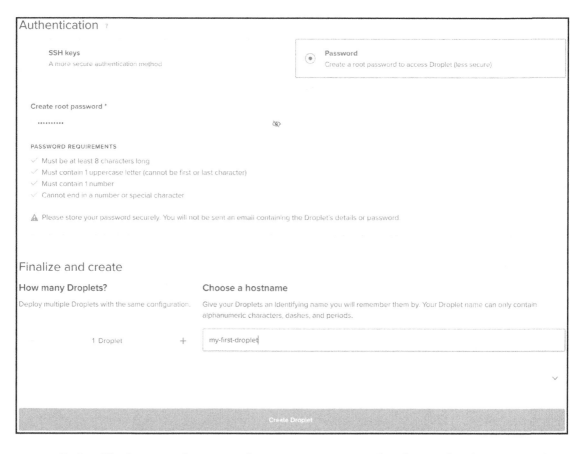

7. It will take around 30 seconds to create your Droplet. Once it has been created, you will be able to see it:

8. Now, in your Terminal, you can access the Droplet by using the following command:

```
ssh root@THE_DROPLET_IP
```

9. The first time you access it will ask you for the fingerprint, you just need to write Yes, and then it will require your password (the one you defined when you created your droplet).

```
→  ~ ssh root@144.126.222.17
The authenticity of host '144.126.222.17 (144.126.222.17)' can't be established.
ECDSA key fingerprint is SHA256:j/SZ4/nXy9t5yD9VnC3fC4mqoFdgKZbKQCvpKQopOgA.
Are you sure you want to continue connecting (yes/no/[fingerprint])? yes
Warning: Permanently added '144.126.222.17' (ECDSA) to the list of known hosts.
root@144.126.222.17's password:
Welcome to Ubuntu 20.04.1 LTS (GNU/Linux 5.4.0-51-generic x86_64)

 * Documentation:  https://help.ubuntu.com
 * Management:     https://landscape.canonical.com
 * Support:        https://ubuntu.com/advantage

  System information as of Tue May 11 06:31:54 UTC 2021

  System load:  0.0                Users logged in:       0
  Usage of /:   5.1% of 24.06GB    IPv4 address for eth0: 144.126.222.17
  Memory usage: 18%                IPv4 address for eth0: 10.48.0.5
  Swap usage:   0%                 IPv4 address for eth1: 10.124.0.2
  Processes:    98

1 update can be installed immediately.
0 of these updates are security updates.
To see these additional updates run: apt list --upgradable


The list of available updates is more than a week old.
To check for new updates run: sudo apt update


The programs included with the Ubuntu system are free software;
the exact distribution terms for each program are described in the
individual files in /usr/share/doc/*/copyright.

Ubuntu comes with ABSOLUTELY NO WARRANTY, to the extent permitted by
applicable law.

root@my-first-droplet:~#
```

Now we are all set to install Node.js, which we will be covering in the next section.

Installing Node.js

Now that you're connected to your Droplet, let's configure it. First, we need to install the latest version of Node.js using a Personal Package Archive. The current version of Node at the time of writing this book is 14.16.x. Follow these given steps to install Node.js:

1. If, when you are reading this paragraph, Node has a new version, change the version in the `setup_14.x` command:

   ```
   cd ~
   curl -sL https://deb.nodesource.com/setup_14.x -o
   nodesource_setup.sh
   ```

2. Once you get the `nodesource_setup.sh` file, run the following command:

   ```
   sudo bash nodesource_setup.sh
   ```

3. Then, install Node by running the following command:

   ```
   sudo apt install nodejs -y
   ```

4. If everything works fine, verify the installed version of Node and `npm` with the following commands:

   ```
   node -v
   v14.16.1
   npm -v
   6.14.12
   ```

If you need a newer version of Node.js, you can always upgrade it.

Configuring Git and GitHub

I created a special repository for helping you to deploy your first React application to production (`https://github.com/D3vEducation/production`).

In your Droplet, you need to clone this Git repository (or your own repository if you have your React application ready to be deployed). The production repository is public, but normally you will use a private repository; in this case, you need to add the SSH key of your Droplet to your GitHub account. To create this key, follow these steps:

1. Run the `ssh-keygen` command and then press *Enter* three times without writing any passphrase:

```
root@my-first-droplet:~# ssh-keygen
Generating public/private rsa key pair.
Enter file in which to save the key (/root/.ssh/id_rsa):
Enter passphrase (empty for no passphrase):
Enter same passphrase again:
Your identification has been saved in /root/.ssh/id_rsa
Your public key has been saved in /root/.ssh/id_rsa.pub
The key fingerprint is:
SHA256:FzejHaIZaY88/wlVUDocpeEjV+wjwY/RfBowIQenWts root@my-first-droplet
The key's randomart image is:
+---[RSA 3072]----+
|         ooXO+   |
|        . B+O= . |
|       + * &*.+  |
|      o O @oB=   |
|       S = E. .  |
|        + .      |
|         o       |
|        o .      |
|         o       |
+-----[SHA256]-----+
root@my-first-droplet:~# 
```

> If you left your Terminal inactive for more than five minutes, your Droplet connection will probably be closed, and you will need to connect again.

2. Once you have created your Droplet SSH key, you can see it by running the following command:

```
vi /root/.ssh/id_rsa.pub
```

You will see something like this:

```
ssh-rsa AAAAB3NzaC1yc2EAAAADAQABAAABgQCzz49rPKe+dctYr3UG8F+vr3uKZS
rqVKbJjypIzOc2OrrEPyjulL0GEYBRLYNDVFHjmhAhQo45Y86xlIfQn4aC9QODiDcj
sDJZwc+bQ91NqvhP4q5+RHK/yizlcVBZKCw5RIx9AzpQt8bFRWWlP188cnvXhHlBxL
b0eej5xtaL6afdAEUh5z/klXGQO6kIzZlnyEnvqqKfUmUHDyLOyqB1xjkY/Shgf5o1
YdNk2hAFfC4r96mIyfVRR23tYPPE06OqZ1M= root@my-first-droplet
```

3. Copy your SSH key and then visit your GitHub account. Go to **Settings** | **SSH and GPG Keys** (`https://github.com/settings/ssh/new`). Then, paste your key in the text area and add your title to the key:

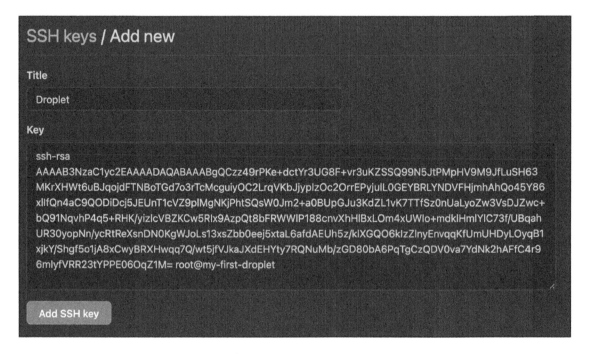

4. Once you click on the **Add SSH key** button, you will see your SSH key, like so:

5. Now you can clone our repository (or yours) using the following command:

    `git clone git@github.com:FoggDev/production.git`

6. When you clone it for the first time, you will get a message asking you to allow the RSA key fingerprint:

```
root@my-first-droplet:~# git clone git@github.com:D3vEducation/production.git
Cloning into 'production'...
The authenticity of host 'github.com (192.30.255.113)' can't be established.
RSA key fingerprint is SHA256:nThbg6kXUpJWGl7E1IGOCspRomTxdCARLviKw6E5SY8.
Are you sure you want to continue connecting (yes/no/[fingerprint])?
```

7. You have to write yes and then hit *Enter* to be able to clone it:

```
Warning: Permanently added 'github.com,192.30.255.113' (RSA) to the list of known hosts.
remote: Enumerating objects: 188, done.
remote: Total 188 (delta 0), reused 0 (delta 0), pack-reused 188
Receiving objects: 100% (188/188), 217.06 KiB | 1.07 MiB/s, done.
Resolving deltas: 100% (61/61), done.
root@my-first-droplet:~#
```

8. Then, you have to go to the `production` directory and install the `npm` packages:

    ```
    cd production
    npm install
    ```

9. If you want to test the application, just run the `start` script:

    ```
    npm start
    ```

10. Then open your browser and go to your Droplet IP and add the port number. In my case, it is `http://144.126.222.17:3000`:

11. This will run the project in development mode. If you want to run in production mode, then use the following command:

```
npm run start:production
```

You should see PM2 running, as shown in the following screenshot:

```
^Croot@my-first-droplet:~/production# npm run start:production

> production@1.0.0 start:production /root/production
> npm run stop && npm run build && NODE_ENV=production pm2 start --interpreter babel-node src/backend


> production@1.0.0 stop /root/production
> pm2 kill


                    ------------
__/\\\\\\\\\\\___/\\_____/\\\___/\\\\\\\\\____
 _\/\\\/////////\\\_\/\\_____/\\\\\___/\\\///////\\\___
  _\/\\_____\/\\\_\/\\\/\\_____/\\\/\\\_\///_____\//\\\__
   _\/\\\\\\\\\\\\\/__\/\\\\\\\\\\____/\\\/\/\\_____/\\\/___
    _\/\\\/////////____\/\\\/////\\\___/\\\/__\/\\_____/\\\//_____
     _\/\\_____\/\\\___\//\\\_/\\\____\/\\\_____/\\\//_____
      _\/\\_____\/\\\____\//\\\\\\_____\/\\\___/\\\/_____
       _\/\\_____\/\\\_____\//\\\\\_____\/\\\__\///\\\\\\\\\\\_
        _\///_____\///_____\/////_____\///____\///////////__


                        Runtime Edition

        PM2 is a Production Process Manager for Node.js applications
                    with a built-in Load Balancer.

                Start and Daemonize any application:
                $ pm2 start app.js

                Load Balance 4 instances of api.js:
                $ pm2 start api.js -i 4

                Monitor in production:
                $ pm2 monitor

                Make pm2 auto-boot at server restart:
                $ pm2 startup

                To go further checkout:
                http://pm2.io/


                    ------------
```

12. If you run it and you view the **Network** tab in your Chrome DevTools, you will see the bundles being loaded:

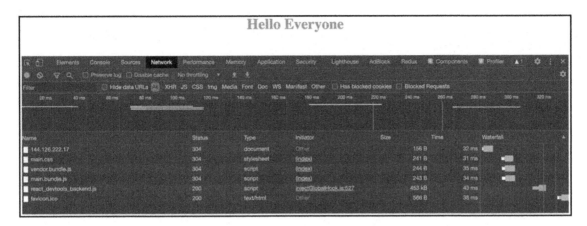

We now have our React application working in production, but let's see what else we can do with DigitalOcean in the next section.

Turning off our Droplet

To turn off the Droplet, follow these steps:

1. If you want to turn off your Droplet, you can go to the **Power** section, or you can use the **ON/OFF** switch:

2. DigitalOcean will charge you only when your Droplet is **ON**. If you click on the **ON** switch to turn it off, then you will get the following confirmation message:

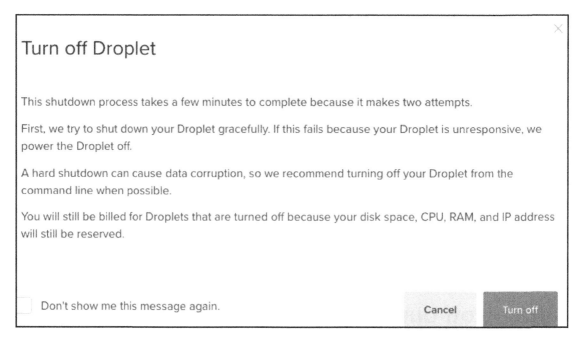

In this way, you can control your Droplet and avoid paying unnecessarily when you're not using your Droplet.

Configuring nginx, PM2, and a domain

Our Droplet is ready to be used for production, but as you can see, we are still using port `3000`. We need to configure nginx and implement a proxy to redirect the traffic from port `80` to `3000`; this means we won't need to specify the port directly anymore. **Node Production Process Manager** (**PM2**) will help us run the Node server in production securely. Generally, if we run Node directly with the `node` or `babel-node` commands, and there is an error in the app, then it will crash and will stop working. PM2 restarts the node server if an error occurs.

First, in your Droplet, you need to install PM2 globally:

```
npm install -g pm2
```

PM2 will help us to run our React app in a very easy way.

Installing and configuring nginx

To install nginx, you need to execute the following command:

```
sudo apt-get update
sudo apt-get install nginx
```

After you have installed nginx, then you can start the configuration:

1. We need to adjust the firewall to allow the traffic for port 80. To list the available application configurations, you need to run the following command:

   ```
   sudo ufw app list
   Available applications:
     Nginx Full
     Nginx HTTP
     Nginx HTTPS
     OpenSSH
   ```

2. Nginx Full means that it will allow the traffic from port 80 (HTTP) and port 443 (HTTPS). We haven't configured any domain with SSL, so, for now, we should restrict the traffic to be sent just through port 80 (HTTP):

   ```
   sudo ufw allow 'Nginx HTTP'
   Rules updated
   Rules updated (v6)
   ```

   If you try to access the Droplet IP, you should see nginx working:

144.126.222.17

Welcome to nginx!

If you see this page, the nginx web server is successfully installed and working. Further configuration is required.

For online documentation and support please refer to nginx.org. Commercial support is available at nginx.com.

Thank you for using nginx.

3. You can manage the nginx process with these commands:

```
Start server: sudo systemctl start nginx
Stop server: sudo systemctl stop nginx
Restart server: sudo systemctl restart nginx
```

Nginx is an amazing web server that is getting very popular nowadays.

Setting up a reverse proxy server

As I mentioned previously, we need to set up a reverse proxy server to send the traffic from port 80 (HTTP) to port 3000 (React app). To do this, you need to open the following file:

```
sudo vi /etc/nginx/sites-available/default
```

The steps are as follows:

1. In the location / block, you need to replace the code in the file with the following:

```
location / {
  proxy_pass http://localhost:3000;
  proxy_http_version 1.1;
  proxy_set_header Upgrade $http_upgrade;
  proxy_set_header Connection 'upgrade';
  proxy_set_header Host $host;
  proxy_cache_bypass $http_upgrade;
}
```

2. Once you have saved the file, you can verify whether there is a syntax error in the nginx configuration with the following command:

```
sudo nginx -t
```

3. If everything is fine, then you should see this:

```
root@my-first-droplet:~# sudo nginx -t
nginx: the configuration file /etc/nginx/nginx.conf syntax is ok
nginx: configuration file /etc/nginx/nginx.conf test is successful
root@my-first-droplet:~#
```

4. Finally, you need to restart the nginx server:

```
sudo systemctl restart nginx
```

Now, you should be able to access the React application without the port, as shown in the following screenshot:

We are almost done! In the next section, we are going to add a domain to our Droplet.

Adding a domain to our Droplet

Using an IP to access a website is not nice; we always need to use a domain to help users find our website easier. If you want to use a domain on your Droplet, you need to change the nameservers of your domain to point to the DigitalOcean DNS. I normally use GoDaddy to register my domains. To do so using GoDaddy, follow these steps:

1. Go to `https://dcc.godaddy.com/manage/YOURDOMAIN.COM/dns`, and then go to the **Nameservers** section:

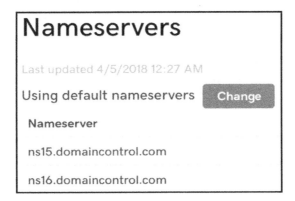

2. Click on the **Change** button, select **Custom**, and then specify the DigitalOcean DNS:

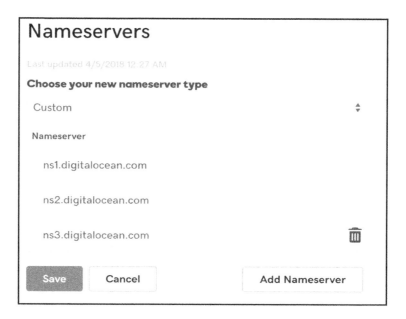

3. Normally, it takes between 15 and 30 minutes for the DNS changes to be reflected; for now, after you have updated your **Nameservers**, go to your Droplet dashboard, and then choose the **Add a domain** option:

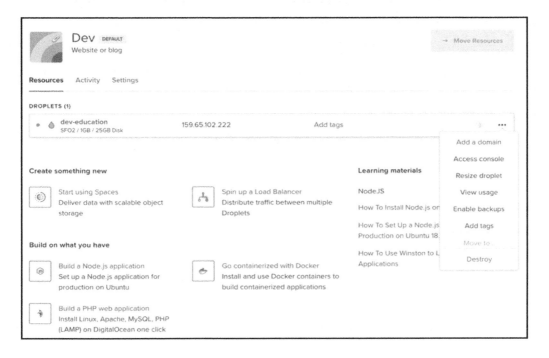

4. Then, write your domain name, select your Droplet, and click on the **Add Domain** button:

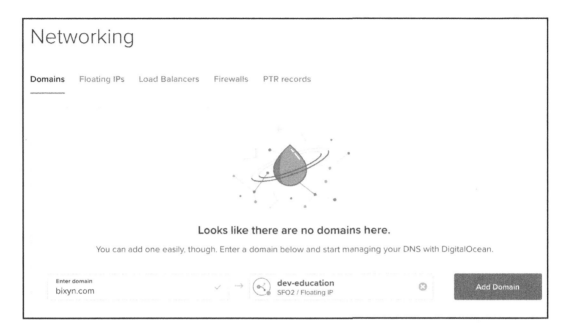

5. Now, you have to create a new record for **CNAME**. Select the **CNAME** tab, and in the **HOSTNAME** write www; in the alias field write @; by default, the **TTL** is 43200. All of this is to enable access to your domain using the www prefix:

If you did everything correctly, you should be able to access your domain and see the React application working. As I said before, this process can take up to 30 minutes, but in some cases, it can take up to 24 hours depending on the DNS propagation speed:

Amazing, now you have officially deployed your first React application to production!

Implementing CircleCI for continuous integration

I've been using CircleCI for a while and I can tell you that it is one of the best CI solutions: it is free for personal use, giving you unlimited repositories and users; you have 1,000 build minutes per month, one container, and one concurrent job; if you need more, you can upgrade the plan with an initial price of $50 per month.

The first thing you need to do is sign up on the site using your GitHub account (or Bitbucket, if you prefer). If you choose to use GitHub, you need to authorize CircleCI in your account, as shown in the following screenshot:

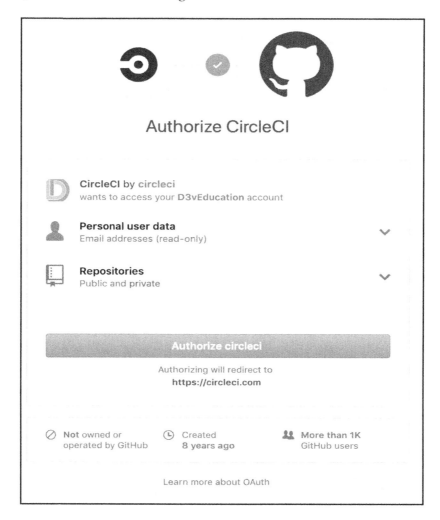

In the next section, we are going to add our SSH key to CircleCI.

Adding an SSH key to CircleCI

Now that you have created your account, CircleCI needs a way to log in to your DigitalOcean Droplet to run the deploy script. Follow these steps to complete this task:

1. Create a new SSH key inside your Droplet using the following command:

```
ssh-keygen -t rsa
# Then save the key as /root/.ssh/id_rsa_droplet with no password.
# After go to .ssh directory
cd /root/.ssh
```

2. After that, let's add the key to our authorized_keys:

```
cat id_rsa_droplet.pub >> authorized_keys
```

3. Now, you need to download the private key. To verify that you can log in with the new key, you need to copy it to your local machine, as follows:

```
# In your local machine do:
scp root@YOUR_DROPLET_IP:/root/.ssh/id_rsa_droplet ~/.ssh/
cd .ssh
ssh-add id_rsa_droplet
ssh -v root@YOUR_DROPLET_IP
```

If you did everything correctly, you should be able to log in to your Droplet without a password, and that means CircleCI can access our Droplet too:

4. Copy the content of your `id_rsa_droplet.pub` key and then go to your repository settings (`https://app.circleci.com/settings/project/github/YOUR_GITHUB_USER/YOUR_REPOSITORY`):

5. Go to **SSH Keys**, as follows:

Overview
Advanced
Environment Variables
SSH Keys
API Permissions
Jira Integration
Slack Integration

6. You can also access the URL `https://app.circleci.com/settings/project/`
   `github/YOUR_GITHUB_USER/YOUR_REPOSITORY/shh,` and then click on the **Add**
   SSH Key button at the bottom:

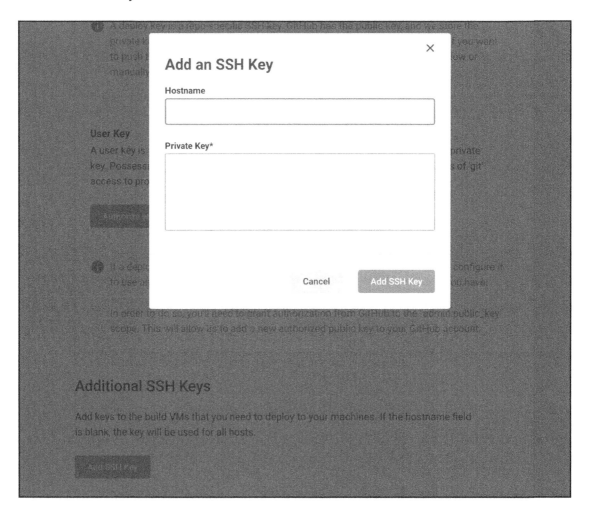

7. Paste your private key, and then provide a name for the **Hostname** field; we will
   name it `DigitalOcean`.

Now let's configure our CircleCI instance in the next section.

Configuring CircleCI

Now that you have configured access for CircleCI to your Droplet, you need to add a config file to your project to specify the jobs you want to execute for the deployment process. This process is shown in the following steps:

1. For this, you need to create the .circleci directory and add the following inside the config.yml file:

```yaml
version: 2.1
jobs:
  build:
    working_directory: ~/tmp
    docker:
      - image: cimg/node:14.16.1
    steps:
      - checkout
      - run: npm install
      - run: npm run lint
      - run: npm test
      - run: ssh -o StrictHostKeyChecking=no
$DROPLET_USER@$DROPLET_IP 'cd production; git checkout master; git
pull; npm install; npm run start:production;'
workflows:
  build-deploy:
    jobs:
      - build:
          filters:
            branches:
              only: master
```

2. When you have a .yml file, you need to be careful with the indentation; it is similar to Python in that if you don't use indents correctly, you will get an error. Let's see how this file is structured.

3. Specify the CircleCI version we will use. In this instance, you are using version 2.1 (the latest one at the time of writing this book):

```yaml
version: 2.1
```

4. Inside jobs, we will specify that it needs to configure the container; we will create it using Docker, and also outline the steps to follow for the deployment process.

5. The `working_directory` will be the temporal directory we will use to install the npm packages and run our deploy scripts. In this case, I decided to use the `tmp` directory, as follows:

```
jobs:
  build:
    working_directory: ~/tmp
```

6. As I said before, we will create a Docker container, and in this instance, I selected an existing image that includes `node: 14.16.1`. If you want to know about all the available images, you can visit `https://circleci.com/docs/2.0/circleci-images`:

```
docker:
  - image: cimg/node:14.16.1
```

7. For the code case, first do a `git checkout` to `master`, then on each run sentence, you need to specify the scripts you want to run:

```
steps:
  - checkout
  - run: npm install
  - run: npm run lint
  - run: npm test
  - run: ssh -o StrictHostKeyChecking=no $DROPLET_USER@$DROPLET_IP
    'cd production; git checkout master; git pull; npm install; npm run
    start:production;'
```

Follow these steps:

1. First, you need to install the npm packages using `npm install` to be able to perform the next tasks.
2. Execute the ESLint validation using `npm run lint`. If it fails, it will break the deployment process, otherwise, it continues with the next run.
3. Execute the Jest validations using `npm run test`; if it fails, it will break the deployment process, otherwise, it continues with the next run.
4. In the last step, we connect to our DigitalOcean Droplet, passing the `StrictHostKeyChecking=no` flag to disable the strict host key checking. We then use the `$DROPLET_USER` and `$DROPLET_IP` ENV variables to connect to it (we will create those in the next step), and finally, we will specify all the commands we will perform inside our Droplet using single quotes. These commands are listed as follows:

`cd production`: Grants access to the production (or your Git repository name).

`git checkout master`: This will check out the master branch.

`git pull`: Pulls the latest changes from our repository.

`npm run start:production`: This is the final step, which runs our project in production mode.

Finally, let's add some environment variables to our CircleCI.

Creating ENV variables in CircleCI

As you saw previously, we are using the `$DROPLET_USER` and `$DROPLET_IP` variables, but how do we define those? Follow these steps:

1. You need to go to your project settings again and select the **Environment Variables** option. Then, you need to create the `DROPLET_USER` variable:

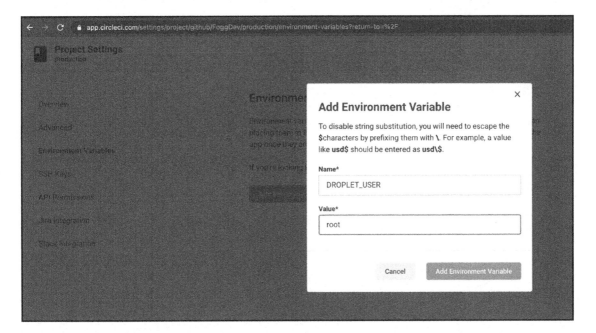

2. Then, you need to create the `DROPLET_IP` variable using your Droplet IP:

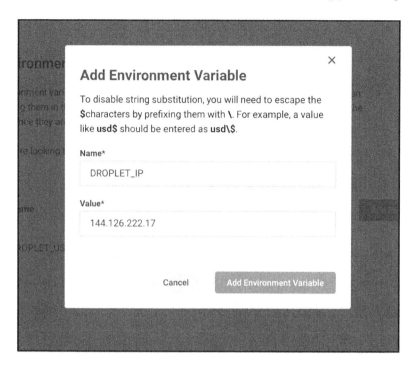

3. Now, you need to push the `config` file to your repository, and you will be ready for the magic. Now that CircleCI is connected to your repository, every time you push changes to master, it will fire a build.

   Normally, the first two or three builds can fail due to syntax errors, indent errors in our config, or maybe because we have linter errors or unit test errors. If you have a failure, you will see something like this:

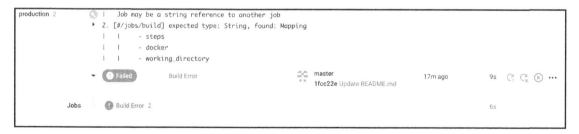

4. As you can see from the preceding screenshot, the first build failures at the bottom say **Build Error**, and the second one says **workflow build-deploy**. This basically means that in the first build I had a **syntax error** in the config.yml file.

5. After you fix all the syntax errors in the config.yml file and all the issues with the linter or the unit tests, you should see a **SUCCESS** build, like this:

6. If you click on the build number, you can see all the steps that CircleCI executed before publishing the new changes in your Droplet:

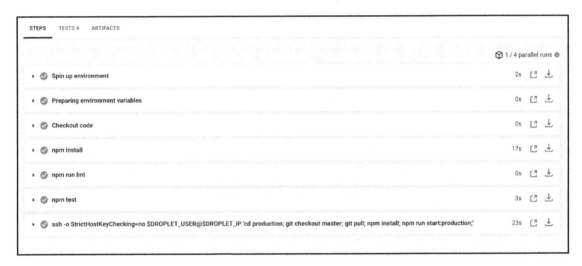

7. As you can see, the order of the steps is the same as we specified in our `config.yml` file; you can even see the output of each step by clicking on it:

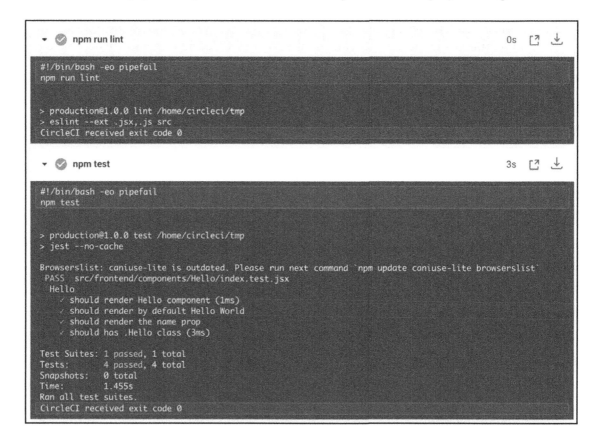

8. Now, let's suppose you have an error on your linter validation or in some unit tests. Let's see what happen in that case, as follows:

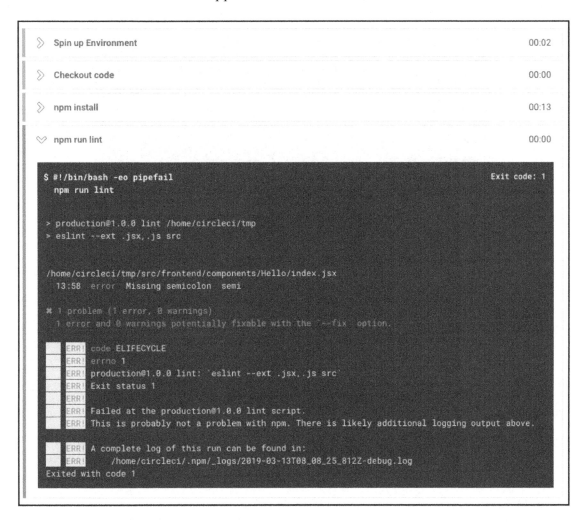

As you can see, once an error is detected, it will exit with code 1. This means it will abort the deployment and will mark it as a failure, and as you can see, none of the steps after `npm run lint` are executed.

Another cool thing is that if you now go to your GitHub repository and check your commits, you will see all the commits that had a successful build and all the commits that had a failed build:

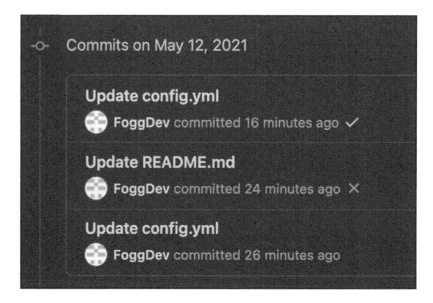

This is amazing – now you have your project configured to do deployments automatically and it is connected to your GitHub repository.

Summary

Our journey through the deployment process has come to an end, and now you know how to deploy your React application to the world (production), and also how to implement CircleCI for continuous integration.

In the next chapter, we will learn how to publish npm packages.

15
Next Steps

React is one of the most amazing libraries that has been released in the last few years, not only because of the library itself and its great features but also, most importantly, due to the ecosystem that has been built around it.

Following the React community is very exciting and inspiring; there are new projects and tools to learn about and play with every single day. Not just that, there are conferences and meetups where you can talk to people in real life and build new relationships, blog posts that you can read to improve your skills and learn more, and many other ways to become a better developer.

The React ecosystem encourages best practices and love for open source developers, which is fantastic for the future of our careers.

In this chapter, we will cover the following topics:

- How to contribute to the React library by opening issues and pull requests
- Why it is important to give back to the community and share your code
- How to publish an npm package and how to use semantic versioning

Technical requirements

To complete this chapter, you will need the following:

- Node.js 12+
- Visual Studio Code

Contributing to React

One thing that people often want to do when they've used React for a while is to contribute to the library. React is open source, which means that its source code is public and anyone who's signed the **Contributor License Agreement** (**CLA**) can help to fix bugs, write documentation, or even add new features.

 You can read the full terms of the CLA at the following URL: `https://code.facebook.com/cla`.

You need to make sure that any bug you post in React's GitHub repository is 100% replicable. Once you verify this, and if you want to file an issue on GitHub, you can go to `https://github.com/facebook/react/issues/new`. As you'll see, the issue comes with some pre-filled instructions, with one of those being to set up the minimal demo. The other questions help you to explain the problem and to describe current and expected behaviors.

It is important for you to read the *Facebook Code of Conduct* before participating or contributing to the repository, at `https://code.facebook.com/codeofconduct`. The document lists good behaviors that are expected from all community members and that everyone should follow. Once the issue is filed, you have to wait for one of the core contributors to examine it and tell you what they've decided to do with the bug. Depending on the severity of it, they might fix it, or ask you to fix it.

In the second case, you can fork the repository and write code to solve the problem. It is important to follow the coding style guides and write all the tests for the fix. It is also crucial that all the old tests pass to make sure the new code does not introduce regressions in the code base. When the fix is ready and all the tests are green, you can submit a pull request, and wait for the core team members to review it. They may decide to merge it or ask you to make some changes.

If you did not find a bug but you still want to contribute to the project, you can look into the issues tagged with the **good first issue** label on GitHub: `https://github.com/facebook/react/labels/good%20first%20issue`. This is a great way to start contributing and it is fantastic that the React team gives everyone, especially new contributors, the possibility of being part of the project.

If you find a good first bug issue that has not already been taken by someone, you can add a comment on the issue saying that you are interested in working on it. One of the core members will get in touch with you. Make sure to discuss your approach and the path you want to take with them before you start coding so that you do not have to rewrite the code multiple times.

Another way of improving React is by adding new features. It is important to say that the React team has a plan to follow, and the main features are designed and decided by the core members.

 If you are interested in knowing the next steps that the library will take, you can find some of them under the **Type: Big Picture** label on GitHub: `https://github.com/facebook/react/labels/Type%3A%20Big%20Picture`.

That said, if you have some good ideas about features that should be added to the library, the first thing to do is open an issue and start talking with the React team. You should avoid spending time writing code and submitting a pull request before asking them, because the feature you have in mind might not fit into their plans, or might conflict with other functionalities they are working on.

Distributing your code

Contributing to the React ecosystem does not only mean pushing code into the React repository. To give back to the community and help developers, you can create packages, write blog posts, answer questions on Stack Overflow, and perform many other activities.

Suppose, for example, you created a React component that solves a complex problem, and you think that other developers would benefit from using it instead of investing time in building their solutions. The best thing to do is to publish it on GitHub and make it available for everyone to read and use. However, pushing the code to GitHub is only a small action within a big process, and it comes with some responsibilities. So, you should have a clear idea in mind about the reasons behind your choice.

The motivation behind why you want to share your code contributes to improving your skills as a developer. Sharing your code, on the one hand, forces you to follow best practices and write better code. On the other hand, it exposes your code to feedback and comments from other developers. This is a big opportunity for you to receive tips and improve your code to make it better.

Other than the suggestions related to the code itself, by pushing your code to GitHub, you benefit from other people's ideas. In fact, you might have thought about a single problem that your component can solve, but another developer may use it in a slightly different way, finding new solutions for it. Moreover, they might need new features and they could help you implement them, so that everyone, yourself included, can benefit from it. Building software together is a great way to improve both your skills and your packages, and that is why I strongly believe in open source.

Another significant opportunity that open source can give you is letting you get in touch with smart and passionate developers from all around the world. Working closely with new people who have different backgrounds and skillsets is one of the best ways to keep our minds open and improve ourselves.

Sharing code also gives you some responsibilities and it could be time-consuming. In fact, once the code is public and people can use it, you have to maintain it.

Maintaining a repository requires commitment because the more popular it gets and the more people use it, the higher the number of questions and issues. For example, developers may encounter bugs and open issues, so you have to go through all of them and try to reproduce the problems. If the problems exist, then you have to write the fix and publish a new version of the library. You could receive pull requests from developers, which could be long and complex, and they need to be reviewed.

If you decide to ask people to co-maintain the project and help you with issues and pull requests, you have to coordinate with them to share your vision and make decisions together.

Knowing the best practices when pushing open source code

We can go through some good practices that can help you make a better repository and avoid some of the common pitfalls.

First of all, if you want to publish your React component, you have to write a comprehensive set of tests. With public code and many people contributing to it, tests are very helpful for many reasons:

- They make the code more robust.
- They help other developers understand what the code does.
- They make it easier to find regression when new code is added.
- They make other contributors more confident in writing the code.

The second important thing to do is add a README with a description of the component, an example of its use, and documentation of the APIs and props that can be used. This helps users of the package, but it also avoids people opening issues and asking questions about how the library works and how it should be used.

It is also essential to add a LICENSE file to your repository to make people aware of what they can and cannot do with your code. GitHub has a lot of ready-made templates to choose from. Whenever you can, you should keep the package small and add as few dependencies as you can. Developers tend to think carefully about size when they have to decide whether to use a library or not. Remember that heavy packages have a bad impact on performance.

Not only that, depending on too many third-party libraries can create problems if any of them are not maintained or have bugs.

One tricky part in sharing React components comes when you have to decide on the styling. Sharing JavaScript code is pretty straightforward while attaching the CSS is not as easy as you may think. In fact, there are many different paths you can take to provide it: from adding a CSS file to the package to using inline styles. The important thing to keep in mind is that CSS is global and generic class names may conflict with ones that already exist in the project where the component is imported.

The best choice is to include the fewest possible styles and make the component highly configurable for end users. In this way, developers will be more likely to use it because it can be adapted to their custom solutions.

To show that your component is highly customizable, you can add one or more examples to the repository to make it easy for everyone to understand how it works and which props it accepts. Examples are also useful so that you can test new versions of the component and see whether there are unexpected breaking changes.

As we saw in *Chapter 3*, *React Hooks*, tools such as **React Storybook** can help you create living style guides, which are easier for you to maintain and for the consumer of your package to navigate and use.

An excellent example of a highly customizable library that uses Storybook to show all these variations is react-dates from Airbnb. You should take that repository as the perfect example of how to publish React components to GitHub.

As you can see, they use Storybook to show the different options of the component:

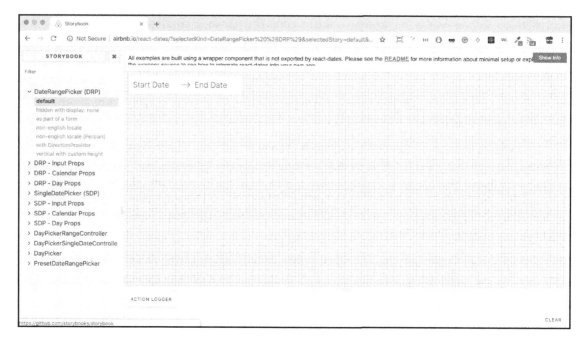

Last but not least, you might not just want to share your code – you may also want to distribute your package. The most popular package manager for JavaScript is npm, which we've used throughout this book to install packages and dependencies.

In the next section, we will see how easy it is to publish a new package with npm.

Other than npm, some developers may need to add your component as a global dependency and use it without a package manager.

As we saw in *Chapter 1, Taking Your First Steps with React*, you can easily use React by just adding a script tag pointing to https://unpkg.com/. It is important to give the users of your library the same option.

So, to offer a global version of your package, you should build the **Universal Module Definition (UMD)** version as well. With webpack, this is pretty straightforward; you just have to set libraryTarget in the output section of the configuration file.

Publishing an npm package

The most popular way of making a package available to developers is by publishing it to npm, the package manager for Node.js.

We used it in all the examples in this book and you have seen how easy it is to install a package; it is just a matter of running the npm install package, and that is it. What you may not know is how easy it is to publish a package as well.

First of all, let's say you move into an empty directory and write the following in your terminal:

```
npm init
```

A new package.json file will be created and some questions will be displayed. The first one is the package name, which defaults to the folder name, and then the version number. These are the most important ones because the first is the name that the users of your package will refer to when they install and use it; the second helps you release new versions of your package safely and without breaking other people's code.

The version number is composed of three numbers separated by a dot, and they all have a meaning. The last number of the package on the right represents the patch, and it should be increased when a new version of the library that contains bug fixes is pushed to npm.

The number in the middle indicates the minor version of the release, and it should be changed when new features are added to the library. Those new features should not break existing APIs. Finally, the first number on the left represents the major version, and it has to be increased when a version containing breaking changes is released to the public.

Following this approach, called **Semantic Versioning (SemVer)**, is good practice and it makes your users more confident when they have to update your package.

The first version of a package is usually 0.1.0.

To publish an npm package, you must have an npm account, which you can easily create by running the following command in the console, where $username is the name of your choice:

```
npm adduser $username
```

Once the user is created, you can run the following command:

```
npm publish
```

A new entry will be added to the registry with the package name and the version you specified in `package.json`.

Whenever you change something in your library and you want to push a new version, you just have to run `$type`, where one patch is minor or major:

```
npm version $type
```

This command will bump the version automatically in your `package.json` file and it will also create a commit and a tag if your folder is under version control.

Once the version number is increased, you just have to run `npm publish` again, and the new version will be available to users.

Summary

In the last stop on this trip around the React world, we have seen some of the aspects that make React great – its community and its ecosystem – and how to contribute to them.

You learned how to open an issue if you find a bug in React, and the steps to take to make it easier for its core developers to fix it. You now know the best practices when making code open source, and the benefits and the responsibilities that come with it.

Finally, you saw how easy it is to publish packages on the `npm` registry, and how to choose the right version number to avoid breaking other people's code.

About Packt

Packt.com

Subscribe to our online digital library for full access to over 7,000 books and videos, as well as industry leading tools to help you plan your personal development and advance your career. For more information, please visit our website.

Why subscribe?

- Spend less time learning and more time coding with practical eBooks and Videos from over 4,000 industry professionals

- Improve your learning with Skill Plans built especially for you

- Get a free eBook or video every month

- Fully searchable for easy access to vital information

- Copy and paste, print, and bookmark content

Did you know that Packt offers eBook versions of every book published, with PDF and ePub files available? You can upgrade to the eBook version at www.packt.com and as a print book customer, you are entitled to a discount on the eBook copy. Get in touch with us at customercare@packtpub.com for more details.

At www.packt.com, you can also read a collection of free technical articles, sign up for a range of free newsletters, and receive exclusive discounts and offers on Packt books and eBooks.

Other Books You May Enjoy

If you enjoyed this book, you may be interested in these other books by Packt:

The React Workshop

Brandon Richey, Ryan Yu, Endre Vegh, Theofanis Despoudis, Anton Punith, Florian Sloot

ISBN: 978-1-83864-556-4

- Use JSX to include logic in the view layer of applications
- Get familiar with the important methods and events in the React lifecycle
- Distinguish between class and functional component syntaxes
- Create forms with Formik and handle errors
- Understand the React Hooks API and the problems it can solve
- Fetch outside data using the Axios library and populate the data to the app

Full-Stack React, TypeScript, and Node
David Choi

ISBN: 978-1-83921-993-1

- Discover TypeScript's most important features and how they can be used to improve code quality and maintainability
- Understand what React Hooks are and how to build React apps using them
- Implement state management for your React app using Redux
- Set up an Express project with TypeScript and GraphQL from scratch
- Build a fully functional online forum app using React and GraphQL
- Add authentication to your web app using Redis
- Save and retrieve data from a Postgres database using TypeORM
- Configure NGINX on the AWS cloud to deploy and serve your apps

Packt is searching for authors like you

If you're interested in becoming an author for Packt, please visit `authors.packtpub.com` and apply today. We have worked with thousands of developers and tech professionals, just like you, to help them share their insight with the global tech community. You can make a general application, apply for a specific hot topic that we are recruiting an author for, or submit your own idea.

Leave a review - let other readers know what you think

Please share your thoughts on this book with others by leaving a review on the site that you bought it from. If you purchased the book from Amazon, please leave us an honest review on this book's Amazon page. This is vital so that other potential readers can see and use your unbiased opinion to make purchasing decisions, we can understand what our customers think about our products, and our authors can see your feedback on the title that they have worked with Packt to create. It will only take a few minutes of your time, but is valuable to other potential customers, our authors, and Packt. Thank you!

Index

Made in the USA
Monee, IL
31 July 2021